QUALITY LEADERSHIP
THROUGH EMPOWERMENT
Standards of Leadership Behavior

RICHARD W. LEATHERMAN, Ph.D.

Published by HRD Press, Inc.
        22 Amherst Road
        Amherst, Massachusetts 01002
        1-800-822-2801

First Printing

ISBN 0-87425-171-0

Production Services by Susan Kotzin

Editorial Services by Lisa Wood

Cover Design by Old Mill Graphics

This book is dedicated to Nancy Leatherman

A loving parent to our seven children
A caring physician
My beloved wife

Preface

Today's organizations are putting quality first! To help do so, they are downsizing, reducing the middle management population ("flattening"), delegating responsibility downward, and giving the responsibility for quality to front-line employees.

Significant shifts in organizational focus have begun. For example, many organizations now utilize work teams. Others are creating employee involvement programs under such names as "Total Quality Performance," "Total Quality Management," or "Continuous Quality Improvement."

What behavioral science has advocated for the past 30 years is now being instituted—not only for the leadership within our organizations, but with our non-exempts as well. Traditionally, Human Resources Departments have focused on providing leadership training for only our supervisors and managers. And in that training we talked a lot about "participative" leadership.

But more often than not, the supervisors and managers would leave the training department to enter a world of work that did not encourage or allow participation! So we payed mere lip service to good management practices. And vast segments of this country's businesses became noncompetitive in the world market.

But today, in a growing number of organizations across the country, the President says: "Executive Vice President Jones, we are going to win that quality award for excellence!" The Executive V.P. replies, "Right, boss."

Vice President Jones then calls in the Senior V.P. of Human Resources and says, "The chief wants us to win that award for excellence. What do we have to do to make it happen?"

The Senior V.P. replies, "I don't know, boss. But I'll find out." And he calls in his V.P. of Training and Development and states, "The chief wants us to win that prize for excellence! What do we need to do?"

The training department V.P. responds, "Let our supervisors and managers do what they have been trained to do. In other words, create an environment that supports participative management practices. And while you're at it," he continues, "give the non-exempts training in how to take on the new responsibility that participative management creates."

But what about the budget?" cries the Senior V.P of HR. "Where are we going to get the money to continue our regular supervisory and management training—and train all the employees at the same time?"

"Use one of the oldest teaching tools in the trade," replies the training manager. "Buy them a book!"

"You're nuts!" snorts the Senior V.P. "You mean you expect me to tell my boss to buy books for our supervisors and managers?"

"Yep," replies the training manager. "I do."

This book is part of the answer to today's need for quality performance. It is a practical how-to-do-it manual that explains the basic leadership tasks in a simple, step-by-step manner. As such, it is an important update for those who have been trained and retrained—and trained again—in leadership principles. It is also a key manual for new and future leaders.

And it's easy to use. Would you like to know how *really* to empower your employees so that they will take greater charge over their own careers? To teach your employees how to take more responsibility for their performance appraisal interviews? To learn how to effectively delegate work to employees? Do you understand that the old saying, "You can't delegate responsibility, only authority" is 99% myth?

In the chapters that follow, you will find clear directions on how to empower your employees. And the exciting thing about empowerment is that you and your employees will produce more, better, and faster—and enjoy doing it, too!

Table of Contents

Introduction

A machine is easy to run. Hit this button, and it starts! Push that one, and it stops. And it usually produces more, better, and faster than a manual worker could ever hope to do. So we have automated most of our highly skilled jobs in a continuous effort to make everything bigger, better, and faster.

But there is one high-skill area that can never be automated: interactions between people. And especially those between a leader and his or her team members.

Somehow we know that it often takes more skill than we have to deal with the great variety of employee needs and problems we encounter. Remember your feelings of discomfort when you had to handle that discipline problem? You're not alone! Most of us have had those same feelings in dealing with employee situations—over and over.

The fact is that it's good that we experience these uncomfortable feelings, because they serve as motivation—motivation to learn more about leading our employees effectively.

A number of years ago I felt like a very lucky supervisor. I had not just one, but four very competent employees. It was fortunate for them that they were outstanding—because I was the original "gutless" supervisor!

I found it very easy to praise my employees on their good work. But it was extremely difficult for me to tell them how I felt they could improve.

So, I didn't! I didn't give them feedback on improvement because it made me feel uncomfortable. And as a result, they were deprived of important opportunities to develop and grow—because they didn't receive accurate information from me.

Then one day I was asked by my management if one of these employees was ready for a promotion. "Not yet," I replied. "There are a couple of areas she needs to work on. Let's give her another year."

The next morning, the employee stood in my office doorway and said, "Can I see you for a minute, Dick?"

"Sure," I replied.

She stepped inside—and shut my door. "Dick," she asked, "did you turn me down for a promotion?"

"Yes," I quietly replied.

"Why?" she asked.

"Because," I said, "I feel you aren't ready."

"Why not?" she responded.

"Well, there are two particular areas I feel you need to work on." And I lamely spelled out the problems.

"But you never told me this," she replied. And she was right!

Two months later, she quit our organization.

At that point in my career, I had a great need to know how to truly lead my employees. Much of what I have learned since then has come the hard way: by making mistakes. And learning from my mistakes.

I have also watched other leaders closely—both good ones and poor ones. Further, I regularly read books on leadership, and attend leadership programs. And I've learned much from 20 years of teaching leadership skills.

This book is my learning process—put in writing for you. It is for leaders who want common sense ideas on how to handle the often-bewildering array of employee problem situations they face.

It is a very special "how-to" book, with step-by-step instructions; a book that gives practical advice, not just theories. Throughout, it presents clear standards of performance for every leader. Its chapters show you how to handle the many day-to-day interactions that are key to empowering your employees—to helping them be more productive, and fulfilled!

1
Establishing Standards
of Performance

Sometimes an employee may quite honestly say, "I didn't know I was supposed to do that!" When this happens, someone has let the employee down by not communicating exactly what was expected.

Or an employee may continually run into problems because the leader has failed to communicate what the employee should not do. This results in a worker who begins to "play it safe" by not seeking out additional tasks or responsibilities.

In addition, most employees are constantly faced with questions such as, "What is a good job?" or, "When am I not doing this job well enough?" and, "Am I spending too much time and energy on this task?" A leader must be able to state specific performance standards for each part of an employee's job. This key task is called "communicating standards of performance."

Why Standards?

Performance standards are useful for a number of purposes. They can help to:

1. Plan and schedule work.

When standards properly define how much work is to be produced by an employee, it is possible to plan total output by combining the output of several employees. For example, maintenance work can be scheduled based on downtime of standby equipment, which, in turn, may be based on production output over time.

2. Estimate budget needs.

Quantity of materials and labor can be estimated by knowing the amount of work to be produced by using data from performance standards. Then budgetary needs can be estimated by applying labor and material costs to quantity.

3. Handle disciplinary problems and grievances.

Information obtained from standards that is compared with actual performance can provide proof that an employee is performing below standard.

4. Provide feedback to the employee on his or her performance.

The comparison of what's expected—the performance standards—to actual employee performance provides job performance feedback to both the leader and employee. The leader can use the information to provide positive feedback to employees who exceed standards, and the employee can use the information to monitor his or her performance.

5. Find the cause of a performance problem.

Because performance standards address each task, the leader can isolate a problem to one or two tasks. Task isolation will provide a starting point for problem analysis, since it helps a leader to avoid vaguely worded observations such as, "You're not doing as well as you should," or "Your production is not satisfactory."

6. Compare and evaluate changes in methods.

Suggestions for improving methods often result in improved quantitative and qualitative output over time. If standards are in effect, we can compare each suggestion to the standard and obtain information on the relative value of that suggestion to the standard.

7. Determine staffing needs.

Standards frequently indicate how much one employee can produce in a given time. If increased output or workload is desirable, this is pertinent when considering additional staffing needs.

Conducting Performance Standards Meetings with Employees

Now let's look at a step-by-step approach that will help you and your employee communicate in establishing performance standards. This method involves meeting with each employee at least once each year, at which time together you analyze the employee's job, and mutually agree upon appropriate standards of performance. Here's how to use this approach:

1. Plan and conduct an initial discussion with the employee.

The better prepared the employee is before a performance standards meeting, the easier it will be for him or her to discuss the job. Approximately one week before the standards meeting, you should meet briefly with the employee to:

- Explain what performance standards are, and why they need to be established.
- Ask the employee to provide information needed to establish such standards and measure performance.
- Help the employee begin by:
  - selecting a critical job task
  - determining the standards that will measure performance, expressed in quality, quantity, cost, or time
  - analyzing any problems that may prevent optimum performance
  - explaining the employee's authority level to complete this task.
- Give the employee a copy of the form shown on the following page, and ask him or her to complete it before the standards meeting.

Job Analysis Work Sheet

Job Summary _____

_____

_____

List the Main Tasks of Your Job:	Set Priorities A = High B = Medium C = Low	Write Standards – Quality – Quantity – Cost – Time	Identify Problems	Establish Authority 1=Complete 2=Act; Then Report 3=Act After Report

_____

_____

_____

_____

_____

_____

_____

_____

_____

_____

_____

_____

(A complete *Job Analysis Work Sheet* is located at the end of this chapter.)

The objective in this pre-standards meeting is to make sure you and the employee have the needed information for your next meeting when you will determine the standards. Ideally, these standards should be proposed by the employee. The employee should know what tasks the job includes, and what he or she can do. The last part of this preparatory step is to set a time and place for the actual standards meeting.

2. Complete your copy of the *Job Analysis Work Sheet.*

You will also complete a copy of the *Job Analysis Work Sheet* before the standards meeting, describing your perceptions of the employee's job. This will help you to provide more specific input during the meeting and to relate the employee's job standards to your own standards or unit objectives.

3. Review the job summary.

Begin the performance standards meeting by discussing and then agreeing upon the general description and content of the job. An agreement upon such a job summary is necessary before you and the employee can analyze and specify individual job tasks—the next step.

4. Ask the employee to describe each job task.

Ask the employee to identify the first job task and its relationship to the total job, how this task might be measured, any problems he or she may have with the task, and his or her perceived authority levels. This step is the heart of establishing performance standards. The employee is telling you what he or she should do, how much, and how well.

Here is the employee's opportunity to tell you how he or she perceives the job. So let the employee do the talking! But as the employee talks, listen carefully to make sure that suggested standards are stated clearly. Eliminate vague or unclear terms. Be especially attentive when he or she identifies quantity or quality and assist in being as specific as possible.

If the employee has problems while completing a task, your job is to help him or her develop solutions. Sometimes employees bring up a problem that is internal—i.e., one that is under the leader's control. For example, if the employee says, "I'm supposed to consolidate the manpower reports, but I can't figure out how to do it," you are dealing with a lack of knowledge. This is an internal problem that you and your employee can do something about. In the other case, the problem may be external: e.g., "The other department sends its reports in late every month. That means I can't make my deadline." Here you are dealing with a problem solving/decision making situation. You may have to delay establishing this standard, or temporarily set one lower than you wish.

A management maxim states, "Try to get the decision making done by the person who has the most information." The message is: listen carefully to what your employee says about authority level. The employee may be telling you that he or she can and wants to make some decisions without having to get your prior approval. And that may be a good idea! Sure, it's difficult at times to give up some control. But remember, you are also responsible for training and developing your employees. By letting an employee take on more responsibility, you are encouraging him or her to become more valuable to the organization.

5. Share your perceptions of the task identified by the employee.

Now is your opportunity to provide input by discussing and resolving any differences in the way you and the employee see the task. Your job is to reduce the employee's tension and to create a good climate for mutual development of standards, joint problem solving, and common agreement throughout the process. Here, you and the employee are attempting to answer these questions clearly:

- What are the job tasks?
- Which tasks are most important?
- How will each task be measured?

- What problems impede task completion?
- What are possible solutions for these problems?
- Who has what authority in each task?

6. Reach a consensus.

A consensus greatly increases the chance that the employee will feel that the performance standards are fair, and will be motivated to achieve them. It also tells the employee that if he or she meets a standard, then performance on that task is satisfactory.

Try to picture yourself as a trouble shooter, guide, coach, or facilitator. Don't get trapped in an evaluative, judgmental role. That will make the employee feel defensive, frustrated—and deceived. He or she will feel that, in spite of your request for input, you really have your own preset agenda—and it doesn't make any difference what he or she says. A successful leader once stated: "When it gets right down to it, I feel my job is to make it easier for my people to do their jobs." So help your employee in these ways:

- Identify any job tasks, particularly critical ones, that the employee may have omitted.
- Make sure that performance is measured quantitatively or qualitatively, preferably both.
- Clarify vague terms.
- Ask the employee for his or her thoughts and recommendations on problems that are identified.
- Clarify any confusion about authority levels.

Look at and listen to the employee carefully. Notice nonverbal communication—frowning, nervousness, hesitation, or relief and relaxation. Such nonverbal signals can tell you quite clearly whether or not you and your employee are really reaching agreement.

7. Ask the employee to make a composite of both work sheets after the meeting.

Give the employee a copy of your *Job Analysis Work Sheet* and ask the employee to make a composite of his or her work sheet and yours after the meeting. This puts the collaborative information into final form, as well as fostering a sense of ownership by the employee.

8. Thank the employee for his or her efforts.

Since the employee has likely invested significant time, energy, and concern in preparing for this meeting, close the meeting by sincerely thanking the employee for his or her efforts. By thanking him or her, you are expressing deserved appreciation, as well as reinforcing productive future behavior.

9. Follow up by reviewing the composite work sheet with the employee.

Obtain a copy of the employee's composite work sheet, and briefly review it with the employee. This is an important opportunity for any final clarification and adjustment. And you should both keep copies of the final agreement.

10. Agree upon a trial period.

Agree upon a trial period and set a future meeting date and time for a review of the employee's standards. This allows:

a. A reduction in potential tension if the employee feels irrevocably committed to an untried plan of action, about which he or she may feel somewhat unsure.

b. A correction of any problems that may surface between you and your employee before they become serious.

c. A specific meeting date and time to communicate to the employee that standards are important to you, and that you will be following up.

On the following pages are: 1) a meeting checklist that you can use to assist you in conducting a standards meeting, and 2) a *Job Analysis Work Sheet* that you can copy and use to set standards with your employees.

Establishing Standards Meeting Checklist

The following suggestions describe what you might say to an employee in a performance standards meeting. They are just that—suggestions.

Prior to the Performance Standards Meeting

1. Plan and conduct an initial discussion with the employee.

- Explain what performance standards are and why they need to be established.

  "A performance standard is simply a statement that describes a job task and how well it is to be performed. I'd like you to propose the standards for your job. We'll discuss and agree on them at the next meeting."

- Explain the *Job Analysis Work Sheet* by analyzing one key job task, explaining criteria for good performance standards, and discussing authority levels.

  "This form will make it easier for you to write your standards. Notice that I've written one job task as an example just to give you the idea. Let's go through this task completely to give you a better idea of how to develop the rest of your standards."

2. Complete your copy of the *Job Analysis Work Sheet.*

During the Performance Standards Meeting

3. Review the job summary.

  "Let's go over this paragraph that sums up the job. Do you feel it is accurate? Is there anything you would like to add or change?"

4. Ask the employee to describe each job task.

> "OK, read your first critical job task."

- Ask the employee to state how he or she sees the task being measured.

  > "How do you think we ought to measure performance?"

- Ask the employee to list problems he or she may have with the specific task.

  > "Are there any problems that are causing slowdowns or trouble?"

- Ask the employee to state perceived authority levels.

  > "Do you think this task is one that requires my prior approval, or one whose completion should be reported to me?"

5. Share your perceptions of the task identified by the employee.

- The task and its relationship to the job.
- How you see the task measured.

  > "This task might be difficult to measure. What are some of the indications that the job is done the way it ought to be done?"

- Problems and possible causes that might prevent the task from being completed.

  > "A concern that I have is...."
  > "Another possible cause of this problem might be...."

- Possible solutions to any problems.

  > "Here is an idea you might consider."

- Differences in your perception of authority.

  > "In this task, I feel that you have complete authority to do the task, but I would like to know how it turns out for you."

6. **Reach a consensus.**

> "If you agree that you can achieve this standard, I'll consider it satisfactory performance."

7. **Ask the employee to make a composite of both work sheets after the meeting.**

> "Please put what we've agreed to on a single *Job Analysis Work Sheet.* When you have completed it, please see that I get a copy for my records."

8. **Thank the employee for his or her efforts.**

> "Thanks for your efforts. I'm looking forward to seeing the composite."

9. **Follow-up by reviewing the composite work sheet with the employee.**

10. **Agree on a trial period.**

> "OK, we'll use these standards for one month. Do you think that will give us enough time to test them thoroughly? We'll get together at that time, say the 16th at 10:00 AM, to see if any changes are needed. Will that time be convenient for you?"

NAME _____ JOB TITLE _____ DATE _____

JOB ANALYSIS WORK SHEET

JOB SUMMARY: _____

LIST THE MAIN TASKS OF YOUR JOB:	SET PRIORITIES A = HIGH B = MEDIUM C = LOW	WRITE STANDARDS — QUALITY — QUANTITY — COST — TIME	IDENTIFY PROBLEMS	ESTABLISH AUTHORITY 1 = COMPLETE 2 = ACT; THEN REPORT 3 = ACT AFTER REPORT

2
Improving Employee Performance Through Counseling

Employees who are constantly late for work, keep dirty work areas, and take too much time for breaks and lunch are a "pain in the neck" for their leaders. The employee usually knows better—so, the problem isn't normally a lack of knowledge of your policies or regulations.

The cause of most poor performance often lies elsewhere. You may have said, "He is just lazy," or "She really should want to stop doing that." But somehow these feelings—especially when expressed to the employee—don't bring about much change. We end up giving formal warnings, and even suspensions. And still little permanent change may take place.

Why? Possibly it has something to do with us—the leaders!

Have you ever seen a leader who had a special knack for handling his or her employees' problems? A super leader who could take marginal workers and turn them around? Very likely you have. For there are many effective leaders who consistently take performance problems and solve them so that they stay solved.

When we look closely at such leaders we see certain things they all do—common sense ways that they handle their people problems. Somehow they have an ability to tell the employee what is expected, to get the employee involved to discover a solution, and to develop with the employee a plan of action that really seems to work.

This is how they do it.

1. Describe specifically the employee's performance problem.

An employee must be made aware of what he or she is presently doing that is improper or incorrect before being expected to improve. In a few cases, of course, the employee may be unaware that his or her performance is poor. It doesn't make much sense to chew out an employee who honestly doesn't know a rule, regulation, or what is required. It would be more appropriate to reprimand ourselves for doing a poor job of training in the first place. When you discuss a situation with the employee, describe performance—not the employee's personality. Stay away from statements such as "You don't work fast enough" or "You have a bad attitude." "Fast enough" is not really specific, and "bad attitude" attacks the employee, rather than giving needed information about the performance.

First, use the "We" technique in describing the situation. It is better to say, "We have a problem," rather than "Your problem is...." After all, if you are the leader, it's your problem too!

Second, talk about performance in specific terms. For example, say "We have a problem because the number of errors has increased 6% during the past month." Or, "Today was the third time this week you were over five minutes late coming back from break."

Often this is not as easy as it sounds. You may know what is wrong, but find it difficult to express the "wrongness" in words. It's usually easier to make a general statement about "poor attitude" or "poor performance" than to be specific.

So stop and ask yourself some questions: "Why do I think this employee has a bad attitude? What has he or she said or done that makes me feel this way?"

Questions like these lead to understanding employee behavior. Behavior is what an employee says or does. If you can define the behavior specifically, you have gone a long way toward solving the performance problem. But this means you must do your homework by giving the performance problem sufficient thought before meeting with the employee.

2. Describe the expected standard of performance.

In Step 1, describe specifically the actual performance. Then, by telling the employee exactly what you expect, you have clearly defined the performance gap.

Actual Performance	Performance Gap	Expected Performance

Here, as before, being specific is the goal. Avoid statements such as, "I expect better performance," "You really need to work harder," and "You ought to change your attitude." "I expect better performance," for instance, is a wishy-washy expression that avoids the "How much is better?" question. "Work harder" and "change your attitude" are not only nonspecific statements, they are also solutions that ignore possible causes.

"What do I expect from this employee?" is the question that needs to be considered carefully before the meeting. Examples of clear performance expectations are:

- "Under standard operating conditions, the maximum error rate allowed is zero."
- "Breaks are ten minutes long."
- "Horseplay of any kind is not allowed."
- "All employees are due at work by 8:00 AM."

3. Explain why the expected standard is important.

"Because it's organization policy" is not a very good justification for a performance standard—at least not from the employee's point of view. It's all right to indicate that something is organizational policy; but go on to give the rationale behind the policy. Most policies exist for good reasons. (If you don't know the reasons, find out before the meeting!)

So consider the regulation or policy from the employee's perspective. Why should the employee arrive at work on time? Why should he or she want to keep his or her area clean? Why is it important for the employee to get back on time from breaks? Why is it critical that employees earn a return on the organization's investment in terms of salary and benefits?

Chances are that your reasons for your concern about the employee's performance (increased production, looking good to your boss, a better raise for you in the future, etc.) are not the same as the employee's. His or her motivation might be fear of losing a job and/or wages, of pressure from fellow workers, of disciplinary action, or of lack of recognition from you, the boss.

Your objective is to foster an internal desire within the employee to improve his or her performance. You can, of course, impose external force to require him or her to change (or to say that he or she will change). And in some cases this may be necessary. But far better results come when the employee decides to improve his or her performance because of a clearly perceived reason.

4. Indicate your concern for improved performance.

It is important that you tell the employee that you, personally, are greatly concerned about the poor performance. After all, you are his or her leader. If the employee feels that substandard performance is "no big deal" to management, he or she probably won't take the situation very seriously.

But poor performance is serious, and in this step you should say so clearly. This lets the employee know exactly what you expect. Leaders with a high level of expectations generally increase the chances of getting high performance.

5. Tell the employee that the situation must change.

Next, express your expectation that the employee's performance will change. If an employee believes that his or her boss is not that concerned about performing to standard, then he or she is not going to be very concerned either. In the press of our duties as leaders, we often don't take the time to spell out how we feel. Thus the employee may not really perceive our concern. So now is the time for you to say exactly what you expect.

6. Determine why performance is below requirements.

A basic law of troubleshooting is, "Don't do anything until you have identified the probable cause of the problem!" This is also sound advice for performance problems. Explore probable causes. Think through the situation in detail before meeting with the employee. Determine what facts you have, and what facts you need. Be clear about the specific questions you should ask during your discussion with the employee.

Look at past records. Is there an observable pattern? Has the problem always existed—or is it recent? Do you have enough information? Do you need to talk with others? What is the employee's record compared with others in your section? In the department? In the organization?

Questions like these may not always tell you with certainty what is causing the performance problem. But they will often give clues to the important questions to be asked during the meeting.

It is remarkable how often we think we know the cause of a performance problem, and then find out during a counseling meeting that there's another reason. The "problem" hasn't changed. We have! This is because new information from the employee can greatly alter our understanding of the problem. Nothing is more frustrating to an employee than to be told to "work harder" when the cause of a problem is something he or she can't control. You will learn much about what the real difficulty is by taking the time to explore the cause. Any solution that's going to work must be based on a sound grasp of this cause. Therefore, before the meeting think through possible causes by asking yourself the following questions:

- Is the employee aware of his or her below-standard performance?
- Does he or she know what is expected?
- Are there any factors this employee cannot control?
- Does he or she lack ability or knowledge?
- Is there a lack of motivation?

Thinking through probable causes before the meeting will give you a chance to get additional information if needed. But remember that these probable causes are only tentative—because your information is incomplete until you talk with the employee. Also remember that your goal is to help the employee discover the cause of the problem during the interview. And you will greatly help the employee understand the problem by asking questions to explore possible causes.

During the meeting, try to ask "open" questions. Open questions begin with the key words "Who," "What," "Where," "When," "How," and "Why." Open questions draw out more information than "closed" questions do. Closed questions open with "Do you...?" "Have you...?" and "Did you...?", and are usually answered with a "Yes" or "No." For example, the question, "What relationship do you see between absenteeism and performance?" is likely to obtain much more information than "Do you see any relationship between absenteeism and your performance?" Though they seem to be the same question, the first one will tend to elicit the desired information, while the second will probably get only a less helpful "yes" or "no" response. You need information to determine causes—and open questions are best for getting it!

To help the employee take a better look at all sides of a problem, you can also ask, "What other things might be causing this situation?" Solutions (the next step) only work if they're aimed at the right cause. That's why you need to spend some quality time in this step. The cause of the problem must be accurately identified before you will have any chance of really correcting the performance problem.

7. Ask the employee for his or her suggested solutions.

There are several reasons why it's important to ask for the employee's solution to the problem.

- The employee might think of a solution that you have not considered that's even better than yours.
- The employee is more likely to change his or her behavior when the solution comes from him or her.

- The employee will see that his or her leader is really concerned about him or her. And this will result in greater trust and better future relations.

Asking for the employee's solution is difficult for many leaders. You were probably promoted to leadership because you were good at solving problems. Naturally, you often have some strong ideas about what an employee should do in order to improve. But you nonetheless need to first ask the employee for his or her solution, while also holding on to your own.

Note also that if you begin by stating your solution, you are likely to initiate the "Yes, but..." game! A "Yes, but" game opens by the leader telling an employee what he or she should do to improve performance. The employee then replies, "Yes, but..." —and gives the leader a number of reasons why the solution will not work. But few people "Yes, but" their own ideas. That's why if you can get the employee to suggest a solution to the problem, you stand a better chance of seeing real change.

Furthermore, although one person may be able to develop several solutions to a problem, two people can often come up with many more. This is because one person's ideas trigger new thoughts in the other. Thus, when you have two people "bouncing ideas off each other," you greatly increase the chances of reaching a good solution.

Remember here that what is important is not so much what the employee says at the meeting, but what he or she does after the meeting to improve performance. And if the employee suggests the solution or is a part of the solution plan, he or she is more likely to view the idea as workable, and accept the responsibility to make sure that the solution is implemented on the job. So ask questions in the meeting such as, "What do you think we should do about this situation?" or "What other things could we do?"

A final suggestion: It is easier to change the environment around a problem than it is to change the employee. For example, if the employee has a "trashy" work area, it may be better to fix the problem by putting a trash can closer to the employee's area!

8. Discuss each solution and offer assistance.

If the employee offers general solutions such as, "I guess I'll just have to try harder," request him or her to be more specific. Thus, ask "How are you going to do that?" or "What are you going to do to improve your performance?" Instead of accepting, "I'll try to improve my performance," inquire, "How much can you improve?" The more specific the improvement target or goal, the better the employee's chances of producing real results.

Now is your opportunity to offer your own ideas if appropriate. This can be done two ways. You might make suggestions to improve the quality of his or her solution. Or even better, you can ask "How to" questions to help enhance the employee's solution: "What would that accomplish?", "How do you see this being done?" or "What can you do to help make that happen?" Such questions will lead the employee to improve the quality of his or her solution. Thus your job in this step is to help the employee develop a specific solution by asking key questions and then offering your assistance.

Few employee ideas are perfect. On the other hand, completely useless solutions are also rare. Most ideas and solutions fall somewhere between perfection and "zero."

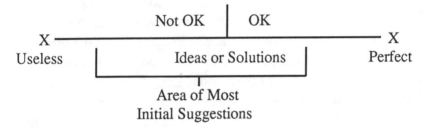

An effective leader recognizes the above situation and focuses the discussion upon the positive values of the employee's suggestion.

Refrain from immediately emphasizing what's wrong with a solution. First, ask questions and discuss the positive points about the employee's idea. Then make suggestions that might improve his or her solution, if you have them.

9. Agree on specific action to be taken by the employee.

Action summaries at the conclusion of the meeting will help produce commitment and will reduce the possibility of later misunderstanding. An action summary makes clear the leader's future expectations by communicating to the employee the specific action that is to be taken. It's called "ensuring follow-up"!

Some leaders make notes on their calendar—in the presence of the employee—showing a follow-up date and the improvement expected. Other leaders have the employee write out a short summary of what he or she will accomplish during the improvement period, with both parties keeping a copy. Whatever method you use, do make a summary—and do follow up!

On the following page is a "Leader's Checklist" that will help you plan and conduct your next employee performance counseling interview.

LEADER'S CHECKLIST
PERFORMANCE COUNSELING INTERVIEW

In reviewing the following checklist, plan what you will say at each step. The examples given are only that—illustrative examples!

1. Describe specifically the employee's performance problem.

- Do your homework; get the facts.
- Use the "We" technique:

    "We have a situation that concerns me."

- Be specific. Ask yourself, "What has the employee done or not done, said or not said, that makes me believe he or she is performing poorly?" For example:

    "Today was the third time this week that you were over five minutes late coming back from break."

- Describe the poor performance; do not attack the employee. Examples:

    "The number of errors has increased 6% during the past month."
    "The records show there have been ten days of absenteeism during the past three months."
    "There are materials all over the floor around your work station."

2. Describe the expected standard of performance.

- Tell the employee exactly what is expected. For example:

    "Under standard operating conditions, the maximum allowed error rate is 1 error per 1000."
    "Breaks are ten minutes."
    "Material should not be on the floor."
    "Horseplay of any kind is not allowed."

3. **Explain why the expected standard is important**.

- Provide the reasons for a policy, regulation, or performance standard.
- Provide "employee" reasons, if possible, i.e., identify reasons that relate to the employee's personal interest. For example:

    "This much absenteeism causes a real hardship for the other people in your section."

    "The policy of 'no horseplay' is for your protection. It could prevent you from having an accident that might cripple you for the rest of your life."

    "We must meet performance standards so that the organization will continue to stay in business, and you will continue to have a job."

4. **Indicate your concern for improved performance**.

    Example: "I am—and always will be—deeply concerned about performance. It's important to the organization, it's important to me, and it's important to you."

5. **Tell the employee that the situation must change**.

    For example, "To me, excellence is a way of life. The organization believes in it; and my employees must not only believe in excellence, but practice it!"

6. **Determine why performance is below requirements**.

- Before and during the meeting, ask yourself:

    "How does this employee's record compare with those of others in the section or department?"

    "Are there any observable patterns in this employee's poor performance?" (e.g., Mondays or Fridays? Holidays? A particular time of year?)

    "How long has this problem existed?"

"When did it start?"

"Where is the problem occurring?"

"When and where does this employee *not* have the problem?"

"Have any changes occurred that might have caused the problem?"

"Are there any other symptoms of this problem?"

- Ask the employee

    "What do you feel is causing this situation?"

    "What other major reasons do you see?"

    "What are the things that interfere with your performance?"

7. Ask the employee for his or her suggested solutions.

"What are your ideas about this situation?"

"What suggestions do you have for increasing your performance?"

"What can you do to resolve this situation?"

"What else could you do?"

8. Discuss each solution, and offer assistance.

- Focus on specific solutions, not general ones.

    "What would that accomplish?"

    "How do you see this being done?"

    "What can you do to help make that happen?"

    "What can be done to make this work?"

    "Do you see any problems that might occur in carrying that out?"

- Offer your assistance.

    "How can I help?"

9. Agree on specific action to be taken by the employee.

> For example: "This has been a good discussion. I appreciate your ideas and solutions. We have agreed that you will..., and I will...(summarize the solution). Is that correct? Good. We'll get together in 2 weeks (making a note of date and time on your calendar), and discuss your progress. I feel good about your commitment to improve and I know you can do it."

3

Following Up Persistent Employee Problems

When initially dealing with a problem employee, you can use all the proper techniques—but sometimes they don't work. The employee shows little or no improvement, and you are still faced with the problem.

It could be that when you first talked with the employee you missed the real cause of the problem, and thus the remedy you developed was the "right solution for the wrong problem." Or it might have been more rewarding for the employee not to improve—maybe he or she likes taking off a couple extra days per month. Or, improvement may involve negative social consequences. For example, an employee might have received a lot of heat from a buddy for not calling in "sick" to go fishing.

Or the initial cause of the problem could even have been you, his supervisor! You may have good intentions of following up a problem and giving positive feedback at the first sign of improvement. But somehow time slips away and you just never get around to it. So, you've still got the same problem to face. Again!

Another reason for persistent problems with an employee is that we tend to let the problem continue long past the point when the employee should have been counseled or disciplined. Maybe we hope the problem would just correct itself. But more often than not it won't go away so easily!

The fact is that most of us avoid doing things we dislike; and few of us enjoy counseling an employee or taking disciplinary action. Yet often these are necessary steps. If we don't follow through, we become part of the problem. And we can even make the situation worse by not following up on a persistent problem. Other, more conscientious employees are usually aware of the breakdown and wonder why "somebody" doesn't do something. Delayed action by a leader can affect the work of everyone. So when follow-up action is necessary, do it! And in following up, take an extra hard look at the probable cause of the problem, and, if possible, develop some new solutions. An im-

portant factor in dealing with persistent problems is the leader's emotions. We are human beings with feelings. One feeling we have in
employee problem situations is disappointment: disappointment with
the employee, and disappointment with ourselves because we failed to
handle the problem successfully the first time. And with disappointment comes anger—anger that is often directed at the employee. It's
this feeling of anger that must be controlled in the counseling meetings, for becoming angry at the employee solves nothing. In fact, it
usually makes the situation worse. But there is a tested way we can
productively deal with both our negative emotions and the employee's
need for help. This method is as follows:

1. Describe the situation and state what is expected.

In specific, exact terms, describe the problem you have observed.
One of the best techniques known to effective leaders is to describe
the situation that has occurred and not to attack the employee as a person. To tell your employee that he or she is "lazy" or a "real goof-off"
is neither specific nor descriptive of the situation. Your feelings about
the employee may be in part correct; but that is not the point! Attack-
ing the individual rather than addressing the situation will not produce
change. Remember, the purpose of counseling is to change the
employee's behavior on the job. It is not to punish him or her.

After describing the problem in specific terms, tell the employee,
again, exactly what is expected. Stay away from making comments
such as, "You're not working hard enough," "You're taking too many
days off," or "You can't be tardy as often as you are." These statements are too general and don't specifically describe the standard of
performance.

2. Review previous discussions.

Before the counseling meeting, review the employee's file. Then in
your meeting, briefly summarize for the employee the previous discussions you have had with him or her. Include in your summary both the

problem cause(s) that was identified, and the previously agreed-to solutions(s).

3. Express concern over insufficient improvement.

Let the employee know exactly how you feel about the lack of improvement. If you don't communicate your concern, the chances are that he or she won't be very concerned either!

4. Explain the consequences of continued lack of improvement.

Since this is probably the second time (at least) that you have talked with this employee, the consequences of nonperformance should be greater. Determine the consequences, or disciplinary action, before meeting with him or her so you are prepared for this step. Remember, there may be a payoff for the employee not to change. Therefore, the consequences of continued lack of improvement must be clearly stated. This step lets the employee know that improved performance is absolutely necessary.

5. Listen and then respond to feelings.

At this point the employee may become defensive, argumentative, or even hostile. And your job now is to listen for feelings. Establish rapport by telling the employee you understand how he or she feels. You probably won't agree that the employee should be angry; but you can understand why he or she is upset. Get the employee's feelings out in the open by saying, "You seem to be..." (name the feeling you observe--angry, upset, sad, etc.). Again, listen, and then say, "I can understand how you might feel that way." If the employee has a chance to vent his or her feelings without criticism, he or she is usually more receptive to the problem-solving steps that follow.

6. Ask why performance has not improved.

Since you may have missed the cause of the problem during past meetings with the employee, it is now extremely important to help him or her determine the most probable actual cause of the problem. Before the meeting, carefully analyze the situation to discover any possible clues for the continued difficulty. These clues can help you formulate questions to be used to explore the cause with the employee. You might say, "We have reviewed this situation in the past, but nothing seems to have worked. Though we tried to analyze the cause of the problem, we may have missed it. What additional causes do you see for this continued problem?"

7. Ask employee for possible solutions, and discuss them.

It's much better if you can get the employee to suggest a new solution. Or in light of new and tougher consequences, he or she may reaffirm the previous solution. But whatever solution is reached, it should if possible come from the employee. This will greatly increase the employee's acceptance of the action he or she must take after the meeting. If an employee says, "I'll just have to try harder!", don't simply accept that as the solution. Ask additional questions to help the employee specify how—what he or she will do—to "try harder." Help the employee be as specific as possible regarding the future action that will be taken.

8. Agree on a solution, and a timetable for improvement.

Discuss the employee's ideas for improvement; add your own suggestions if you have any. And if appropriate, set up a timetable with specific targets for improvement.

9. Indicate additional disciplinary action that will be taken if there is no improvement.

In this step, communicate to the employee the negative consequences if significant improvement does not occur. Be very specific, not general, while describing the future disciplinary action. Avoid statements such as, "If you don't improve, things are going to get a lot worse for you." Instead, state exactly what the action will be, and when it will occur.

10. Express confidence that the employee will improve.

Let the employee know that you think he or she can improve! Employees often rise to the expectations of their supervisor. This will also end the meeting on a positive and encouraging note.

The *Leader's Checklist* on the following page provides examples of a leader's responses at each of the key steps outlined above.

LEADER'S CHECKLIST
FOLLOWING UP PERSISTENT PROBLEMS

1. Describe the situation and state what is expected.

- Describe the present unsatisfactory performance

    Example: "The client complaint rate at your work station for the past two weeks has been consistently above our minimum acceptable standards. We received two complaints this week: one concerning the telephone ringing excessively before being answered, and another from a client who was placed on hold for over five minutes without being checked on."

- State desired performance

    "As you know, we cannot exceed one complaint per 100 contacts. In addition, the client should not be left on hold for more than one minute without an acknowledgement."

2. Review previous discussions.

"Four weeks ago, we met and discussed the high client complaint rate at your work station. At that time you felt the problem was caused by insufficient training. I spent extra time with you the following week and your rate improved. Now two weeks later, unfortunately, the complaint rate is right back where it was."

3. Express concern over insufficient improvement.

"This situation deeply concerns me!"

4. Explain the consequences of continued lack of improvement.

"Continued client complaints will not be tolerated. If we cannot make rapid improvement in this situation, then...(describe specific consequences)."

5. **Listen and respond to feelings.**

   - Name the feelings observed

     "You seem to be..." (angry, upset, sad, etc.).

   - Listen—and do not interrupt
   - Acknowledge the employee's feelings

     "I can understand why you might feel that way."

6. **Ask why performance has not improved.**

   "Why do you think this situation recurred?" "How do you see that as causing the situation?" "Is there anything else that could be causing this situation?"

7. **Ask employee for possible solutions, and discuss them.**

   "What can we do about this?" "What else could be done?" "How are you going to do that?"

8. **Agree on a solution, and a timetable for improvement.**

   "Then you have agreed to.... Let's get back together on the 27th at 10:30 a.m. to see how you are doing."

9. **Indicate additional disciplinary action that will be taken if there is no improvement.**

   "If the complaint rate is not reduced to an average rate at or below the required standard during the next four weeks, you will be placed on formal probation."

10. **Express confidence that the employee will improve.**

    "I'm confident that you will be able to make the needed changes in order to perform even better than standards. Let me know if there is anything else I can do to help."

4
Handling Employee Complaints

When an employee charges into your office or area furious about something you did, it is hard to remain calm. And when an employee is upset, unhappy, or angry about something, it is easy for him or her to use language normally considered inappropriate. At this point, some leaders assert their authority and chew out the employee for being "disrespectful." But look at the cost of this approach.

An employee who leaves your area with a chip on the shoulder can create ill will among other employees, negatively affect morale and efficiency—and may be a potential safety problem "looking for a place to happen"!

The best way to handle this kind of situation is to deal immediately with the employee's feelings. Before taking action on the situation he or she is concerned about, take action that considers his or her emotions. Take the right kind of action—action that produces positive results.

Here is a method that works:

1. Listen! Listen! Listen!

Real listening is hard work! If someone else is angry, it's difficult to keep from taking it personally and becoming angry ourselves. You may think you already know what the employee should do. And this makes it doubly difficult to keep from jumping in, cutting him or her off, and telling the employee what you think or feel.

But if you bite your tongue and listen, without interrupting, you can:

a. Learn more about the situation.

b. Demonstrate to the employee that you really care about him or her.

c. Give yourself more time to think about how the situation can best be handled.

    d. Give the employee an opportunity to express his or her feel-
       ings, thus reducing the emotional level.

As you listen, be sure you have stopped doing whatever it was you
were doing, make good eye contact, nod your head appropriately, and
respond with, "I see" or "Uh huh." Encourage the employee to continue to talk as long as is necessary to "ventilate" his or her feelings.

2. Summarize what you think you heard.

In this step, you repeat to the employee, in your own words, what
you think you heard—and then ask whether what you heard was correct. This accomplishes three things:

    a. What you thought you heard may not be what was really said.

    b. You show the employee that you do care about him or her.

    c. You let the employee know you really do understand what he
       or she is upset about.

For example, if an employee bursts into your office and starts shouting
about a new job assignment, listen first. Then, when the employee has
finished talking, you repeat what you think you heard. For example,
you might say, "Let me see if I understand. You're upset because you
were assigned to another location when you were prepared to go to
your regular work? Is that correct?"

But this is not as easy as it might seem. It's sometimes hard to listen
to even one or two minutes of emotional statements without interrupting. It's even harder to remember all that was said. But this practice
forces you to listen, because you know that you will have to sum up
and repeat what you just heard. And when you summarize, you will
show the employee that you listened, that you understand, and—most
important—that you do care about him or her!

3. Acknowledge the employee's feelings.

Acknowledging your employee's feelings by saying "I understand how you feel" lets the employee know that you care about the way he or she feels. It is not agreement, but understanding. You're not saying, "Yes, you should be mad," but rather that you respect his or her right to have such feelings.

4. Ask diagnostic questions.

An effective leader is also a good troubleshooter. And good trouble-shooters ask questions to diagnose the cause of a problem. In some cases you may already know the full details of the situation. But in other cases, the employee may not know that you know. Thus asking questions at this point may not only provide you with some additional information, the employee will also know that you really do understand the situation.

When you ask the employee for additional information, ask "open" questions that begin with the words, "Who, What, Where, When, How and Why?"

Open questions can give you more information for diagnosing the situation. And asking open questions can not only give you additional facts and communicate to the employee that you really do understand the situation, they also help the employee to better understand the problem.

5. Ask for the employee's suggestions.

By this time you probably feel you have a good idea of what should be done to remedy the situation. And that's what makes this step so difficult! It is hard not to jump in with your solution! But it is a great deal better, in the long run, if you can get the employee to tell you what should be done. Employees are usually more open to their own ideas than to yours. And if the employee's solution is in line with yours, why not let him or her suggest it? In fact, leaders who use this technique say that many times the employee's idea or solution turns out to be better than their own.

6. Present your position.

If you agree with the employee's idea or solution to the problem, say so. If you don't, clearly state your position, and give the reason(s) why. Try to stay away from the "It's organizational policy" kind of answer. Most policies exist for a reason. Employees respond better if you give common sense reasons for your position.

7. Decide on specific follow up.

At this point, summarize the discussion, and agree on the action that will be taken. This helps to prevent later misunderstanding by making sure you and the employee agree on what will happen after the discussion.

8. Thank the employee.

Thank the employee? Thank an employee who barged into your office and raised his or her voice? Yes!

For it's far better that the employee talked to you than not. Angry or upset employees are poor workers. They can cause reduced production and create lower morale. Thanking the employee for coming to see you helps to:

　　a. make sure that he or she feels free to see you again.

　　b. improve your image as a leader who cares about your
　　　　employees.

　　c. end the meeting on a positive, morale-building note.

This eight-step method for handling complaints comes from the experience of leaders who care about their employees—leaders whose main responsibility is to get the job done through others. It's from leaders who know their organizations don't run by themselves—they need employees. Using this method will help you be a better leader, not just "a boss."

On the following page is a *Leader's Checklist,* with suggestions for your role while handling your employees' complaints.

HANDLING COMPLAINTS
LEADER'S CHECKLIST

1. Listen! Listen! Listen!

- Focus attention on the employee.
- Nod your head to show understanding.
- Say "Yes," "I see," or "Uh huh," as the employee talks.

2. Summarize what you think you heard.

"Let me see if I understand. You are upset because..."
Repeat in your own words what you heard. "Is that correct?"

3. Acknowledge the employee's feelings.

"I understand how you feel."
"I can appreciate your concern."

4. Ask diagnostic questions.

"Who is—and isn't—involved?"
"What has occurred?"
"Where is the problem occurring?"
"Where is the problem not occurring?"
"When did it start?"
"When was everything OK?"
"Why do you feel it happened?"

5. Ask for the employee's suggestions.

"What do you think we should do about the situation?"
"What other suggestions do you have?"

6. Present your position.

If the employee's suggestion in Step 5 is acceptable, say, "That sounds like a good idea." If the suggestion does not seem appropriate, present your position. "I'm sorry; I really wish we could do that. But we can't, because....
What I suggest we do is...."

7. Decide on specific follow up.

"Now let's see. I will.... And you will.... Do we agree?"

8. Thank the employee.

"I really appreciate your coming to me with your concerns. And if you have any other questions about this, please feel free to talk with me about them."

5
Motivating Employees

Employees are motivated to excel for many different reasons. Thus it is difficult to establish hard and fast motivational rules. But because people are similar in so many ways, we can make some general statements about motivating our employees.

For example, if your boss informs you that she is going to give you a big raise because of your outstanding contributions during the past year, you will probably feel—at least for the moment—highly motivated.

However, suppose you are already making big bucks in your job, yet you feel unappreciated because your boss never takes the time to tell you how much she appreciated your work. Then odds are that a sincere compliment might mean just as much—maybe even more—than a bigger paycheck.

Yet, some people feel uncomfortable receiving compliments. For these employees, something different, like a more challenging job, or even a different job, might be a better motivator. In short, employees are motivated by their needs, not ours.

So how do you motivate your employees? First, by knowing something about the dynamics of motivation. And second, by using this knowledge appropriately. Let's look, then, at some general theories of motivation.

Theories of Motivation

Of the many persons who have contributed to our knowledge about motivation, Douglas McGregor, Abraham Maslow, and Frederick Herzberg have been particularly helpful.

The figure on the next page suggests how the three main theories contribute to our understanding of motivation.

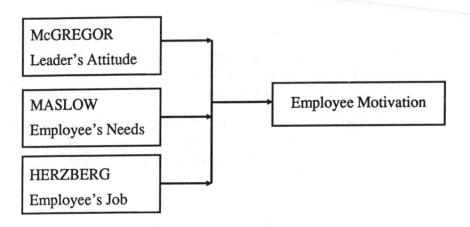

Figure 1. Theories of motivation.

Douglas McGregor studied the relationship between a **leader's attitude** toward his or her employees and the resultant employee behavior. Maslow investigated **employee needs**. And Herzberg looked at how the **employee's job** affects his or her motivation. All three of these factors—the leader's attitude, the employee's needs, and the employee's job itself—greatly affect employee motivation.

Douglas McGregor: The Leader's Attitude. McGregor believed that there are two types of leaders. One type believes that an employee works hard only because he or she has to, and will goof off if given a chance. McGregor labeled this type of leader "X." He also felt there is a second group of leaders, who believe that employees work productively because they enjoy their work. He labeled these leaders "Y."

McGregor emphasized that a leader's attitude toward employees affects the way he or she manages. For example, if you believe that your people work only because they are made to work, you will probably be a very controlling boss. That is, you will establish strict job standards, set up job controls, observe and monitor your people carefully, and let them know that they are being watched. On the other hand, if you believe that your employees can be trusted to do their jobs, you will tend to be less controlling. You won't need to control your people because they will control themselves. Now whether or not your employees need to be controlled is not the point—it's whether or not you believe they do. What you believe to be true tends to result in your employees becoming what you expect. It's a little like raising children. If you expect children to be dishonest and therefore treat them as if they were dishonest, they often become dishonest.

The same thing is true with adult workers. If you believe that employees have to be watched, monitored, controlled, and forced to work, then they tend to become that way. But if you expect your people to do their work, then they usually will. A lot of what happens in terms of an employee's morale is simply due to your attitude about him or her.

Let's look at an example. Suppose an employee takes excessive time for his morning break. An "X" type leader will say to this employee, "You're late. Don't you know that breaks are only ten minutes? Get back to work—and in the future, I'll be watching you!" Here, the leader believes that he or she has to keep a close eye on this employee in order to prevent future problems. In short, there is a lack of trust that employees will behave appropriately on the job. And this lack of trust is due to the way this particular leader views his or her employees. As a result, the employee, not feeling trusted, is more likely to behave in untrustworthy ways in the future.

A less controlling leader might say to this employee, "I'm surprised that you are late from break. What happened?" Here, the implication is that there may be a legitimate reason why the employee was late returning from break, and that the employee is self-motivated in wanting to return to his job on time. The leader has clearly communicated his or her standards ("I'm surprised that you are late returning from break") and has demonstrated his or her concern for the employee's situation ("What happened?").

But your attitudes and beliefs about how your employees feel about work is only part of the motivational puzzle. Another piece of the puzzle involves your employees' needs and how they are motivated to fulfill those needs.

Abraham Maslow: Employee Needs. Abraham Maslow studied highly motivated people to determine why they are successful. He discovered that individuals have a series of needs, and that they can be arranged in a hierarchy of ascending order. These are: physiological needs, safety needs, the need to belong and/or be loved, esteem needs, and self-actualization needs.

Figure 2. Maslow's hierarchy.

Let's look at these needs in more detail.

Physiological needs are the most basic; they include the needs for food, water, sleep, warmth, and sex. Maslow suggested that employees are motivated to meet these primary needs before they are motivated by the needs at the next level. For example, if you are walking across a desert and haven't had water in two days, you are going to be most strongly motivated to satisfy your thirst. Until you obtain water you are not going to be interested in other needs. On the job, physiological needs can be satisfied by paying employees fair salaries that enable them to pay their water bills, purchase food, and keep their houses warm.

Safety needs include both the need to be free from imminent danger and the need for security. On the job, safety needs include a work environment that is not hazardous to health, safe equipment, and freedom from worry about losing one's job. Thus, if you are genuinely worried about losing your job, you are not going to be motivated by higher-level needs. But if you are dying from lack of water (physiological need), you are not going to be much concerned about losing your job.

Belonging and/or love needs include the need to feel a part of a group, to receive affection from others, and to be in a loving relationship. For example, do you remember what it was like when you first came to work for your organization? Remember the feelings of uneasiness when you first arrived? No one knew you, and you didn't feel included as a part of the work group. The lack of belonging produces strong needs that most people are motivated to fulfill. Maslow believed that all individuals will try to satisfy the need to belong—but only when their physiological needs and safety needs have already been satisfied.

Esteem needs. Maslow stated that all people have a need for the esteem of others, as well as a need for self-esteem. On the job, this need is usually met by different forms of recognition. Examples are giving an employee a sincere compliment for a task well done, providing him or her with a private parking place, asking an employee's advice, or assigning him or her to a special task group.

Esteem given by others, especially when received in the employee's formative years, usually results in self-esteem. If an employee does not receive positive feedback as a child, then he or she may become either a person who is never able to get enough compliments, or one who seems uncomfortable receiving compliments. In either case, it is necessary for a leader to attack such a deficiency with sincere positive feedback.

Self-actualization needs are seen by Maslow as the highest or "peak" experience. This level results from having all of our other need levels met while we are engaged in a satisfying job.

As an example, at the turn of the century there were a number of companies that still manufactured old-fashioned pump organs. But as pianos became more and more popular, pump organs in the "parlor" went out of style. Today you would be hard-pressed to buy a new pump organ.

But there is still a man in Virginia's Shenandoah Valley who makes pump organs—one at a time. He cuts his own walnut, and spends hours sanding, rubbing, and finishing each by hand. This man is happy doing what he does. In other words, he is self-actualized because his work is personally interesting, rewarding, challenging and important to him.

When your employees come to work because they take joy in what they do, they can become self-actualized. Part of your job as a leader is to make sure, as much as possible, that their other need levels are being met so they can operate at this peak level of being. One last point: employees don't arrive one day at their highest level of functioning and simply remain there forever. Suppose you are in the middle of an exciting, challenging and joyful task. The phone rings, and it's your boss. She is not happy. She wants to see you in her office—now! Suddenly, you no longer feel self-actualized. You are now concerned about your safety needs.

Frederick Herzberg: The Employee's Job. Herzberg interviewed many employees. First, he asked them to think of the times that they were happy on the job and to describe the events that made them feel happy. Next he asked them to think of times when they had been unhappy on the job and again, to describe the events that produced those feelings.

From these interviews Herzberg discovered something remarkable: the things that made people happy on the job were not necessarily the same things that made them unhappy! Herzberg learned that employees listed five factors that led to the most happiness and satisfaction on the job. He called them "Satisfiers." They were:

1. Achievement

2. Recognition

3. Work itself

4. Responsibility

5. Advancement

But the factors that created the most unhappiness on the job were, except in the area of "Recognition," different. Herzberg called these "Dissatisfiers." They were:

1. Poor organizational policy and administration

2. Technically incompetent supervisor

3. Lack of recognition

4. Salary perceived as being unfair

5. Poor interpersonal relations with supervisor

Thus Herzberg discovered that having good organizational policy, technically competent supervisors, and a fair salary didn't in themselves make people happy. Having these items satisfied just kept them from being unhappy. He believed that it is necessary to improve the way that the employee is treated, eliminating dissatisfiers, so the employee can be motivated by using the satisfiers. Note that the factors that employees said made them happy were those that had to do with the job—i.e., achievement in the job, recognition for a job well done, the job itself, more responsibility, and advancement to a higher level. But the factors that made people unhappy had to do with how they were treated. Only "Recognition" appeared in the top five of both lists as a factor causing happiness, or, in its absence, unhappiness. That is why, as we will see later, employee recognition is a very powerful motivational tool.

Application

Theories of motivation can give you important clues as to how to motivate your employees and yourself. In the following section you will see how to apply motivational theory to the question of what you as a leader can do to increase employee motivation, with reference to the employee's job, the organization, and your actions toward your employee.

The Employee's Job. You can have a significant positive impact on the morale of your employees by matching their jobs to them as much as possible. An effective leader modifies jobs to fit people, not people to fit jobs. And small changes in a job can result in large changes in motivation! You can look for ways to make your employees' jobs more interesting, create challenging and responsible jobs for them, reduce the stress level as much as possible, protect their status, organize the work so one task is completed before another is started, and make sure that their jobs provide visible feedback of results.

1.   Create interesting jobs for your employees. Granted, there are restrictions as to what you can do in restructuring an employee's job. But if you believe that there is nothing you can do to make a job more interesting for an employee, then that is exactly what will happen to his or her motivation—nothing. So take the time to talk with your employees to learn about their likes and dislikes regarding job tasks. You may find that it is quite possible to enhance an employee's job and make it more interesting.

Sometimes you can reverse specialization by consolidating tasks being done by several people into one person's job. You can also consider cross-training people within your section or department to jobs that, because of their newness, are more interesting. A key question to ask is, "What can this employee do uncommonly well?" Chances are that what an employee does well is also something that he or she enjoys doing. If you can modify a job so that the employee can better utilize his or her strengths, you can probably produce a motivated employee.

2.   Create challenging jobs for your employees. It is possible to have an interesting job that is not especially challenging. A job tends to be interesting because it is something that the employee likes to do. A job is challenging when it allows the employee to work to his or her full potential. The best job for an employee is both interesting and challenging. To create a challenging job, assign tasks that provide opportunities for growth and development.

3.   Create responsible jobs. Do everything you can to make the job of each employee in your section or department appear special in the eyes of all employees. Never refer to an employee's job as being "simple," or "a job that anyone can do," or a "no-brainer job"! To the employee, the job may not be simple at all.

Think through the reasons why each employee's job is important to the organization. Then make sure the employee understands those reasons and, thus, the real importance of his or her job.

4.   Reduce the stress level in your employees' jobs. Impossible deadlines, excessive workloads, and constant interruptions all create unhealthy stress for your employees. If you are part of the stress problem, then it is up to you to become part of the solution.

Make sure that deadlines are realistic. If the work load is excessive, document the need for additional people, or say "No!" to unrealistic demands that ask your employees to do more than is possible. Help your people to manage interruptions by having them keep a log of when and how they are interrupted. Then examine this log to determine if there are patterns that can be changed to help the employee reduce unnecessary interruptions.

In the long run, continuous stress is extremely unhealthy for your employees. It is up to you to monitor them to make sure that their job requirements are reasonable.

5.   Protect your employee's status. Being reprimanded in private for something you did is bad enough. Being chewed out in public is even worse—for it affects the employee's status. It can be difficult, at times, if an employee does something you think is especially bad, not to reprimand him or her on the spot. But unless there is a safety problem, it is usually better to wait until you can talk with the employee in private. And when you do, take the time to find out why the employee behaved as he or she did before reprimanding him or her. You may discover that, from the employee's point of view, there was a legitimate reason for doing what was done. An employee's morale is seriously undermined by leaders who don't take time to listen actively.

Another way to diminish an employee's status is to give him or her a task to do, and then step in and do it yourself. If you take over a previously delegated task, you are demonstrating to his or her fellow workers that you lack confidence in this employee.

6.   Organize the employee's work so that he or she can complete one task before moving on to another. One of the things that gives an employee good feelings on the job is to complete a task before moving on to another. If the work is set up so that this rarely happens, a great opportunity for motivation is lost. As much as possible, you should try to arrange the work flow so that your employees can complete each task before moving on to the next one.

7.   Provide visible feedback on the results of task completion. Try to structure the work flow so that your employees can see the results of their completed tasks. If an employee does not receive visible and immediate feedback on his or her efforts, it is not only detrimental to the employee's morale, but it also prevents the employee from correcting his or her behavior.

The Organization. The organization and its policies and procedures have a great impact on your employees' motivation. Following are some suggestions that are often helpful in reducing the impact of organizational problems that hinder morale.

1.   **Make the value of organizational benefits clear.** Although there is not much that you can do about your organization's benefits, the way that they are presented has a great deal to do with how they are viewed by your employees. Do you know how much employee benefits cost your organization? Do your employees understand what their benefits are worth? Most employees don't really know how much it costs today to fund their retirement and pay for their vacation time, holidays, sick time and medical insurance.

In most cases it is fairly easy for you to find out what employee benefits cost. Talk to your personnel people, add up the figures, and make sure that your employees know exactly what their benefit costs are per year. It is usually true that if employees don't know the expense involved they won't fully value the benefits.

2.   **Enhance opportunities for salary increases.** You may not have complete control over your employees' salaries. But there are ways to compensate. You can carefully evaluate your people and develop them in areas where improvement may be needed. Then as much as possible make sure that they are paid fairly for their performance. And even where there is not much chance to obtain additional money for a specific employee, the fact that you tried will enhance this employee's feelings of worth.

One of the best ways to ensure that your employees are paid fairly is to document their accomplishments. Keep an anecdotal file for each employee as a place to record key accomplishments during the year. Then at the end of the year, you will have the necessary information to conduct a fair analysis of the employee's performance, and you will be able to suggest appropriate salary increases.

The anecdotal file will also help you to explain to your employees why they did or did not receive raises, to justify the amount of salary increase, and to suggest areas for needed improvement. Remember that it isn't so much the amount of the employee's pay increase that is important as it is the employee's perception of the fairness with which he or she has been treated. It is far easier for the employee to accept less than what is expected if there are clear reasons why it is less, and if the employee is not taken by surprise.

3.   Encourage technological growth in the employees' jobs. In recent years there has been tremendous growth in job technology. Innovation is rampant with new, faster computers, computer networking, robotics, FAX and FAX systems tied to computers, and miniaturization. These are just some of the changes that are having a major impact on our employees' jobs. Not only are the tools they use to do their jobs changing, but their jobs are changing too.

One of your key tasks as a leader is to ensure that your employees are involved in lifelong learning. This means that you need to be a lifelong trainer! Not that you will always have to do the training, but you will need to manage the employees' training.

For example, make sure that your employees receive journals that publish articles relevant to their jobs. Send people off site for training when appropriate. Bring in technical representatives and set up mini-training sessions where needed. Get help from your training department to obtain needed resources. Whatever it takes, keep your employees up-to-date on the changes that they will encounter in their jobs.

4.   Help your employees make a difference in the organization. The basic question that must be answered here and then communicated to your employees is, "How does each person's job affect the organization's success?" Do your people clearly know how their jobs help make the organization prosperous? It makes no difference if the end result is a product or a service. Your employees must feel that what they do or don't do makes a real difference. Your job as a leader is to determine the relationship between your employees' jobs and the organization's final output—and then to share this information with each employee.

5.   Make sure that co-workers are friendly and supportive. You can establish a friendly and supportive work climate. For example, with new employees, first determine their outside interests or hobbies. Then when you introduce them to their co-workers, establish "interest" links between the new employees and their fellow employees. You can also set up a "buddy" system by assigning each new employee to a senior employee. You can also ask your people to play a part in the selection of new employees who will be a part of their work team.

With existing employee groups, develop their team spirit by working with them to create overall team goals. When individuals within a team work together to produce their group's goals, they become much more motivated to succeed. You can also train your employees in interpersonal communication skills. Of course it is nice when you can get the training department to conduct a half-day communications program for you. But if you can't, then do it yourself! Select any good book on interpersonal communications skills (or read Chapter 15 in this book). You will find information on asking questions, paraphrasing, summarizing, and listening skills. After you have studied these techniques, look for opportunities to teach them to your employees, either individually or in small groups.

Last, for truly effective work teams, make sure that they are taught problem-solving and decision-making skills. Problem-solving skills like Situational and Causal Analysis, and decision-making skills such as Determining Alternatives, Force Field Analysis, the Herringbone Technique, and Potential Problem Avoidance are all tools that will help your team work together more cooperatively and effectively.

Remember that long-term happiness and high morale are as much the result of what your employees experience with each other as how you treat them. You can't just say, "Be happy!" Instead, you must create a climate where they can support and help one another. And you must teach them the skills to do so.

6.   Arrange acceptable working hours. Today's work force is a great deal different from what it was in the past. Single-parent families, working mothers, and different values all add up to the need for more flexible work hours. You may not be able to change the working hours of your employees or allow them to work out of their homes using computers and modems because of your organization's policies. But if you can, it may make your job easier—and also more difficult. It is easier because it can reduce the amount of your time spent in direct supervision, lessen overcrowding in your section or department and provide you with employees you may not have been able to hire before.

But it is harder because it will be very difficult for you to observe both good performance and problem areas. In addition, employees who work out of their homes need solid works habits and self-discipline to maintain productivity. Employees also have social needs, and when they work alone these needs may result in lower morale.

7.   Provide good physical working conditions. Inadequate temperature control, excessive noise level, unpleasant surroundings, and an unsafe environment are just a few of the things that can create poor morale in your section or department. Even though working conditions are really an "organizational" factor, you can often effect improvements that may be needed. With strong legal penalties for unsafe working conditions, and much organizational experience in creating pleasant environments for employees, it is often fairly easy to obtain funding for better working conditions. But it is still up to you to make this happen! You are the one who will need to write up problems for upper management to consider. And you are the one who will need to follow up to make sure that things get done. But remember that improving the area where your people work will not make them happy, it will only keep them from being unhappy.

8.   Help your employees obtain deserved promotions. It doesn't take long for the word to get around that you are concerned about the future promotional opportunities of your employees. It also doesn't take long for them to learn that you would rather not have them promoted because you might lose them to another section or have to train their replacements.

So spend time meeting one-on-one with each of your employees and determine their job goals. If promotion is a realistic goal for a particular employee, then your job is to do everything possible to help him or her to achieve that promotion.

There are many things you can do in the present to help prepare employees for the future. You can assign them to special tasks such as leading one of your meetings, training a new employee, or being the team leader on a special project. If organizational exposure is important in order to obtain a promotion, you can "volunteer" an employee to serve on a special organizational task force or committee. You can also assign special jobs to the employee that require him or her to interact with people in other departments in the organization.

Organizational restrictions on promotions may keep you from promoting an employee even if he or she deserves a promotion. But if you have demonstrated a genuine concern for your employee's future by doing what you can do, you will find that the employee is much more accepting of the realities of the organization's restrictions.

The Leader's Direct Actions. Your direct actions toward your employees have a tremendous effect on their motivation, often more than the job or organizational modifications described above.

1. Share your expectations. Employees will tend to live up to your expectations. If you expect a lot, you will usually get a lot. On the other hand, if you don't expect much from an employee, that's what you will probably get! If you feel that your employees are not very creative, you're not likely to ask for their suggestions or ideas. But if you expect them to have ideas about their jobs, you are more likely to get good ideas—simply because you ask for them. Leaders who ask for better ideas develop employees who think of them.

2. **Be fair.** Employees expect to be treated fairly. And what's fair in their view is defined by them, not you. The problem of fairness is complicated by the tension between the need to treat all employees the same, while recognizing that all employees are different. Nonetheless, there are important things you can do to increase the chances that you will be perceived as fair.

Look at two examples:

a. Joe works for you. He is one of the nicest people you know. He has been with the organization about two years, and he has a very positive attitude about his job, the organization, and you. You find that it is easy to give him much of your time and attention, because he is so nice to be around.

b. Betty works for you. She has worked for your organization for 35 years, and she is nearing retirement. You find it is similarly easy to give her special time and attention, since she has been a loyal and dedicated employee for so many years.

In examining these two examples, you may feel that your actions in both cases are fair. Your other employees may feel that your conduct in the first case is unfair, while they accept your preferential treatment of the 35-year veteran. Some basic principles underlie the examples above:

a. A leader simply cannot treat everybody the same. People are different. They have different needs. Give to each what you perceive he or she needs at the time, but don't play favorites! This means, "Give to each what he or she needs", not "Give to each what you need." Playing favorites to meet your needs is, in fact, discrimination.

Communicate your rationale to your group when you are giving particular individuals what may appear to be preferential treatment. And don't get trapped by the employee's question, "Well, you did it for Mary. Why can't you do it for me?" Mary, in all likelihood, has different needs, and different needs require different treatment.

b. When resources are limited, use the laws of probability to determine who gets a desired resource. For example, flip a coin, draw straws, or draw names to find out who will receive a desired assignment, who has to work overtime, or who has to operate the phones on Christmas or Hanukkah.

c. Rules and policies are created to help make jobs easier. But they may have to be temporarily altered in order to be truly fair to particular employees in specific circumstances.

3.   Involve your employees in goal setting. Effective leaders usually set goals *with* their employees, rather than *for* them. If you know that your employees like what they do for a living, then you will more likely feel comfortable allowing them to determine some of their own goals. But, if you believe that your employees don't like to work, then you will be more apt to set goals for them.

This doesn't mean that it isn't perfectly appropriate for you to set goals for an employee occasionally. If, for example, your employee is new to his or her job and doesn't have enough experience to create his or her own goals, then you will probably need to determine them. Or you may choose to set goals for a problem employee who has demonstrated an unwillingness or inability to do so. In fact, you may need to give your employees goals that are required by the organization. But the best underlying philosophy is that employees can be trusted to work toward their full potential if given a chance. There is considerable payoff when you allow your employees to develop their own goals. First, you will find that they are more committed to fulfilling their own goals than those given to them. And second, motivated employees will often determine better and more challenging goals than their leader.

4.   Keep your employees informed. Some leaders believe that since information is power, giving information to their employees is giving away power. But this is not true. In fact, the benefits to you of sharing as much information as possible with your employees are enormous.

Consider these facts: 1) employees who know what is going on make better decisions; 2) they are more accepting of present and future actions that management may be required to make; 3) they are more prepared for future changes; and, 4) most importantly, they feel more a part of the organization. For these reasons, let your people know what is going on in their organization as much as possible.

5. Listen to your employees. It isn't enough just to keep your employees informed. You also need to listen to them. And when you listen, listen without interrupting. Unfortunately, this basic rule of communication and courtesy is often violated. In conversation you may be so interested in what *you* want to tell the employee that you don't listen to what *he* or *she* is saying.

By listening actively, you not only communicate to the employee the fact that you care about him or her, you also obtain new information. You may discover what works or doesn't work—and why. You can locate problems and elicit suggestions for solving them. Helpful information can then be spread to other levels of management that need it. If you don't learn the power of listening, you will not get needed information. Remember, it is the listener who controls the conversation, not the speaker.

6. Consult your employees about decisions that affect them. This powerful way of leading not only improves the quality of decisions, but also increases your employees' acceptance of those decisions. The quality of your decisions is likely to be enhanced for several reasons: your employees may well see additional decision alternatives beyond the one that you proposed; they will often identify additional factors that need to be considered while evaluating a decision, and they can often identify unanticipated risks in choosing a particular action. Employees naturally like to feel that they are a part of decisions that affect them. Asking for their input before making a decision will usually increase their acceptance of it when it is made.

7. Delegate appropriately to your employees. Delegating work to your employees has many advantages. It will enrich your employees' jobs, develop better employees, give you more time for tasks that only you can do, and, most importantly, increase the morale of your employees.

Considering these clear advantages, you might wonder why most of us are not already excellent delegators. The main reason seems to be that we don't delegate because we don't want to! Delegation may heighten our fear of losing control, of giving up parts of our job that we like doing, of spending additional time training employees to do delegated tasks, or of burdening our employees with additional work.

You can overcome your fear when you realize that delegating a specific task doesn't mean that you have lost control of that job. Although you won't be physically doing a job that you delegated, you will still be able to provide quality follow-up with your employee to ensure that the job is properly completed.

It is true that in delegating you may be giving up parts of your job that you enjoy doing. But the payoff in terms of employee morale makes it well worth it. In addition, you will find that you have extra time to spend on other quality tasks that will provide even more payoff than the one that was delegated.

Delegation will require much of your time at first. Odds are that you will receive a return on the time you invest that far exceeds the amount of time invested.

If you are concerned about delegated tasks becoming a burden to your employees, note the word "appropriately" used in the heading of this section. Delegating appropriately means being concerned not only about your needs, but also about your employees' needs. Placing excessive work on an employee, or simply giving more routine work to him or her, is not delegation.

To delegate, you need to first evaluate your job by listing your major tasks. Then, determine your authority level in each of the tasks.

"A" = You have complete authority to do the task
"B" = You can do the task but you must then report
        what you did
"C" = You need to obtain permission from your boss
        before doing the task

When you have listed each task in your job and determined your level of authority for each one, you may be able to delegate a number of your "A" tasks. Some of these "A's" will be opportunities for both you and your employees.

After determining which tasks can be delegated, evaluate your people to see which of them would benefit most by assuming the responsibility for specific tasks on your list. Finally, set up mini-training programs for the tasks that you have delegated. (For more information on delegation, see Chapter 6.)

8. Avoid over-supervising your employees. Here are some examples of over-supervising:

    a. Delegating a task—and then doing it yourself.

    b. Training an employee in exactly how to do a task, and then continually monitoring him or her.

    c. Giving an employee too much detail about how to do a task.

    d. Asking for too many—or unnecessary—reports.

As a leader, you walk a fine line between being available for your employees and over-supervising them. If you delegate a task, let the employee do it! Instead of giving an employee too much detail on how to do a task, define the end goal or results, and then ask the employee how he or she plans to complete the task. Avoid asking for unnecessary reports, or too many reports.

9. Conduct career counseling sessions with your employees. A key component of any system for motivating an employee is the career counseling interview conducted by the leader with his or her employees. In years past, if an employee were willing to work hard, success would come almost automatically because of the many opportunities that existed within most organizations.

Today this is largely no longer true. The idea that "hard work will ensure success" has become more myth than truth. Look at the facts. In the 1950s and 60s, the chances of being promoted were 1 in 5. Today the odds are 1 in 30. In other words, an employee is six times less likely to be promoted today than in the recent past. But unfortunately, our employees expect the same opportunities for advancement that their parents enjoyed. And this is not going to happen in the way, or with the same frequency, that it used to. Therefore, you need to manage differently. And one solution is to conduct career counseling sessions with your employees. In providing career counseling, you will need to help the employees explore their strengths, areas of needed improvement, knowledge, skills, likes and dislikes, values, and career goals. A counseling interview should be conducted to discover what the employee wants to do in the future, what needs to be done by the employee to get there, and how well the employee's goals meet the needs of the organization. (See Chapter 15 for more information on career counseling.)

10. Provide honest ongoing recognition for tasks well done. As Frederick Herzberg's research demonstrated, recognition is a major motivator. Conversely, lack of recognition is a powerful demotivator. And recognition becomes even more important to an employee when other rewards, such as salary, are restricted by regulations and policy.

We all know that recognition is important to most people. Yet, some of us still don't take the time to give our employees a needed pat on the back. Of course we have nice words for our superstar performers. But very few people are superstars! Most employees fall somewhere in the middle of the performance range.

The key to motivating your average employees is their natural need for recognition. If they don't receive recognition in their work, they will put their energy into seeking it elsewhere—often to the detriment of their jobs.

Fortunately, there are three ways to provide recognition to your average performers.

a. An employee's performance is never absolutely consistent. Like everyone, he or she has good and not-so-good days. Be alert to those times your employees are performing at an above-average level, and provide rapid recognition for such performance.

b. An employee's job is normally made up of a series of small operations. And the employee is likely to perform certain of these tasks better than others. Here, offer positive feedback on the operations the employee does well.

c. You can give recognition for strengths that may not be directly related to the job. An employee who is only an average performer but who arrives early may be good at orienting new employees or maintaining his or her area in a clean and orderly way. Your job is to reinforce the habit of excellence with positive recognition wherever you see it.

Remember: An employee may be "average," but there is nearly always something that the employee does well. Genuine recognition given for whatever that employee does well produces greatly improved motivation and self-esteem.

You might ask here: How should we handle the recognition of slight improvement in a problem employee? Suppose you recently counseled an employee who has a job-related problem and, as a result, the employee makes minimal improvement—to a "just acceptable" level. Do you immediately tell this employee how pleased you are with his or her present performance?

Some leaders will answer, "No! Why should I give an employee a pat on the back when his performance is only barely acceptable? Besides, it was only last week that I chewed him out for his sloppy work. It's still too soon to tell if he has really changed."

Two questions are being raised here. One deals with the amount of improvement necessary before feedback is given, and the other, when the feedback should be given. Let's look at the first point.

Suppose we turn the question around and ask, "Will recognition increase the chances that this employee will keep up improved performance?" The answer to this question is probably "Yes," simply because sincere recognition is one of the strongest motivators affecting any employee. To reduce the chances that a marginal employee will lapse into unacceptable performance, an insightful leader recognizes that it is not so much the amount of change that is required before giving an employee positive feedback, but rather the direction of that change. If it's a change for the better, positive feedback will tend to maintain improvement.

The second point raised concerns timing. When should we give positive feedback? If an employee did something poorly, you wouldn't wait several months to tell him or her about it. The same is true with positive feedback. If you want to reinforce an employee's positive behavior, give feedback as soon as you see positive change. An effective leader hopes for improvement, expects improvement, and, at the first sign of improvement, quickly reinforces the positive change in the employee's performance.

What if you give immediate positive feedback to a marginal employee who has improved slightly, and he or she gets worse? Now you are really disappointed—and maybe even angry! You gave the employee positive recognition, and the employee let you down. Sometimes this is going to happen. But more times than not, it won't. So don't let one or two negative results prevent you from improving your career average as a motivating leader. Continue to provide positive recognition to your low-performance employees when they show small improvements. Do it as soon as you see change, and you will see your batting average start to climb.

The way that you recognize employees is also very important. For example, general compliments such as, "You did a good job" or "I'm proud of your improvement" are not in fact the best motivators. A better way is shown in the following step-by-step method.

1. Describe the positive situation in detail.

Vague compliments are sometimes perceived as being insincere. Be specific: describe in detail the positive behaviors you observed. Don't just say, "You did a good job." Instead, spell out what you mean by "a good job"—and then watch the employee smile.

This approach works because the employee most likely knows he or she did well—and your recognition of the specifics will be perceived as observant, accurate, and genuine. For example: "Your desk looks great! All the extra files are put away, there's nothing out of place, and your desk looks completely organized."

2. Tell the employee why the positive performance is important.

You can add meaning to a compliment by emphasizing the importance of his or her performance. The opportunity for high-impact recognition is lost if you say only, "You did a good job," not only because you aren't being specific, but also because you haven't said why the positive performance was important.

There are three types of reasons you can mention as to why a positive performance has been a significant one.

- Why is the performance important to the employee?
- Why was it important to the section, department, or organization?
- Why is it important to you?

3. Tell the employee you have confidence in his or her ability.

An employee who works for two different leaders will often exhibit two different levels of performance. One reason for this discrepancy has to do with what the leader expects. Leaders with high levels of expectation usually obtain better overall employee performance. When you tell an employee that you have confidence in his or her ability, you are communicating strongly your future expectations. By expressing confidence in an employee's ability following improved performance, you increase the employee's motivation to continue to fulfill your growing expectations.

4. Ask the employee if there is anything you can do to support his or her improved performance.

When employees do something better today than in the past, they have made some changes in what they are doing, whether it is a matter of coming to work on time, organizing their work more efficiently, or something else. And when an employee changes, even for the better, there is a likelihood that he or she will encounter some new problems—even that of being teased by co-workers.

All kinds of problems can arise with changes, and an alert leader anticipates problems. So check out the situation by asking the employee if there is anything you can do to help in supporting his or her progress.

5. Emphasize your appreciation.

Conclude by expressing clearly and warmly the appreciation you feel. We all respond to others' feelings. If you feel good about what an employee has done, say so! You can say, "I really appreciate your efforts!" or "Thanks! I'm very pleased with your progress!" This reinforces what has been expressed and ends the discussion on the desired positive note. After your meeting, be sure to make a note of your conversation with the employee, and place it in the employee's anecdotal file.

On the following page is a survey that you can use with your people. It asks an employee to rate you in the three major areas covered earlier—the employee's job, the organization, and you as his or her leader. After you receive the completed surveys from your people, examine them to determine if a particular employee has important areas of motivational need. Then tally each of the responses to see if there are any group needs. After evaluating individual and group needs, refer to the text for ideas for taking action to improve the morale of your area of responsibility.

APPLICATION ON THE JOB

List the people who report to you in column 1 and identify areas in which they have needs in column 2. Next, in column 3, identify specific actions that you will take during the next four weeks to enhance each employee's morale. When you have completed your action for a specific employee, insert a completion date in column 4. Then, in column 5, make a brief note of the employee's reaction. At the end of the four-week time period, discuss the results with your boss.

1. Employee's name	2. Area(s) of need	3. Action(s) taken	4. Date(s) completed	5. Employee's reaction(s)

6
Delegation

OK, it's quiz time! See how many of the following questions you answer with a "yes." Do you . . .

   _____   1. Take work home at least once a week?

   _____   2. Often feel overworked and overstressed because you have too much to do?

   _____   3. Keep missing your important deadlines?

   _____   4. Have to deal with constant, recurring crises?

   _____   5. Find you don't have time for important issues such as long-range planning?

   _____   6. Spend significant time putting band-aids on symptoms of problems, rather than fixing the problems themselves?

   _____   7. Think that if you don't do it, it won't get done?

   _____   8. Enjoy doing things for others, especially your employees?

If you answered "yes" to one or more of these questions, you may have a problem. And possibly a very serious problem. A problem that could kill you—figuratively *and* literally!

Not being able to delegate is a killer. The stress from it can stop your heart! And even if you survive the stress, it can kill your chances of ever being considered suitable for more responsibility.

It's an organizational reality that the more responsibility you are given as you move up the promotional ladder, the more you must delegate. In fact, a promotion is a formalized, ritualistic way that organizations take all of your work and delegate it to someone else. So if you can't delegate, your chances of being promoted are slim.

Of course there are some tasks that can't be delegated. For example, it's tough to delegate a task that can't be taught, or leadership aspects of your job that only you can do, or a task that has an unacceptable risk of failure. But in most cases, you not only can delegate—you *should* delegate.

Reasons for Not Delegating

Unfortunately, there are lots of reasons why leaders don't delegate. Some are good reasons. And some are not good. When we group them, there are personal reasons, task reasons, staff reasons, and organizational reasons. So let's examine some of the common reasons why leaders who ought to know better don't delegate when they should.

Personal Reasons for Not Delegating

"I can do it better myself." No doubt! If you have always done the task, then obviously you are probably able to do it better than an employee who has never done it. So what do you do? Keep taking on more work as you become evermore experienced on the job, or as your boss delegates more and more to you? Somewhere along the line, you will *have* to delegate—you will have no choice. At this point, you must assign some of your work to your people and teach them how to do it—or collapse.

"I don't trust my people." If this is your reason, you had better back up and ask "Why?" Why don't you trust them? If the answer points to a psychological problem—like an inability to trust anybody—then you should seek professional help. But if the answer is simply that your people are new or inexperienced, then the solution is clear—and with time the problem will resolve itself: your employees are going to grow with experience. So you can best help them grow by providing them with ongoing training. You can delegate small tasks to them, and then offer appropriate training and follow-up. You can reward them for good performance—and then give them slightly larger tasks to do. It's called "developing subordinates." And it is a big part of your job as a leader.

"I like doing it." Now here's an honest reason! When I was a kid growing up in the mountains of Virginia, I never got any mail. So as an adult there is still this little mail-deprived kid inside of me that wants to get mail. And guess who opens all of the mail that comes to

my office? You're right—me! We have extremely competent employees who could be opening and routing the mail. In fact, some of them can likely do it better than I do. But I like opening the mail. It's the highlight of my day. So I sacrifice about thirty valuable minutes daily because I am unwilling to delegate this job to the people who should be doing it.

If you are laughing at my stupidity, think about the things in your job that you do just because you like doing them. What are those tasks that you like to perform so that you can have the satisfaction of scratching them off your "to-do" list? These are the little things that feel good to do—but eat up your time. When you have identified some of them, figure out the cost of not delegating them to others.

"My subordinate might take over my job." This reason for not delegating is frequently listed in books on delegation—though it is difficult for me to imagine that leaders actually worry about losing their jobs to subordinates because they delegated work. If delegation is a necessary part of leadership, you are really failing in your job if you do *not* develop your employees by delegating appropriate tasks. Also, how are you ever going to get promoted if you 1) can't delegate, and 2) don't train your replacement? It is the leader who doesn't delegate that should worry about a subordinate taking over his or her job!

"I won't get credit for doing the job." This is one I can relate to better. But certainly not enough to withhold delegating because of it. I used to produce all the videotapes for our organization. You know—I was the big-time producer. I wrote the scripts, hired the actors, and directed the productions. Real exciting. Action! Take 1! And when the videotape is played, it reads, "Directed by Dick Leatherman." Nice. Good for the old ego!

But as the organization grew, new things needed to be done, such as long-range planning, and managing a team of employees. So I gave up the excitement of being the producer. Now my name isn't on the videotapes. I still feel some loss over not being recognized. But our videos are better. And the quality of my work is better, because I have more time to devote to the tasks that really matter for me to do in our organization.

"If I delegate to others, I give up my power." We need to recognize that this reason is mostly "bunk." In 40 years in the business world I have never seen a leader lose power because he or she delegated properly. (Though I have seen some who lost power—were demoted or fired—because they *didn't* delegate.) You may know of a leader, somewhere, who lost power because he or she delegated tasks to a subordinate. But 99% of the time, when you delegate, you don't lose power—you gain it. The more you appropriately delegate, the more work can and will be done by your section or department, and the more time you will have to devote to other, more important tasks. And the more quality work gets done, the more real power you have. In fact, you will be well on your way to becoming irreplaceable—and promotable!

"I'll lose control if I delegate. When I'm in control, I feel safer." This reason for not delegating is true—but only when the leader mishandles the delegation process through ignorance of how to do it. That's why I've used the term "appropriate delegation" so far in this chapter. Presently, you'll see a step-by-step process that will help you delegate tasks effectively—without losing control.

"I'm a perfectionist and I know that my employees can never do it to my satisfaction." If this is your real reason for not delegating, you need help that this chapter can't give you. Leaders who are perfectionists to the point of not being able to delegate are doomed to a lifetime of miserable, mediocre leadership. If in fact you don't delegate because you can't stand to see your employees make mistakes as they learn, we are back again to the need for professional help. "Perfectionist" tendencies will not only drive others crazy, they can also destroy you.

When I see a perfectionist, I see a frightened person desperately trying to maintain security by keeping tight control of everything— and ultimately failing. But with help, a perfectionist can figure out why he or she is so afraid, what or who caused the fear, and begin to move to a new paradigm for living. It's not easy. But it can be done. And when this happens, life becomes a lot easier for everyone—especially for the leader.

Task Reasons for not Delegating

Task reasons for not delegating have to do with the assignment itself. Let's look as some of them.

"It takes too long to train someone else to do it." Sure, it does take time to train employees to do delegated tasks. But look at it as a return-on-investment decision. If the benefits you gain by delegating a specific task exceed the cost of delegating—then delegate.

Certainly you will need to weigh the factors that affect your decision to delegate. For example: How long will it take you to train this particular employee to do this task? Is this the right employee to do the task? Will the employee's morale be enhanced by taking on this responsibility? And of course, how much time will it save you that can be devoted to more important tasks?

"I really don't have the time to delegate." If this is true, and it might be, you are probably in this situation because you didn't delegate as you should have in the past. But it is almost never too late to start. Look at your job. Select a task to delegate that won't take huge amounts of your time in employee training. Then take the time to delegate the task. Next, with the time you have saved through delegating this task select another task to delegate—one which has a greater payoff for you, even though it will take time initially to train the employee. And enjoy the payoff! Busy, "pressed and stressed" leaders will never experience the great benefits of delegation until they make it happen.

"The task cannot be delegated." There are tasks that can't be delegated. Tasks concerning your leadership responsibilities are usually ones that you will have to do yourself. For instance, you will probably not be able to delegate the task of conducting a counseling

session with an employee who has an attendance problem. Also, it's part of your job to provide positive feedback to your employees on an ongoing basis.

On the other hand, you might be surprised at some of the things you can delegate. For example, in some organizations today, new employees are hired by a team of other employees rather than by the leader. Other organizations are having their employees' performance appraisals conducted by a group of peers instead of the leader. At the least, you can share the performance appraisal responsibility with the employee by asking him or her to fill out the appraisal form in advance, and to come prepared to do most of the talking in the interview. Or if you are hiring someone for the section or the department, it makes good sense to include in the interview and selection process some of the key people who will be working with this individual.

Generally speaking, there is not much that you can't delegate. Many of your interactions with your boss—or boss's boss—can be delegated to your subordinates for their growth, development, and increased motivation. Special reports, budgets, trips, visits to clients, and professional shows can appropriately be delegated. In fact, you'll be hard-pressed to come up with any task in which part of it can't be delegated. And at the least, someone else could look at the task to see how it might be delegated either entirely or in part. We sometimes have trouble seeing the "parts and pieces" of our jobs in terms of tasks that could easily be delegated. And we tend not to because we don't *want* to!

Staff Reasons for not Delegating

Another reason we don't delegate has to do with our perception of the people to whom we would be delegating. I call them "staff reasons." Let's look at some of the important ones.

"My people are too inexperienced." In some cases, this is a legitimate reason. There may well be situations where your staff really

is too inexperienced to be given additional responsibility at that moment. The solution here is obvious—train, and then delegate.

"My employees lack confidence in themselves." Uh, oh! This statement tells more about you as a leader than it does about your employees. Don't give this reason to your upper management; they will look at you and wonder how you 1) got your job, and 2) keep your job! If you said, "I've got an employee who lacks confidence," then the cause of the problem might not be you. But if you believe that all of your people are lacking confidence, you do have a severe problem—and that problem is you!

There are a couple of ways to look at this situation. If you think that your people don't have adequate confidence, then you will tend not to delegate additional responsibilities. And guess what? They will not develop confidence in themselves. Or if you have trouble delegating and then tolerating less than perfect results, you may have a tendency to jump in and "save the day" by doing the delegated task yourself. About the second time you do this, you will be convinced that 1) the employee can't do the job, and 2) you may as well not delegate anymore tasks to him or her. Both of these problems—not delegating when you should, and performing delegated tasks when you shouldn't—are symptoms of lack of trust in your employees—a key problem already mentioned.

"No one reports to me, so it's kind of hard to delegate." This is another one of those reasons that sounds legitimate, but isn't. For even if you don't have direct reports, you can still delegate a great deal. Think about the people you work with in your section or department, and the ways in which your job and its tasks overlap their jobs and tasks. Next, imagine who would perform your work if you were no longer employed in your organization, and weren't replaced? This exercise suggests that there are people around you who can do at least some of what you do—and also what tasks might be delegated first. So if you are overwhelmed with work, the chances are good that you can ask for help from your co-workers—and get it.

You can even practice "reverse delegation" if absolutely necessary. That's when you ask your leader to give you a hand with a specific job task. Leaders are usually happy to help out on a temporary basis (sometimes only too glad, for the reasons already mentioned!).

"I don't have anyone else who can do it." If the meaning of this statement is that everyone truly is that overworked, then there may be validity to it (but see the next paragraph). Or if the task is such that no one is actually capable of doing it, and that would be a *very* unusual task, then you would be justified for the time being in not delegating. But if this statement actually means that you don't *think* you have anyone capable of doing the task, read again what has been said concerning the leader's "trust," and employee "lack of confidence."

"My people are already overworked and don't have time to do additional work." As just indicated, if this is true, it is a genuine problem— and one that you are going to have to resolve creatively. So think about how your people got to be overworked. Did a budget crunch cause the organization not to replace those who were promoted, quit, retired, or died? Has your organization grown faster than the number of employees available to handle the work? Has the work changed as to require more people? Are other departments or sections dumping more work on your employees?

Are your people using antiquated ways of doing their jobs? Could they be more effective? Could the work be reorganized so that they would be less overworked?

Have you spent time analyzing the causes of the overload and creating solutions to resolve them? To handle this kind of situation you must spend *quality* time doing some heavy-duty thinking about the problem. You need to generate a list of possible causes of the "overwork," and then create specific solutions for the most probable causes.

One thing is certain: the problem is not going to go away. It is only going to get worse! And the problem will probably not be entirely fixed simply by hiring more people—even if you have the money to do so. But fortunately, a full analysis of the causes of the problem will normally suggest workable solutions.

The bottom line is twofold: you *can* do something to resolve problems of overwork, and then begin to delegate. And whatever needs to happen won't occur until you take the initiative and make it happen!

"If I give my employees more responsibility, they'll ask for more money. And more money isn't available." This reasoning is, to speak plainly, hogwash—and as you can see, I don't have much patience when I hear it! If you believe this idea, then you need to re-examine your personal values, as well as your perception of others. Let's take an example. Think of the people who have joined the Peace Corps. As a rule, these individuals have made little or no money, toiling in places that you probably wouldn't want to go, under marginal living conditions, and likely working a lot more hours than you work. Do you think they ask for more money? And what about teachers, priests, ministers, and rabbis? Why do they stay in jobs in which many are typically underpaid and overworked? Because they *like* what they do.

Now consider your employees. If you enrich their jobs by delegating more responsibility, they will find more joy in their work. And when their work is joyful, they normally will not go around grumbling and complaining about money. Not that we all don't need money to pay the bills. But when employees earn a fair income, more money is as much as anything a form of recognition. And delegation is equally a form of recognition. When you delegate, in effect you are telling your employees that you trust them, that you see them as being competent, and that you care about their continued growth on the job.

If your organization has enough money in its budget to reward employees who have become more valuable through your delegation of responsibility, then naturally you need to recognize their new worth momentarily. But if you really don't have the money in your budget, you will find that most employees understand this fact of life—especially if they like what they are doing, and you make their jobs more meaningful and productive through delegation.

Organizational Reasons for not Delegating

"My boss doesn't delegate and doesn't want me to either." Granted, this is a difficult situation to deal with—but not impossible. It *isn't* easy to work for a boss who doesn't delegate. But at some point, "the buck stops here." You simply will have to find the old-fashioned guts to do what needs to be done for your employees in spite of the fact that your boss doesn't see the need to delegate to you. So, do it quietly. Delegate aspects of your job that aren't highly visible. And encourage your people to do it with their subordinates.

Or do it noisily! Stand up to your boss. (Note that I'm not using the word "leader" here. Bosses that don't delegate are not leaders). Tell him or her to "get a grip," "get with the program;" or, at least, get out of the way and let you do what needs to be done with your employees. And give him or her this book to read with this chapter marked. I don't mean to sound flippant—for I couldn't be more serious. Somewhere along the line, a real leader has to take a stand. If my boss wouldn't delegate to me, I would take that stand. We really don't have much choice—not only so that we can "look at ourselves in the mirror" each day, but also to be able to look at our employees in good conscience.

"A strong union prohibits delegation." (i.e., "It's not in my job description!") This reason used to have some validity. Today, however, tremendous changes are occurring everywhere. And organizations are flattening, downsizing, putting quality first, and giving responsibility for quality to all employees.

Total Quality Performance. Total Quality Management. Continuous Quality Improvement. Statistical Process Control. Quality Circles. Leaderless Work Teams. Employee Empowerment Programs. Everywhere we look we find overwhelming evidence that times indeed are changing. Today we see world markets, not regional ones. We see the very survival of organizations threatened by foreign competition. And as a result, we see front-line employees—and their unions—working hand-in-hand with management to keep their organization competitive and in business.

So if your employees belong to a union—you can still delegate. Sure, you'll have to take it a little slower, and play by the rules. But stick with it. The results achieved in unionized organizations through delegation of major responsibilities to employees have been remarkable. It's worth the extra effort!

Reasons for Delegating

As we've seen in answering a variety of objections to delegation, there are many important reasons to delegate work to your subordinates. They fall under two different kinds of reasons: yours—and theirs. Let's look at them from this viewpoint.

Leader Reasons for Delegating Work

- You need to develop your subordinates.
- You are so overworked that you have no choice but to delegate.
- You're ambitious, and know that the higher up you move in your organization, the more you will have to delegate.
- You need to free yourself to do more critical and important tasks.
- You don't want to do a task. In fact, you can't stand doing it!

It's the last reason for delegating that gets us in trouble. There may be something you do that you hate doing—but that one of your people would love to do. If so, there is no problem—delegate. But sometimes a leader has what medical students call "skut work": a routine task that the leader hates to do, is tired of doing, or is just too proud to do. And nobody else wants to do it, either. If part of your job is to take out the garbage, than delegating that particular task to an employee will not be enriching to him or her either.

There are a couple of tasks like this in my shop. Changing the empty water cooler bottle is one—no fun! Since our organization is not big enough to have the services of a water bottle changer, we have to do it ourselves. So we carry 45 pounds of bottled water up two flights of steps, and try to pour the water into the cooler without spilling it all over the floor. And since nobody looks forward to having the full-time responsibility of carrying water up two flights of steps, we take turns. So here is the CEO of the organization—namely, me—carrying the water bottle up the stairs. Of course, I could delegate this responsibility, but I need the exercise. And my people need a boss who will share the "skut work."

Employee Reasons for Delegating

- It makes more sense to delegate the task to the employee because of the relationship of the task to the employee's job.
- The employee may be better suited to do the job than you are.
- The task may provide the employee opportunities for recognition.
- Delegation usually increases the motivation of your employees in that their jobs become more challenging.
- The task is specialized, and someone else has skills to do it that you don't have.

It is possible, of course, for negative results to come from delegation. But, as indicated, this is most often due to improper delegation. Suppose that your employee screws up a delegated task, and you are blamed for using bad judgment in asking him or her to do it. The real solution to this problem is to ensure that it doesn't happen in the first place, by: 1) selecting the right employee to do the task; 2) properly training the employee to do it; and, 3) following up after the task is delegated. All these things will greatly increase the chances that your employee will succeed. And that is exactly your goal when you delegate: to set up your employee for success!

So let's look at how we can delegate effectively—with a high probability of success.

How to Delegate

The following information on how to delegate for success is not new. In fact, most of the ideas described below have been around a long time. But they are presented in a logical, step-by-step order that will make it easy for new leaders to learn how to delegate—and help those old bosses who don't understand delegation learn how to be true leaders.

1. Prepare to delegate.

The first step in delegation is to answer some questions about your job. You need to determine:

- the key tasks in your job
- your authority level for each task

As an example, let's look at how I would analyze one of the jobs in my organization to determine what could be delegated—using a *Delegation Planning Work Sheet* (found at the end of this chapter). Suppose I am the Director of Program Development. The first thing to do is to list all of the major tasks in my job on a *Job Analysis Work Sheet*:

Job Analysis Work Sheet

1. Task List

- Write proposals, and reply to proposal requests
- Make presentations to key potential clients
- Attend annual training shows (two per year)
- Attend professional meetings (monthly)
- Research content for training modules
- Observe pilot programs conducted by others
- Read books and professional journals
- Negotiate with authors who write for us
- Edit work contracted by us
- Write training modules
- Provide one-on-one coaching and counseling as needed for staff
- Meet with key clients
- Conduct informational meetings with staff
- Drive to the post office to pick up the mail

If you regularly use a planning calendar, or keep a daily "to-do" list, it is easy to go back over the notes you wrote for each day to see the actual tasks on which you spend your time.

The next step is to determine your "authority level" for each of these tasks. In that I'm the real-life CEO of my organization, I don't have a boss to whom I report (except my wife, Nancy!). But since I am here playing the role of Program Development Director in my organization, I will imagine that I have a kind, lovable, wonderful boss named Dick Leatherman—who is terrific at delegating. So as Dick's employee, I review my task list to decide which of the following authority levels I have concerning each task:

> Level 1 = I have total authority to do the task.
> It is a routine part of my job.
>
> Level 2 = I can do the task, but *after* it is done I need to let Dick know that I did it.
>
> Level 3 = I need to check with Dick *before* I do the task.

Next, I carefully evaluate each task to determine: 1) if it's a task that I can delegate; and 2) whether I want to delegate it. It may be that even though I can delegate the task, I choose not to for one reason or another.

At this point my *Job Analysis Work Sheet* looks as follows:

Job Analysis Work Sheet

1. Task List	Authority Level			Delegate Maybe		To Whom?	Notes
	1	2	3	No	Yes		
• Write proposals, and reply to proposal requests		x			x		
• Make presentations to key potential clients		x			x		
• Attend annual training shows (two per year)	x				x	Dan	
• Attend professional meetings (monthly)	x			x			
• Research content for training modules	x				x	Jodi	
• Observe pilot programs conducted by others	x			x			
• Read books and professional journals	x				x		
• Negotiate with authors who write for us			x	x			
• Edit work contracted by us	x				x		But not yet. Too complex.
• Write training modules	x				x		
• Provide one-on-one coaching and counseling for staff as needed	x			x			
• Meet with key clients		x			x		
• Conduct informational meetings with staff	x			x			
• Drive to the post office to pick up the mail	x				x	Sharon	

Notice that I have delegated many of the tasks I rated "1" for authority level (i.e., I have total authority to do the task). However, some I did not. The personal improvement tasks—"Read books and professional journals" and "Attend professional meetings"—are not ones that can normally be delegated. Similarly, tasks that relate to the leadership aspects of my job, such as "Conduct informational meetings with staff," and "Provide one-on-one coaching and counseling for staff as needed," would not usually be delegated.

Other tasks, such as "Make presentations to key potential clients," or "Write training modules," are ones that I might be able to delegate—but probably only portions of them. On the other hand, the task "Drive to the post office to pick up the mail" is, of course, one that should have been delegated six years ago! And I should delegate several other tasks at the point when I have the time to invest in training, and the employees who can take on the responsibility.

After completing a *Job Analysis Work Sheet* to determine which parts of your job to delegate, you need to spend time thinking about how these tasks should be delegated, and to whom (already indicated in my example *Work Sheet*). Ask yourself these questions:

- Which tasks can be done better at a lower level? What is the lowest level that can handle the task?
- Which tasks are leadership tasks that cannot be delegated? (For example, taking disciplinary action, handling confidential issues, or giving rewards and recognition to others as the leader.)
- Are there any problems that stand in the way of delegating a task?
  — Is there time to delegate the task?
  — Does my boss have a problem with my delegating this task?
  — What is the risk if the employee fails in the delegated task? Is the risk acceptable?

— What is the complexity of the task, i.e., can the task be taught in a reasonable amount of time?

- Who is best suited to take on the task?

  — Is there someone who can do it better than I can?

  — Will the individual be overloaded if he or she takes on this additional responsibility? If so, are there aspects of his or her work that could be delegated to others?

  — Does this individual want this additional responsibility?

  — Will performing this task help the individual grow and develop?

- Is it better to split up the task into several subtasks and assign each part to a different employee (lightening the load, and giving each one a chance to show what he or she can do)?

- What should the employee's authority level be for the delegated task?

- What is a successful performance of the task, i.e., how will I and the employee know that the delegated task has been done well?

- What will a specific training plan look like for this employee on this task?

- Who else should be informed that this task is going to be delegated?

At the end of this chapter you will find a *Delegation Planning Work Sheet* that you can copy and use as a guide in thinking through these questions. And as you make decisions about tasks to be delegated, you can note this information on your *Job Analysis Work Sheet* as I did in my example.

In addition, you may need to complete training plans for more complex tasks before meeting with your employees. Here is an example of a plan that I—as the hypothetical Director of Program Development—could use to train one of my employees:

Task to be delegated: Attend annual training shows (two per year)

Employee Training Plan	Date to be completed:
Activities:	
1. Order booklet: "Working the Show"	Today
2. Review and list our show objectives	1 June
3. Design a check sheet for the show	3 June
4. Schedule a meeting with Dan	4 June
5. Meet with Dan to:	6 June

    — Discuss show objectives
    — List items to be taken (books, TV-player
      and monitor, training modules, catalogs,
      business cards, etc.)
    — Review list of workshops to attend
    — Review list of distributors' booths to visit
    — Discuss face-to-face client contact procedure
    — Set follow-up meeting to review Dan's progress

| 6. Follow-up meeting with Dan | 1 July |

2. Describe the task to the employee.

After you have prepared to delegate by identifying what you will delegate and to whom, and have designed a training plan, you need to set up meetings with these employees to discuss the tasks that will be assigned. In this step you will need to tell them:

- What needs to be done
- Why it needs to be done
- How the delegated task fits the overall objectives of the section or department
- *Suggestions* as to how the task could be completed

- Whom he or she needs to contact to complete the task
- Expected results
- Priority of this task relative to other tasks in the employee's job
- When to start on the task, and by what date it should be finished
- Any other needed information—especially things that you know that are not in writing

3. Offer training if necessary.

Step 2 assumes that the employee already knows how to do the task, and needs only general instructions on how to carry it out. But if the employee does not know how to perform the task, you may need to provide additional training. Information on how to train has already been presented in the chapter on one-on-one training skills— an especially important chapter! The thing to note here is that you first need to spend time planning out your employees' training using the *Delegation Planning Work Sheet,* as discussed in Step 1. Then, meet with these employees individually and *tell* them how to do the task. Next, *show* them how to do it. Finally, let them *do* the task while you observe them doing it—showing respect for their intelligence throughout.

4. Offer help.

Good leaders recognize that employees are apt to feel a little anxious about taking on a new responsibility. By offering your assistance, you help to reduce their natural anxiety. You may need to pave the way for an employee by talking to his or her co-workers who will be affected by the delegation of this task. Or you may want to help the employee by delegating part of his or her task to someone else. By offering your help, you demonstrate that you care about the employee and will do everything possible to ensure his or her success in the new task.

5. Determine required interaction points.

This step is designed to avoid trouble. If you have decided how the employee should accomplish the task, you also know when you need to meet with him or her to make sure that everything is going all right. But if you have delegated to the employee the responsibility for how the task will be accomplished, you may need to ask him or her to develop a plan describing how the new task will be done. In such a plan you will be able to spot the "mileposts"—when you and the employee need to touch base to determine how things are going.

It is important, however, that you don't overmanage a delegated task. And it may not be easy for you to "keep your hands off!" After all, you're the expert. You may even feel that you performed the task the best that it has ever been done. But it is far better for the employee that you allow him or her to manage the new assignment. I didn't say "abandon" the employee! But there is a great difference between monitoring an employee's efforts, and breathing down his or her neck. You can walk this line by letting go of the nitty-gritty details of how the task should be done, and scheduling times when the two of you can get together to review the employee's key activities and final results. Managing the delegated task in this fashion will significantly increase the employee's self-confidence. And you may even be surprised to find in the end that the employee has figured out a way to do the task better than you did!

6. Follow up.

Finally, you need to follow up on delegated tasks. When you do, provide feedback on the employee's performance—both good and not so good. Let your employees know, specifically, what they did that you liked, and what you didn't like. Suggest concrete ways in which their performance could be improved; or how a satisfactory performance could be made even better. Ask them what they learned from the experience, and what they will do differently in the future.

Remember, also, that more often than not, you bear some of the responsibility for the employee's performance if things aren't accomplished as well as expected. Therefore, when providing feedback to your employees, be sure to let them know when you see yourself as part of a particular problem. And avoid blaming an employee for what goes wrong. Instead, simply make sure that the employee knows how to do it properly the next time. At the end of this chapter you will find a *Delegation Evaluation Work Sheet* that you can use as a guide in evaluating an employee's performance on a delegated task.

Ask your employees, if you have the courage, how you can improve your delegation skills. What could you have done to make it easier for them to do the tasks that you delegated? Should you have provided more training? Met with them more often? Less often? Did you provide them with the authority to do the task? Did you let them do it? Did you take over, or take back, the job? These and other key questions are listed in an employee's *Delegation Evaluation Work Sheet* at the end of this chapter. Give this *Work Sheet* to your employee to use to provide you feedback—both on what you did well in delegating, and how you could improve the next time.

Summary

We need to delegate every day in little ways! When an employee asks, "What should I do?" respond by asking, "What do you feel you should do? What do you think is the best thing to do?"

And stop rubber-stamping! Are you signing documents just because you're the "boss"? Do you make your employees come to you for your approval because you are "the boss"? Do you make all the contacts with people outside the organization because you're "the boss"? Do you make all the presentations to others in the organization because you are "the boss"? Do you always talk to other bosses because you're a "boss"? If this is you, then you are "a boss,"—not a leader! And you need to begin delegating.

Delegation Planning Work Sheet

Task to be delegated: _____

Task assigned to: _____ Date
assigned: _____

Date task
to be started: _____ Date task
to be completed: _____

1. **Is this person best suited to take on this new responsibility?***

   — Can the individual do the task?_____
   _____

   — Does this individual want the additional responsibility?
   _____

   — Will doing this task help the individual grow and develop?
   _____

   — How does this task play to the employee's strengths?
   _____
   _____

   — What problems might this employee have in completing this
   task? _____
   _____
   _____

   — Will the individual be overloaded if he or she takes on this
   additional responsibility? _____
   If so, can any of his or her present responsibilities be delegated to others? _____
   If so, what work should be delegated, and to whom?
   _____
   _____

— Would it be better to split up this task into several subtasks and assign each part to a different employee (lightening the load, and giving several people a chance to show what they can do)?

_____

_____

*Is there someone else who could perform this task better?

_____

If so, who? _____

State the reasons why the task is assigned to the above-named person. _____

_____

_____

2. **What problems stand in the way of delegating this task?**

— Is there time to delegate this task? _____
If not, how will I be able to find the time?

_____

_____

— Does my boss have a problem with my delegating this task?

_____

— What is the risk if the employee fails in this delegated task?

_____

_____

_____

Is the risk acceptable?_____
How could the risk(s) be reduced? _____

_____

— What is the complexity of this task, i.e., can the task be taught in a reasonable amount of time? _____

_____

— What should be the employee's authority level for the delegated task? _____

_____

3. What is a successful performance of this task?

— How will you and the employee know that the delegated task has been performed well? _____

_____

_____

_____

— What things should *not* happen in doing this task?

_____

_____

_____

4. Who else should be informed that this task is going to be delegated?

_____

_____

5. Employee Training Plan (if needed)

Activities:

Date
completed:

_____   _____

_____   _____

_____   _____

_____   _____

_____   _____

_____   _____

_____   _____

_____   _____

_____   _____

_____   _____

_____   _____

_____   _____

_____   _____

_____   _____

_____   _____

_____   _____

_____   _____

_____   _____

_____   _____

_____   _____

_____   _____

_____   _____

_____   _____

_____   _____

_____   _____

_____   _____

_____   _____

_____   _____

_____   _____

Delegation Evaluation Work Sheet

To be filled out by the *leader* on his or her employee.

Date form
Employee: _____ completed: _____

Person completing this form: _____

Delegated task: _____

_____

_____

What was the quality of the completed task? _____

_____

_____

_____

_____

What did this employee do well in completing this task?

_____

_____

_____

_____

What could have been done more effectively? How?

_____

_____

_____

_____

Was the task accomplished within the allotted time? _____
If not, why not?

_____

_____

_____

_____

How was the employee's other work affected by the delegation of this task?

_____

_____

_____

_____

Was this the right person to do this job? _____
If not, why? _____

_____

_____

_____

Delegation Evaluation Work Sheet

To be filled out by the *employee* on his or her leader.

To: _____ From: _____

Re: Feedback on my delegation of the following task: _____
_____
_____

Date: _____

Please provide me with feedback on my delegation skills by honestly answering the following questions. When you have completed this check sheet, please return it to me. After I have reviewed it, we will meet together to discuss your comments.

1. What did you like about the way I delegated this task to you?
_____
_____
_____
_____
_____

2. How could I have improved? Consider such things as:

   - Were you the appropriate person to do this job? Should I have selected someone else?
   - Did I tell you whom to see, and who else needed to be contacted?
   - Did you know the results that were expected before you started?
   - Should I have provided more training? Less training?
   - Should I have met with you more often? Less often?

- Did you feel I was available to answer your questions as they came up?
- Did I provide you with the authority to do the task?
- Did I let you do it? Did I take over, or take back, the job in any way?
- Did I provide you with positive and/or corrective feedback when you finished the task?
- Did you encounter any problems that I should have foreseen?

Please list below how I might delegate better in the future. Be specific. Note examples where possible.

_____

_____

_____

_____

_____

_____

_____

_____

_____

_____

_____

_____

_____

_____

7
Problem Solving

Some leaders seem to have a knack for coming up with the best solution to a problem. Others—with the same intelligence and experience—seem to come up with solutions before they are even sure what the problems are! We've all seen examples of disasters that occurred when the cause of the problem wasn't analyzed before expensive action was taken: decisions that resulted in wasted time, materials and money; plans that looked perfect on paper, but failed in real life.

This chapter will help you develop skills in problem solving. It will show you logical—and simple—ways to make your problem-solving effective.

A key step emphasized in this chapter is *writing out the problem*! It is amazing what a simple thing like writing down information can do to increase your success with problem solving. You don't always have a clipboard in your hand. But whenever you have a problem, begin by taking a minute to make the problem "visible" in writing.

Visibility does several things:

- First, if a problem-solving process is taking place only in your mind, no one can help you! Others are kept from pointing out oversights, errors, or faulty assumptions.

- Second, if you don't make your thinking visible, you don't have a reliable way to review how you attempted to solve a problem—and therefore to learn from your mistakes.

- Third, writing down the problem will help you see the whole problem rather than just some parts and pieces of it.

- Fourth, part of your job as a leader is to help your people develop. You may be an outstanding problem solver. But if you can't make what you think visible, how can you teach?

- Fifth, in a team meeting, visibility will help keep your group on track and focused on the problem at hand.

SITUATION ANALYSIS

"Situation Analysis" (S.A.) is a problem solving tool that will help you break a large—even messy—situation down into manageable pieces. These pieces become the problems, decisions, plans, and even new problem situations to be analyzed.

So when you have a problem that is big, complex, bulky, and has lots of parts and pieces, this is probably the time for S.A. Issues such as high turnover, low morale, dirty facility, or high cost, are often called problems. Technically they are not problems at all, but statements about symptoms of problems. And for concerns like these, a good tool to reach for is Situation Analysis.

Let's take a messy situation to see how S.A. can be used to break it down.

> "I just don't understand those leaders," thought Old Jake, a senior manager with I.T.A. "Back when I was a team leader, a person took a lot of pride in the fact that he or she was a leader at the best organization this side of the Mississippi. But now if morale were any worse, I'd have to jack my people up with a hydraulic lift. They are grumbling and complaining worse than a bunch of workers who just got an across-the-board pay cut.

> "Now, because I've been here longer than anyone else, the boss wants me to come up with some bright ideas to solve the morale problem. I don't even know where to start on this one. It's a real mess because so many things are causing the situation. Maybe it's because every time there is a dispute between a team leader and a worker, the team leaders get shot down by personnel.

> "Of course, it could be that the team leaders just aren't as tough as they used to be in my time. I mean, after all, we used to be called 'supervisors' or 'foremen.' We had respect! And it seems like the workers can sense when a supervisor—

excuse me, I mean a 'team leader'—is weak. And then they needle him or her constantly until something blows.

"The low morale might also be a result of some team leaders not being able to make that big transition from being a worker to being a leader. I've seen several like that. Tom is a good example. He's the most miserable human being I've ever seen. He loved doing what he was doing, and was good at it. Then he was promoted to leader—and now he can't keep his hands off the equipment."

"Another problem is that there's so much pressure to get high production. A team leader who achieves high production gets a lot of recognition from everybody. But sometimes things happen outside a leader's control that hurts his or her production. Then we've got a morale problem.

"I don't know," thought Old Jake. "Maybe the problem of low morale is caused by the new 'work team' program. Delegating authority and responsibility to workers is fine— I'm all for it. But it seems to me like the workers really weren't ready for all that authority and responsibility. Now the team leaders are having fits trying to get their people to work together as a team, to take charge of their own goals and objectives—and at the same time keep up production. Why couldn't the organization spend some of its dollars on giving the workers some training before dumping a new way of operating on them? It's crazy!

"What a mess!" sighed Old Jake. "I'm usually an optimistic kind of person. But things aren't going well. Something needs to change."

Step 1. Write down the problem.

The first step in using Situation Analysis is to make the problem statement visible. Write it down!

Visible   Visible

Low Team Leader
Morale

Visible   Visible

Step 2. Separate the problem into its related parts.

Separating the pieces of a problem allows you to focus your energy on those areas that most affect the initial problem—and at the same time lets you see the problem as a whole. At this point, you don't have to analyze or conclude anything. Just jot down as many parts and pieces of the problem that you can think of. In the example, Old Jake would ask himself this question: "What are the things that make me think, 'We've got low team leader morale?'"

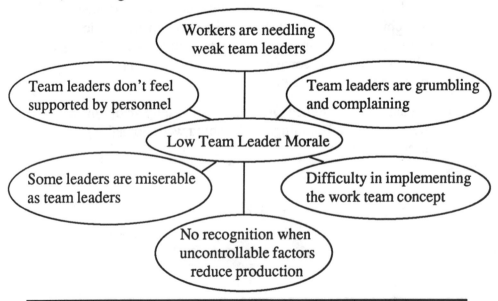

Step 3. Determine which parts of the problem are probable causes and which are probable results.

In Step 3, decide which of the separate pieces are causes, and which are results of causes. To fix a mess, you must attack the causes, not the results. When four people who work for you suddenly quit their jobs, you do have to replace the people. But you don't stop there! In order to fix the cause of the problem, you must find out why they quit. You haven't solved the problem just by replacing the employees. So when you analyze a messy situation, you need to determine the probable causes—and take action on them, not on the results.

You can indicate a probable cause by drawing an arrow pointing toward the problem situation, and a probable result with an arrow pointing away from the problem. Then cross out the "results," and focus your energies on the causes. Here's an example:

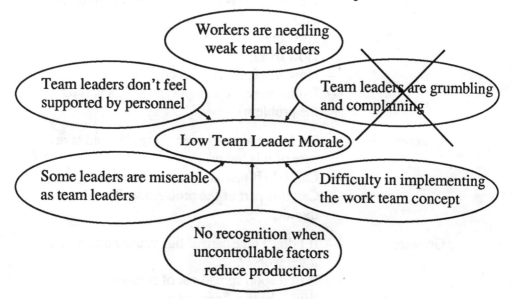

The team leader's grumbling and complaining is probably a result of low team leader morale and should be "X'ed" out. And if a piece of the situation seems to be both a probable cause and a probable result, treat it as a probable cause.

Step 4. Set priorities.

Many problems have a number of related causes, some major and some minor. To be effective, you need to devote your time to the major causes that can be changed. With today's tight schedules, you simply don't have time to do everything. Therefore, fix the things that matter most by making them visible components, determining causes and results—and then assigning priorities only to the causes, not to the results.

A simple way to assign priorities is to use the categories of "Seriousness," "Urgency," and "Growth." Rate each suspected cause as having a high (H), medium (M), or low (L) degree of seriousness, urgency, and growth potential. To do this, ask the following types of questions concerning each cause:

Seriousness:
— How serious is this cause in relation to the other causes?
— How big is it?
— How bad is it?
— How frequently is it occurring?
— Dollar wise, how important is this part of the problem?

Urgency:
— Do I have to drop everything else and take care of this today?
— Can I do it just as well next week?
— Can this part of the problem wait until next month?

Growth:
— If I don't take care of this cause now, will it get worse?
— Will it soon spread out of control?
— Will it have a financial impact?

Old Jake finds that he can now analyze his problem fairly easily by using the "Seriousness / Urgency / Growth" (S.U.G.) system to rate each cause. It seems to work best to rate the "Seriousness" of each cause first, then the "Urgency," and finally the rate of "Growth." Here is what his chart looks like now.

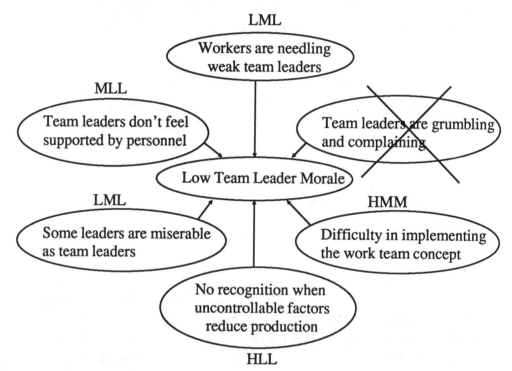

At this point, note that Old Jake rated two parts of his problem as "high" in seriousness: "No recognition when uncontrollable factors reduce production," and "Difficulty in implementing the work team concept." But his urgency rating for these two causes was not "high," but "low" and "medium," respectively. You may feel that if the seriousness of a problem is high, then the urgency must be high, and thus the growth factor will also be high. But be careful not to allow a high seriousness rating influence your ratings of urgency and growth. In Old Jake's case, "Difficulty in implementing work team concept" was serious to him. But he also felt that the urgency of this cause was only medium, and that the growth factor was also only medium.

Likewise, even though he rated "No recognition when uncontrollable factors reduce production" as high in seriousness, he rated it low in urgency. Jake's management needs to do something about this part of the problem. But realistically, it is not something that must be handled today—or even this week. In fact, it might be better to give this cause some time and solid thought before talking to management about it. Jake wisely rated this piece of the problem as low in growth. Yes, the problem is bad. But, no, the problem is not likely to get any worse. It is probably as bad as it is ever going to be right now. Therefore, it has low growth potential.

Step 5. Decide which of the problem causes are problems, decisions, plans, and new messes.

The final step in Situation Analysis is to analyze each of the major causes of the problem situation as follows:

Problems to be diagnosed. For example, "Difficulty in implementing the work team concept" may be a problem to Old Jake because he doesn't really know what the cause is. He thinks it might be lack of worker training. But that is only an assumption at this point. He needs to discover why the teams are not working out. Only when he determines why this is occurring is he ready to take some kind of action to address the problem.

Decisions that must be made. Jake knows why there is no recognition when uncontrollable factors reduce production. And since he knows the cause of this situation, his next step is to make some decisions about fixing it.

Plans to be implemented. Jake also knows why some leaders are miserable as team leaders. He even knows what needs to be done about it. But he feels that determining how to do what needs to be done will require some planning.

New messes (new problem situations that must be further broken down). For instance, team leaders not feeling supported by the personnel department may be a new situation to be analyzed, with its own set of causes and results.

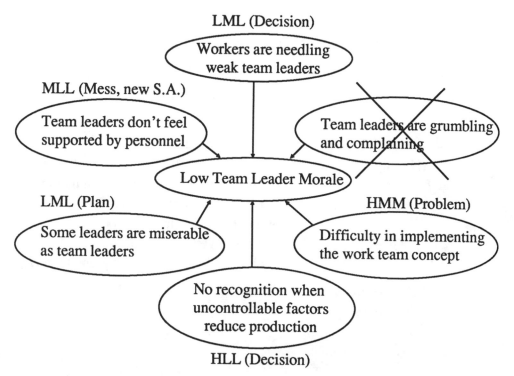

After you have analyzed your problem using Situation Analysis, you are ready to devote your time to the high priority causes. S.A. will not hand you a predetermined solution to your problem. But it does help you with the key task of making the various parts of your problem visible, evaluating each part in a meaningful way, and deciding where to focus your energy.

Each priority part of a Situation Analysis can be regarded as an opportunity—an opportunity to do something differently and better.

On the following page is a *Situation Analysis Work Sheet* that you may duplicate for use to analyze your problem situations.

SITUATION ANALYSIS WORK SHEET

1. Write down the problem.

2. Separate the problem into its related parts.

3. Determine which pieces are probable causes and which are results.

4. Assign S.U.G. priorities for each cause
   (H = high, M = medium, L = low).
Seriousness —	How bad? How big? How much money?
Urgency —	Must it be taken care of today?
	Will next week be just as good?
Growth —	Is the cause getting worse?
	Or is it already as bad as it is going to get?

5. Label the major causes: "Problem," "Decision," "Plan," and "New Mess."

FINDING CAUSES

When trying to remedy a problem, many people jump into action without thinking. They just can't seem to help it: they want to be "doing" something—anything! In fact, taking action without thinking, no matter how unproductive, can become a way of life. Before—repeat, before—you take action to solve a problem, look for causes. When you find the probable causes, fix the cause that is most clearly connected to the problem.

When you problem-solve, you are finding the cause of a problem—not analyzing a situation, making a decision, or implementing a plan. You are problem-solving when:

1. **You have a deviation from the standard.**
   Something should be happening, but it isn't. It was supposed to have happened, but it didn't. It wasn't supposed to happen, but it did. All of these are deviations from the standard.

2. **You are uncertain about the cause of the problem.**
   If you already know the cause, then your next step is to make a decision by selecting the best way to fix the problem.

3. **You are concerned about the problem.**
   If you see a deviation from the standard and you don't know for sure why it happened—but you are not really concerned about it—you have no problem.

You can find the cause of a problem by following these seven steps:

1. **Develop a specific written problem statement.**

In writing out your problem statement, make it specific—and in the negative. Write "Poor Morale in the Data Processing Section," not just "Poor Morale." This not only helps pinpoint the problem, but also highlights what the real issue is.

2. Ask "what, where, and when" the problem is occurring, and "what, where, and when" the problem is not occurring.

At times causes can be located more quickly if you clarify what is not the problem, as well as what is. The better you define the boundaries of a problem by specifying where the problem isn't occurring, the easier it is to determine the most probable causes.

Also, in Step 2 ask: "What is the extent of the problem?" That is, how bad or serious is the problem? This information can keep you from developing a $500 solution to fix a $3.00 problem.

These "what, where, when and extent" questions help you locate and isolate the problem area, and thus show you where to look for causes. An electronics technician calls it "troubleshooting;" a doctor calls it "diagnosing." You might say it's "working smarter, not harder."

For example, suppose you have a bad pain. Now what kinds of questions would your doctor ask before he says, "Take two aspirin and call me in the morning?" He might ask, "Where does it hurt? When does it bother you? When did you first notice it?" And, "How much does it hurt?"

But good doctors don't stop there. They also ask questions about what the problem is not. For example, your doctor might ask, "Have you been experiencing pain anywhere else? Have you ever had this pain before?" and "When don't you notice the pain?"

From asking such questions, your doctor might discover that your problem is only in your right elbow, and not any other part of your body. It hurts all day, not just at certain times of the day. The pain first started six weeks ago. And you didn't have it before then—except when you were in high school.

3. Closely examine the differences between where and when the problem is occurring, and where and when it isn't.

If a problem exists in one area and not in another, the differences between the two areas can produce clues to help locate the cause. So you ask: "What peculiar differences exist between where the problem is occurring, and where it is not occurring?" Or, "What is different about when the problem occurs and when it doesn't?"

In the example of the pain problem in Step 2 above, by specifying what, where, when, and to what extent the problem is and is not occurring, the doctor is able to identify the particular differences. For example, your doctor might discover that you are right-handed, and that you were a softball pitcher in high school. Then, by determining the peculiar differences between what, where, and when the problem is and is not, he or she is then able to look for changes in and around the differences.

4. Look carefully for changes that have occurred in and around the environment of the problem.

Changes can cause problems. In fact, problems—by definition—are always caused by changes. Remember that problems where no change has occurred are not truly problems. They are decisions that must be made or plans that should be implemented. For example, guess what your doctor discovered you were doing with your kid every night after supper for the past six weeks? Right! You have little league elbow.

5. Develop "probable cause statements" concerning the changes discovered in Step 4 by linking each change to the problem.

Every change will produce its own unique probable cause statement.

In the example of elbow pain above, a probable cause statement would be:

> "Pitching softball with your child each night after supper has resulted in tendinitis in your elbow."

6. Test each probable cause statement against all of the IS and IS NOT facts, in order to determine the most probable cause.

For example, your doctor might say:

"If it is tendinitis, would that account for the fact that the pain is in the right elbow and not the left?"

Answer: yes.

"Would it account for the fact that it hurts constantly, and not just certain times in the day?"

Yes.

"That the pain first started six weeks ago—and you never had it before except when you were a pitcher in high school?"

Yes!

Since tendinitis checks out against the known set of facts, your doctor would then move to the next step—verifying that this really is the cause.

7. Verify the most probable cause to make sure it is the real cause.

In this final step your doctor can verify the cause of your pain by gently probing your elbow, or by taking X-rays.

Note that these seven steps of Problem Solving are usually inexpensive. They involve only paper and pencil mental analysis—and sometimes phone calls to gather confirming information. Taking action to remedy the problem, of course, may involve financial commitment—and many lost dollars if you fail to follow the problem-solving process above!

Yet, many people start their problem solving efforts by throwing money into an ill-conceived solution before thinking through the problem. They jump in with both feet to take action. Any action! And they often end up spending much unnecessary time and money—and the problem still isn't solved.

In brief outline the seven-step process above looks like this:

1. PROBLEM STATEMENT:_____

2.	IS	IS NOT	3. DIFFERENCE	4. CHANGES
What?	_____	_____		
– Defect	_____	_____		
– Object	_____	_____		
Where?	_____	_____		
When?	_____	_____		
Extent?	_____	_____		

5. Probable Causes

1. _____
2. _____
3. _____

6. Test the probable cause statements against the initial set of facts.

7. Verify the most probable cause.

Now let's illustrate the seven-step problem-solving technique with a real-life example:

THE CASE OF THE REJECTED PROMOTION

Tom Swift, Director of Marketing, shook his head in amazement. Jean Williams, one of his best telephone salespersons, had just turned down a promotion to outside salesperson. Of course, it would have meant a move outside the close-knit telemarketing group. But the possibility of a substantial increase in salary should have been tempting. It wouldn't have been so bad except that this was the second person to turn down the position. Tom had asked Sue Atkinson first, and, after thinking it over, she said "no."

Tom had asked both of them why they turned down the promotion. Jean and Sue both had similar responses. Jean said that she was happy where she was and didn't want the stress of taking on new responsibilities. "And besides," she said, "I really enjoy the relationships that I have established with my customers." Sue similarly said that she enjoyed her work and the people she worked with—and, like Jean, said that she had made many friends with her customers and didn't want to give them up.

A couple of years ago, Tom would have had to beat off outside sales applicants with a stick! Now, even though the opening had been posted for three weeks, not a single person had applied for it. And since there was a strong policy of promoting from within, it would be difficult to get approval to look outside the organization for a salesperson. Other departments in the organization had no problem finding applicants wishing promotions to other jobs.

"I don't know," thought Tom. "Maybe it's Betty." Betty had been Tom's outside sales manager for about three years, and had a reputation for being the toughest taskmaster in the organization. Firm but fair was her motto. And was she firm! Betty set high goals, and saw to it that her salespeople met them year after year. "Maybe that's the reason I can't get anybody to take this job," Tom thought. "Betty is just too hard to work for. She's not like Bill, the old manager who retired. He was a great leader—his people really liked him."

"Of course," Tom reflected, "it might be the telemarketers are afraid to make sales calls in person. Making sales calls face-to-face is a whole lot different than talking on the telephone. In some ways it's actually easier. You can see the customer's non-verbals and respond to them. As a result, our outside sales-people's call-to-sales-ratio is better than the telemarketers'.

"But in other ways it's harder to make calls in person. I think the salesperson feels rejection more keenly in a face-to-face situation than on the phone. Since neither Jean nor Sue has ever done this, each one may just be afraid to face rejection in person.

"Also, an outside salesperson usually works alone. The telemarketers do work alone on the phone—but they have lots of opportunities to talk with each other during the day.

"The other big difference between in-person and telemarketing sales is the amount of time required on the job," mused Tom. "Sure, the outside people make more sales, and as a result make more money. But it's definitely not a nine-to-five job like telemarketing. They spend more evening and weekend time preparing for their calls. And they leave home earlier, and usually get back later.

"But neither Jean nor Sue has a family, so the extra time shouldn't be that much of a problem—considering how much better the money is. Besides, Sue said she would like to be considered for the telemarketing leader's job if it ever opens up, and that's definitely not a nine-to-five job!

"I just don't know what the problem is," thought Tom. "I do know that the telemarketers feel really good about working together. Ever since last year when we did those three team building training workshops with the telemarketers as a pilot program, they have gotten along so much better. They're such good friends. And it's great to see the way they support each other."

Tom knew that his boss was going to ask him at the afternoon managers' meeting how he was doing filling the outside sales job. And, at this point, Tom didn't know what to say. "I don't want to jump to conclusions—or do anything until I really know what's causing this problem," Tom thought. "But I bet it's Betty. Maybe I should think about what I can do to help her become a more congenial supervisor to work for."

As we examine the above example, we can see many possible reasons why the two telemarketers turned down this promotional opportunity: A tough supervisor, more responsibility, working alone without a support group, extra time required in an outside sales job, and fear of face-to-face rejection. As with most actual cases, there are a number of possible causes—and each cause requires a different solution. If action is taken on the wrong cause, not only will the problem not be solved, but there is a chance of making the problem worse.

So Tom's first job is to get paper and pencil and write out a problem statement. He writes:

1. **"Two telemarketers have turned down a promotion to outside salesperson."**

Next, he lists what the problem is, followed by where, when and to what extent it is occurring, as follows:

2. THE PROBLEM IS:			
WHAT: — Telemarketers refusing promotion — Promotion to outside sales-person			
WHERE: — Telemarketing department			
WHEN: — Now			
EXTENT: — Serious—two people rejected promotion — No applicants			

After Tom has written down what the problem is and where, when and to what extent the problem *is* occurring, he next describes the what, where, when, and extent to which the problem *isn't* occurring.

1. **"Two telemarketers have turned down a promotion to outside salesperson."**

2. THE PROBLEM IS:	THE PROBLEM IS NOT:		
WHAT: — Telemarketers refusing promotion — Promotion to outside sales-person	— Telemarketer's job — Promotion with-in telemarketing department		
WHERE: — Telemarketing department	— Other departments		
WHEN: — Now	— Prior to two years ago		
EXTENT: — Serious—two people rejected promotion — No applicants	— OK (the two telemarketers acceptance of a promotion) — A number of applicants		

In Step 3, Tom determines the difference between the situation in which the problem is occurring, and where it does not exist. That is, what factors are connected with the problem situation that are not present where there is not this problem? Thus Tom notes the factors in the "Difference" column:

1. **"Two telemarketers have turned down a promotion to outside salesperson."**

2. THE PROBLEM IS:	THE PROBLEM IS NOT:	3. DIFFER-ENCE	
WHAT: — Telemarketers refusing promotion — Promotion to outside sales-person	— Telemarketer's job — Promotion with-in telemarketing department	– Hours – Respon-sibility – Established customer relationships – Betty, the boss	
WHERE: — Telemarketing department	— Other departments	– Team building training	
WHEN: — Now	— Prior to two years ago		
EXTENT: — Serious—two people rejected promotion — No applicants	— OK (the two telemarketers acceptance of a promotion) — A number of applicants		

Note that the "Difference" column may—and often will—be left blank in some of the rows (the EXTENT rows in this example). Also note that in solving real problems, there may be many differences between what the problem is and what it is not. Only list those factors (differences) that have a direct bearing on the problem. For example, a key difference between the "Telemarketers refusing promotions" and the "Telemarketer's (present) job" is that the promotion involves an increase in salary. But it doesn't make sense that someone would turn down a promotion to a new job because it pays more. Thus, even though "money" is a major difference between these two positions, it is not listed in the "Difference" column because it is not likely to be a cause of the telemarketers' refusing a promotion to outside sales.

Tom's next step is to look carefully for changes that have taken place or would take place that might affect the thinking of the telemarketers concerning the promotion. So Tom wrote in column 4, "Changes."

2. THE PROBLEM IS:	THE PROBLEM IS NOT:	3. DIFFER-ENCE	4. CHANGES:
WHAT: – Telemarketers refusing promotion – Promotion to outside sales-person	– Telemarketer's job – Promotion with-in telemarketing department	– Hours – Respon-sibility – Established customer relationships – Betty, the boss	– Longer hours – Greater responsi-bility – Loss of valued customers – Tougher super-vision
WHERE: – Telemarketing department	– Other departments	– Team building, training	– Closer relation-ships with peers
WHEN: – Now	– Prior to two years ago		
EXTENT: – Serious—two people rejected promotion – No applicants	– OK (the two telemarketers acceptance of a promotion) – A number of applicants		

After Tom identifies situational differences and critical changes, he is now ready to create probable causes of the problem (called "probable cause statements") related to each of the change factors. For example, in the illustration above, "Longer hours" is one of the changes involved in the promotion. Thus Tom would write a probable cause statement that relates this new change factor to his initial problem statement, as follows:

> "Because a promotion to outside salesperson entails longer hours, two telemarketers turned down the promotion."

Note here that Tom cannot say with certainty at this point, "Eureka, I've found the cause!" What he has identified is a probable cause—not a verified one.

And in fact, Tom finally identified five probable causes of the problem. He then constructs a chart in which he:

1. writes down each of the selected change factors, and

2. relates each change to the problem (rejected promotion) using a common sense link.

Thus he writes:

PROBABLE CAUSE STATEMENTS

Change ⟶ Link ⟶ Problem

Change	Link	Problem
Longer hours	may require telemarketers to give up too much personal time, thus resulting in	their rejection of the promotion.
Greater responsibility	could be a hassle, thus causing	their rejection of the promotion.
Loss of established customers	might be too upsetting, leading to	their rejection of the promotion.
Tougher supervisor	could be very difficult to work for, therefore causing	their rejection of the promotion.
Closer relation-ships with peers	as a result of the team training programs may be the reason for	their rejection of the promotion.

In his next step (shown on page 146), Tom numbers his six pairs of "is/is not" facts concerning the what, where, when, extent of the problem. Then on the right-hand side of his *Probable Cause Statements* chart, he adds six narrow columns corresponding to the six sets of "is/is not" facts (shown on page 147). This makes a grid on which he can test each probable cause against the known facts, by answering the question:

> "Does this probable cause statement account for the 'is/is not' facts concerning the WHAT/WHERE/WHEN and EXTENT of the problem?"

Thus Tom takes the first probable cause statement and asks, "If longer hours require telemarketers to give up too much personal time, thus resulting in their rejection of the promotion, does this explain why the telemarketers are refusing promotions ("is" fact), and there is no problem concerning their job ("is not" fact)? Tom's answer is "Yes." So he puts a "✓" mark in the first box under "#1," as shown on page 147.

Using this same probable cause statement concerning longer hours for outside salespersons, Tom tests it against each of the other five sets of "is/is not" facts, and records his answers in column #1 of the grid. If the cause could explain a set of "is/is not" facts, he records a "✓." If it doesn't explain the pair of facts, he records an "A"—which stands for "Assumption." In other words, he assumes that something else must account for that set of "is/is not" facts. For instance, the first probable cause statement (longer hours) does not check out with set of facts #2—the telemarketers refusing promotion to outside sales, but not within telemarketing department. For Sue had said she would like a promotion to head up the telemarketing group—and that job also requires extra hours. Nor does the first probable cause check out with set of facts #4—the problem is occurring now, but was not present prior to two years ago—because outside sales have always involved longer hours than telemarketing.

Thus Tom checks out each probable cause against each set of "is/ is not" facts, recording "✓'s" when the cause statement checks out, and an "A" when it doesn't. (If you don't have enough information to know whether one of your statements accounts for a set of facts, use a "?" to indicate this.)

After Tom checked all of his cause statements against all six of his sets of "is/is not" facts, only one cause appeared to account for every set of facts concerning the problem: "Closer relationships with peers as a result of the team training programs."

1. **"Two telemarketers have turned down a promotion to outside salesperson."**

2. THE PROBLEM IS:	THE PROBLEM IS NOT:	3. DIFFER-ENCE	4. CHANGES:
WHAT: (1) Telemarketers refusing promotion (2) Promotion to outside sales-person	— Telemarketer's job — Promotion within telemarketing department	– Hours – Respon-sibility – Established customer relationships – Betty, the boss	– Longer hours – Greater responsi-bility – Loss of valued customers – Tougher super-vision
WHERE: (3) Telemarketing department	— Other departments	– Team building training	– Closer relation-ships with peers
WHEN: (4) Now	— Prior to two years ago		
EXTENT: (5) Serious—two people rejected promotion (6) No applicants	— OK (the two telemarketers acceptance of a promotion) — A number of applicants		

PROBABLE CAUSE STATEMENTS

Change of	Link	End Result	Set fact #'s 1 2 3 4 5 6
Longer hours	may require telemarketers to give up too much personal time, thus resulting in	their rejection of the promotion.	✓ A A A ✓ ✓
Greater responsibility	could be a hassle, thus causing	their rejection of the promotion.	✓ A A A ✓ ✓
Loss of established customers	might be too upsetting, leading to	their rejection of the promotion.	✓ ✓ ✓ A ✓ ✓
Tougher supervisor	could be very difficult to work for, therefore causing	their rejection of the promotion.	✓ ✓ ✓ A ✓ ✓
Closer relationships with peers	as a result of the team training programs may be the reason for	their rejection of the promotion.	✓ ✓ ✓ ✓ ✓ ✓

Tom's last step, #7, is verification of the most probable cause statement. Until he verifies that closer relationships resulting from the telemarketers' pilot team training is the key reason for their rejection of the promotion offer, he cannot say that "closer relationships" is the cause, only the most probable cause.

Thus Tom's probable cause grid analysis above has not yet eliminated any causes, but rather tells him which cause to try to verify first—"Closer relationships due to team training." If he cannot verify this as being the cause of the problem, he will then attempt to verify the next most probable cause or causes—in this case, "Loss of established customers," and "Tougher supervisor." The problem solving approach illustrated above is based on recognizing that a problem situation involves effects which, upon analysis, indicate a most probable cause. The effects point to a very particular kind of cause—one that would produce the unique effects (problem) that have been observed.

As we have seen above, the cause of any problem leaves a telltale imprint of clues (effects) that can be investigated along four lines. The first is *identity*. In the "Case of the Rejected Promotion," the problem's identity was the telemarketers' refusal of a promotion to an outside sales position. The second clue is *location*. The problem occurred in the telemarketing department, and not in other departments.

The third clue is *timing*. The problem occurring now was not present prior to two years ago.

And the fourth line of investigation is the *extent* of the problem—its size and severity. In the case above, with two people rejecting promotion to outside sales and no other applicants for the job, the problem is serious—and thus needs attention.

But because this problem was carefully analyzed, probable causes were identified for verification—and any action will be directed to a verified cause.

One final point: problems that fit the criteria of a real problem (deviation from the standard, unknown cause, you are concerned about it) don't stay problems for long. You will normally be motivated to find the cause and fix the problem.

But when you identify a list of existing problems, you will often find that your list includes a number of old problems. And these old problems frequently have known causes—but haven't been solved simply because you have not made decisions about them. These are not true "problems" at all. They are situations requiring decisions (covered in the next chapter), not problem solving.

In this chapter we have seen:

- the importance of thinking through a problem before attempting to solve it

- the need to make the problem visible in writing
- the key role played by a problem-solving process
- the importance of not jumping to conclusions and taking premature, costly action.

The problem-solving technique we have seen in this chapter is as useful in the hands of a group as it is for the individual problem solver. Playing the role of a participative leader, you can use this process with your employees in group meetings by asking the following oral questions:

1. PROBLEM STATEMENT
   "What is wrong?"

2. PROBLEM DESCRIPTION

• WHAT DEFECT?	"What symptoms do we have?" "What symptoms don't we have that we might expect?"
• WHAT OBJECT?	"What/who has failed?" "What/who has not failed?"
• WHERE?	"Where do we have the problem?" "Where don't we have the problem?"
• WHEN?	"When did it start?" "When was everything OK?"
• EXTENT?	"How serious is it?" "How big is it?" "What is normal?"

3. DIFFERENCES?   "What is different/unusual/peculiar about
                      this problem?"
                   "Why is it doing this, and not that?"
                   "Why did this fail, and not that?"
                   "Why did it happen here, and not there?"
                   "Why did it start then, and not before?"
                   "Why is it this much bigger or more serious
                      than normal?"

4. CHANGES?   "What has changed?"
                   "How has it changed?"
                   "When did it change?"

5. PROBABLE   "How could this change cause the problem?"
    CAUSES

6. MENTALLY   "If this is the cause, does it explain all
    TESTING   the facts of our problem-description?"

7. VERIFICATION   "Who else can we talk to, what records can
                      we check, and what evidence can we find
                      to determine that this is the real cause of
                      our problem?"

Try using the seven-step problem-solving grid on the following
page to solve a problem you have. Note that you may have some blank
spaces in the grid. And since many people are task-oriented and want
to solve a problem immediately, these blanks can cause frustration.
This is not only a normal reaction, it is often a positive one—since it
gives you clear direction on where to go and whom to ask for the missing information. In other words, the grid process protects you from
jumping to conclusions and taking the right action on the wrong cause!

By using this seven-step diagnostic process, you will resolve
problems quicker, correct causes—not just effects, solve problems so
they stay solved, and prevent new problems by taking the right action!

PROBLEM SOLVING WORK SHEET

A problem exists when: (1) a deviation from an expected standard has occurred, (2) the cause of that deviation is uncertain, and (3) the deviation concerns you.

STEPS IN DIAGNOSING CAUSE

1. Write a specific, negative problem statement.
2. Describe the problem by writing what, where, when and to what extent the problem IS and IS NOT occurring.
3. Determine any peculiar, pertinent differences between what the problem IS and what the problem IS NOT.
4. Look carefully for changes that have occurred in and around the differences.
5. Write a probable cause statement for each change discovered in Step 4 above.
6. Test each probable cause statement against each specific set of IS and IS NOT facts, and identify the most probable cause.
7. Verify the most probable cause statement, take appropriate action, and monitor results.

1. PROBLEM STATEMENT: _____

		2. PROBLEM IS	PROBLEM IS NOT	3. DIFFERENCE (between IS/IS NOT situations)	4. CHANGES (concerning Difference)
W H A T ?	DEFECT? (symptoms)				
	OR				
	OBJECT? (who/what failed)				
WHERE?					
WHEN?					
EXTENT? (seriousness)					

International Training Consultants, Inc.
P.O. Box 35613
Richmond, Virginia 23235

5. PROBABLE CAUSE STATEMENTS (one for each change from column 4)			6. Test each probable cause statement against each set of "IS/IS NOT" facts. (Probable cause does explain facts = ✓. Does not explain facts = A.)					
CHANGE	LINK (to problem)	PROBLEM	(1)	(2)	(3)	(4)	(5)	(etc.)

7. MOST PROBABLE CAUSE STATEMENT: _____

• What can be done to *verify* that this is the cause? _____

• Given this cause is verified, what *actions* can be taken to correct the initial problem? _____

8
Making Effective Decisions

Charles Kepner and Benjamin Tregoe have greatly influenced the field of modern decision-making. They have formulated their ideas into a four-stage process—called the "Kepner-Tregoe (KT) Decision Analysis." These four steps are:

1. write a decision statement;

2. develop objectives;

3. create alternatives;

4. examine risks.

Let's look at the Kepner-Tregoe process, presented in their book *The New Rational Manager*. We'll begin with some important ideas on how to write a decision statement.

1. Write a decision statement.

As with problem solving, the first step is to make the decision statement visible—write it down. So let's begin by examining how to write this statement.

One mistake that is easy to make when writing decision statements is to write "binary statements." "Binary" is a word used to describe something that has two parts. Binary statements are decisions such as: "Accept or reject that proposal"; "Go to San Francisco or not"; "Vote 'yes' or 'no' on gun control"; or, "Quit job or not." These statements may force your thinking into a premature comparison of only two alternatives.

To make more effective decisions, keep your statements open for more than two alternatives. For example, you could take the binary decision statement, "Accept or reject that proposal," and rewrite it to give you other alternatives. If you start decision statements with the words, "Select the best . . .," you can almost guarantee an "open" decision statement. Thus, the first binary statement above can be written, "Select the best proposal." The second binary decision statement, "Go to San Francisco or not," becomes "Select the best city to visit." Now you are free to choose: to go to San Francisco, New York, New Orleans—or stay home. How would you turn "Vote 'yes' or 'no' on gun control" into an open decision statement? Sometimes it helps to ask yourself a question—"Why would someone want gun control?" (We're not taking a stand here.) Now note that gun control is one possible solution to at least two different problems—reducing crime and preventing gun accidents. But as Peter Drucker said, "Trying to solve two problems with one solution very seldom works."

Rather than limiting your decision statement to only one solution, it is better to find the main problems you face. Then, put each problem's solution in its own decision statement. This allows you to develop a list of alternative solutions for each decision statement.

PROBLEMS:	High crime rate	Gun accidents
DECISION STATEMENTS:	Select best way to reduce crime.	Select best way to reduce gun accidents.
ALTERNATIVES:	1. Gun control 2. Stiffer penalties 3. More police 4. Better security	1. Gun control 2. Education 3. "Safety" ammunition 4. Childproof guns

Notice that many different alternatives are now made available by making the decision statements "open." You can still implement gun control if you wish. But by transforming your initial gun control statement into two pertinent open statements, you now have a variety of possible choices.

2. Developing objectives.

Step 2 in decision-making is to decide what you want to do—your goals, objectives, desired results—before creating alternative solutions. Developing objectives before alternatives counteracts the tendency to choose only those objectives that fit your preselected solutions.

Get help from others in writing out your list of objectives. And include all important items that are considerations in making the decision. The more sound data you have here, the better your final decision will be. Objectives come from questions such as:

"What factors should I consider?"
Examples:
— Time   — Location
— Approvals   — Etc.

"What results do I want?"
Examples:
— Efficiency   — Saving Money
— Safety   — Satisfaction
— Recognition — High Morale
— Etc.

"What resources are available?"
Examples:
— People   — Budget
— Equipment   — Materials
— Skills   — Knowledge
— Etc.

"What restrictions are there?"
Examples:
— Law   — Policy
— Standards   — Values
— Ethics   — Etc.

Before proceeding to the last two steps, let's look at an example of decision-making. Read the following case study, noting what you feel are the important objectives in this situation.

Bill, maintenance team leader for the Wonder Wombat organization located in Craigsville, Virginia, needed to hire a new employee for his section. He called a meeting of his people, and as they watched expectantly, wrote out a decision statement on a flip chart as follows:

1. MAKE A VISIBLE DECISION STATEMENT
"Select best entry-level employee for our maintenance group."

Then Bill said, "As you know, we have been authorized a new entry-level maintenance person. Since the new employee will be working closely with each of you, I thought you should be in on the selection of a replacement. The first thing we need to do is to generate a list of the things we want in the new employee. In other words, what knowledge, skills, or ability does the new person need to do the job? Does anybody have any ideas?"

After a moment's silence, Joan, the electronics technician, said, "It would be good if he or she already had an elementary understanding of basic electricity. You know, if he or she could do things like change a lamp fixture, replace a socket or a switch—and most important, read an electronic schematic."

Tom, the pipe specialist, said, "Yes, it would help if he or she could read a schematic. But how about using simple tools? The new person should be able to solder using a gun or torch, use basic hand tools, know a voltmeter from a pressure gauge, and be willing to take on the nasty jobs that sometimes have to be done. I don't want a prima donna who is too good to unstop a commode!"

"Yeah," said Rick, another member of the group, "handling tools is important. But what he or she doesn't know, we can teach. It seems to me that what's more important is that whomever we hire has a good attitude. You know, gets along well with everybody."

"And with a good attitude," responded Tom, "is the need for good work habits. We need somebody that we don't have to pick up after, gets to work on time, and doesn't hold up the rest of us. In other words, let's get somebody who's a hard worker and doesn't goof off!"

"Say," suggested Joe, a technician, "what about my brother? You all met him at the organizational picnic last month. He's a hard worker and a great guy! He'd fit right in with the rest of us."

Bill who had been writing objectives on the flip chart with a magic marker, paused and said, "Hiring your brother is a good idea, Joe. But personnel won't let us because he is your brother. So let's hold off considering alternatives until we've had a chance to finish the objectives. OK? So what other factors should we consider in hiring a new employee for our section?"

"How about reading and writing?" ask Rick. "I know it sounds silly, but there are people in the job market who can't. Any maintenance person we hire must be able to read!"

"OK," said Bill, "I'll add that to the list. What else? How about you, Chuck—any other ideas?"

Chuck, who hadn't said anything up to this point, thought for a minute and said, "I don't know. The only thing I can think of is whoever takes this job has to be willing to work for the money we can pay."

Bill, writing, said "OK, good suggestion. 'Meets salary requirements.' Anything else?" Bill waits for a moment, and then says, "I've got one. We need to hire someone who is available now, or at least within the next few weeks."

At this point, Bill and his group have developed the following objectives to use to make their decision:

1. MAKE A VISIBLE DECISION STATEMENT
"Select best-entry level employee for our maintenance group."

2. DEVELOP OBJECTIVES

- Understands basic electricity
- Knows how to use hand tools
- Willing to do any type of task
- Gets along with others
- Good work habits
- Able to read and write

- Meets salary requirements
- Available to work

When you finish your objectives, the next step is to decide which of them you require ("must" objectives), and which you desire ("want" objectives). Then when you develop alternative solutions, each solution must meet the required—"must"—objectives, or it is not acceptable. This will save time later by preventing you from considering alternatives that don't meet your required objectives.

Establish "must" objectives by looking at your basic needs—budget, time, policy, rules, law. "Want" objectives are often comparisons, such as low cost, least time, largest, nice, best, etc.

Because "must" objectives limit alternatives, it is wise to restrict their number when possible. Musts also need to be specific and measurable (e.g., "Available to work within 3 weeks," not "Available to work").

Looking at the list, which items do you think were the team's must objectives and which were their want objectives?

If you were making this judgment for yourself, of course, your must and want objectives probably would be different from theirs. In their case, however, they felt that "Available to work within 3 weeks," "Meets salary requirements" (which they specified), and "Reads and writes" were their musts. Bill's group spent considerable time discussing the measurability of the objective, "Reads and writes." They realized that the objective was not a "must" the way they wrote it because it wasn't quantifiable. Thus they developed a simple reading and writing test based on the forms and text that they used within their section. They showed this test to the personnel department and received permission to use it in their evaluation of applicants. Because of their discussions they rewrote this objective to state, "Passes reading and writing test."

At this point, their decision analysis looked like this:

1. MAKE A VISIBLE DECISION STATEMENT
"Select best-entry level employee for our maintenance group."

2. DEVELOP OBJECTIVES

— Understands basic electricity	Want
— Knows how to use hand tools	Want
— Willing to do any type of task	Want
— Gets along with others	Want
— Good work habits	Want
— Passes reading and writing test	Must
— Meets salary requirements	Must
— Available to work in 3 weeks	Must

Obviously some of their "want" objectives are more important than others. Understanding basic electricity may be a great deal more important than knowing how to use hand tools. Therefore, the quality of their selection process will be improved if they assign higher weights to more desirable objectives to reflect their greater relative importance. Using a scale of 1 to 10, and giving the highest number to the most important "want" objective, their list might now look like this:

1. MAKE A VISIBLE DECISION STATEMENT
"Select best-entry level employee for our maintenance group."

2. DEVELOP OBJECTIVES

— Understands basic electricity	9
— Knows how to use hand tools	8
— Willing to do any type of task	6
— Gets along with others	7
— Good work habits	5
— Passes reading and writing test	Must
— Meets salary requirements	Must
— Available to work in 3 weeks	Must

Note that they didn't assign a "10" to any of the want objectives. Usually, avoid assigning "10's" to your objectives. Save them for extremely important objectives that normally would be musts, but can't be because they aren't measurable.

Note also that the assigned weights will differ according to the raters. In a group, obtain a consensus. If you're not leading a group but doing this process by yourself, seek help from others by asking, "How important do you think this objective is compared to that one, and why?" Also note that some must objectives also may have a corresponding want objective. For example, if it had been important to Bill's group, they could have written a new want objective, "Can start work at anytime over the next 3 weeks" and maybe rated it a "2." Here, they felt that it wasn't very important that somebody start immediately, so they did not rewrite the must objective. However, they rewrote the objective, "Meets salary requirements" and added as a want objective, "Satisfaction with salary."

3. Creating Alternatives.

In this step you create alternatives to fulfill your objectives. At this point it is often helpful to think in terms of the following classifications:

- *corrective* alternatives that solve the problem;
- *interim* alternatives that don't remedy the problem, but do buy time; and
- *adaptive* alternatives that allow us to live with the problem.

For example, if the problem is a fire, I can take corrective action by putting the fire out with water. Or I might take interim action, by doing something to restrict air flow to the fire. Or I could take adaptive action by deciding to let the fire burn—and roast hot dogs! By being aware of all three of these classes of alternatives you can significantly increase the number of available approaches.

In developing creative alternatives two things are helpful. First, "brainstorm" a list of possibilities, and later evaluate and combine them to create workable solutions. Second, get help! Talk to people whose opinions and judgment you trust. Talk with employees who are involved in the decision or play a role in carrying it out. Since you wrote out your decision, you can show others both the decision statement and the alternatives you are considering, and ask them for additional ideas.

It is much easier to make good decisions after you have clarified your objectives and created alternatives. For example, consider the example of Bill's team just presented. Suppose Bill and his group were faced with the following applicants. Should they eliminate any of these prospective employees because he or she fails to satisfy at least one of the must objectives?

Applicant #1. Female, 32 years old, with two children. Recently divorced. Great personality. High school graduate. Attended a two-year electronics technical school after high school. New to the job market. States she is willing to do any type of work. Little knowledge of work habits as she has not been employed since school years. Fourteen years ago worked part-time after school as a maintenance person for a local grocery store chain. She says that she was seldom late for work. Unable to check references since organization is now out of business. Reads and writes well, meets the salary requirements. She is unemployed and could come to work tomorrow.

Applicant #2. Male, 44 years old, married, and has two grown children. In interviews, seemed quiet and withdrawn—almost depressed. His job was eliminated when there was a major reorganization at his old company. He has been out of work three months and is having difficulty obtaining employment. He is a highly-skilled maintenance person with 20 years' experience in carpentry, hydraulics, and electricity. His references check out. He has good work habits, but a history of sickness. His old organization would not specify type of illness. He said he needs a job, and would be satisfied with the starting salary though it is less than what he had been making. Also said he doesn't mind doing any type of work, no matter how disagreeable. Reads and writes well. High school education. Could start tomorrow.

Applicant #3. Male, 18 years old. Single but engaged. High school graduate. Worked for his father during the summer while in high school. Father runs a small electrical contracting business out of his home. Father says his son is a hard worker, has good work habits, and never missed a single day from work. Applicant states he is not too proud to do any task that needs to be done. Reads, but writing skills are marginal. His writing sample, full of errors in basic grammar, had many misspelled words, and his handwriting is barely legible. When questioned about his writing, applicant stated that he has always had difficulty with his spelling and thinks he may be dyslexic. He meets salary requirements, and would like to start immediately. Seems like a nice guy, but very serious. Did not laugh or joke during any of his interviews with members of the group even when it would have been appropriate.

Must they eliminate any one of these three alternatives from consideration because he or she fails to meet the objectives of Bill's team?

Bill's group has a difficult decision. They cannot consider applicant #3 because he doesn't meet one of their must objectives—"Passes reading and writing test." We have pointed out that it is not desirable to have must objectives that are not absolutely necessary, because they eliminate alternatives. So unless the group can find a way out of their dilemma by making "reading and writing" a want objective, they cannot select this alternative—and must confine their attention to applicants #1 and #2, both of whom meet all their must objectives.

This decision is typical of the ones you face at work—and at home. You may want to select, or at least consider, a particular alternative—and too often do, even when it doesn't meet a must. Decisions turn out better when you first take the time to determine objectives, rank them, create several alternatives, and then rationally evaluate each in terms of musts and wants. This process produces good decisions because it helps you determine what is really important.

Bill's group is now ready to write down information on how well each applicant meets each objective. Usually, it is probably best to write in data—including a "Yes" or "No"—for the must objectives first. As discussed, applicant #3 is eliminated because he did not meet the "must" reading and writing requirement.

1. MAKE A VISIBLE DECISION STATEMENT
"Select best employee for our maintenance group."

2. DEVELOP OBJECTIVES		3. ALTERNATIVES Applicant #1	Applicant #2	Applicant #3
— Understands basic electricity	9	Two years tech. school	Highly skilled	
— Knows how to use hand tools	8	Part-time maint. person 14 years ago	20 years' experience	
— Willing to do any type of task	6	Says she is willing to do any kind of work	Was a senior craftsman but indicates would do any task	
— Gets along with others	7	Great personality	Quiet and withdrawn, seems almost depressed	
— Good work habits	5	Can't verify work habits	Good work habits but has a history of illness	
— Passes reading and writing test	Must	Yes	Yes	No
— Meets salary requirement	Must	Yes	Yes	
— Available to work in 3 weeks	Must	Yes	Yes	
— Satisfaction with salary	4	Satisfied	Salary may not meet his needs	

Notice that Bill's team could have written "yes" and "no" answers for their objectives. But later, when they compare the alternatives with each other, it will be very difficult to weight a series of "yes's" and "no's." By writing in data or information they can later judge which alternative is best. (Of course, *must* objectives always include "yes" or "no"—i.e., go or no-go, meets or doesn't meet the objective.) For example, in the objective, "Gets along with others," they could have written in "Yes" or "No" for both applicants.

Having previously compared and weighted their want objectives using a value scale of 1–10, Bill's group will now do the same for each alternative. For each objective (each row), they will automatically give the best alternative a "10," and the other alternative something less than 10. (This will keep them from double-weighting an objective.) They will not weight the must objectives, since these objectives are really screening devices that eliminate alternatives that cannot be considered.

1. MAKE A VISIBLE DECISION STATEMENT
"Select best employee for our maintenance group."

2. DEVELOP OBJECTIVES		3. ALTERNATIVES		
		Applicant #1	Applicant #2	Applicant #3
— Understands basic electricity	9	**2** Two years tech. school	**10** Highly skilled	
— Knows how to use hand tools	8	**2** Part-time maint. person 14 years ago	**10** 20 years' experience	
— Willing to do any type of task	6	**10** Says she is willing to do any kind of work	**8** Was a senior craftsman but indicates would do any task	
— Gets along with others	7	**10** Great personality	**4** Quiet and withdrawn, seems almost depressed	
— Good work habits	5	**10** Can't verify work habits	**8** Good work habits but has a history of illness	
— Passes reading and writing test	Must	Yes	Yes	No
— Meets salary requirements	Must	Yes	Yes	
— Available to work in 3 weeks	Must	Yes	Yes	
— Satisfaction with salary	4	**10** Satisfied	**3** Salary may not meet his needs	

Next, Bill's group multiplies the weight of each want objective by the weight of each remaining alternatives (applicants #1 and #2), and records each product (objective weight x alternative weight) in the table.

1. MAKE A VISIBLE DECISION STATEMENT

"Select best employee for our maintenance group."

2. DEVELOP OBJECTIVES		3. ALTERNATIVES Applicant #1	Applicant #2	Applicant #3
— Understands basic electricity	9	x 2 = 18 Two years tech. school	x 10 = 90 Highly skilled	
— Knows how to use hand tools	8	x 2 = 16 Part-time maint. person 14 years ago	x 10 = 80 20 years' experience	
— Willing to do any type of task	6	x 10 = 60 Says she is willing to do any kind of work	x 8 = 48 Was a senior craftsman but indicates would do any task	
— Gets along with others	7	x 10 = 70 Great personality	x 4 = 28 Quiet and withdrawn, seems almost depressed	
— Good work habits	5	x 10 = 50 Can't verify work habits	x 8 = 40 Good work habits but has a history of illness	
— Passes reading and writing test	Must	Yes	Yes	No
— Meets salary requirements	Must	Yes	Yes	
— Available to work in 3 weeks	Must	Yes	Yes	
— Satisfaction with salary	4	x 10 = 40 Satisfied	x 3 = 12 Salary may not meet his needs	
Total product scores:		**254**	**298**	

Bill's group added the product scores and had a tentative first choice—alternative #2. But note that at this point in their analysis their choice is only tentative, because they must now consider the potential risks involved in making their decision.

4. Analyzing Risk.

The fourth and last step in the decision process is to consider carefully the risk involved with each of the leading alternatives. This is the most neglected step in decision-making—because we tend to look at life's new possibilities and beginnings enthusiastically. Thus, you must examine the risks in your decisions before you carry them out. To do this, simply ask, "What can go wrong?" Here again, seek help from others with experience, and talk to your employees who will be involved in carrying the decision, since several individuals can often foresee future problems better than one person working alone.

When first considering potential risks, deal with one alternative at a time. That is, do not initially attempt to evaluate the possibility of each risk occurring in every alternative. Then when you have completed your list of potential risks (problems) for the first alternative, evaluate each potential problem in terms of the probability of it happening, and its seriousness if it does happen. Again, we will use the numerical scale of 1–10 to assign "seriousness" and "probability" weights to each of our risks. Multiply the two weights, add the numbers, and the resultant score will show the amount of risk involved in that particular alternative. Then repeat the process with each of your other leading alternatives.

In our example of Bill's group, two alternatives were left—applicants #1 and #2. Their last step, then, is to evaluate the risks in selecting each of these alternatives by asking: "If we hire that applicant, what could go wrong?" After talking with each other and the personnel department, they developed the following "risk list." (Note that though we show the following risk analysis completed in one chart, each alternative's risks should be analyzed separately.)

RISK

Alternative #1:	Probability (of it happening)	Seriousness (if it happens)	
1. May not be able to do job	1	10	1 x 10 = 10

Total risk for alternative #1 = 10

Alternative #2:	Probability	Seriousness	
1. Because of low salary, he may stay with job only until he finds a job that pays more.	8	10	8 x 10 = 80
2. May be a possibility of significant lost time in the future due to illness	4	8	4 x 8 = 32

Total risk for alternative #2 = 112

Though we can't make the decision for Bill's group, their evaluation of risks suggests that, although applicant #2 scored slightly higher than applicant #1 in terms of objectives, applicant #1 has a much lower estimated risk than applicant #2. Want objective scores like "9 x 9 = 81" and "8 x 9 = 72" are probably a missed must alternative, i.e., they probably should have been must objectives from the start. These "9 x 9" and other high risk scores are rattlesnakes under the bed!

All things considered, applicant #1 appears to be the best candidate.

When you finish evaluating your various alternatives risks, do not subtract the risk score from the objective/alternative scores. They are "apples and oranges"—two entirely different factors. Simply compare the original objective/alternative scores with the risk scores to make a balanced decision.

If you have to make a major decision, try to use a grid analysis similar to the one just shown. But—you don't always have the time. So when you're on the phone, in the hallway, or in the boss's office, you can use the "O.A.R." approach of: 1) developing *objectives*; 2) creating and evaluating *alternatives*; and 3) analyzing *risk*. It is a good way to make a well-balanced decision.

Below is a checklist for using the step-by-step decision-making process.

1. WRITE AN OPEN DECISION STATEMENT.
(Beginning your statement with "Select best . . ." should guarantee an open decision statement.)

2. LIST OBJECTIVES.

- Ask questions:
  — What factors should you consider?
  — What are your resources (money/time/people/equipment)?
  — What results do you want?
  — What restrictions are required?
- Determine "must" objectives
- Weight "want" objectives

3. CREATE ALTERNATIVES.

- Brainstorm a list of alternatives on another sheet of paper. (Do not evaluate alternatives until list is completed.)
- Select three or four best alternatives
- Write in data:
  — Write data in "must" objective boxes for each alternative first
  — Eliminate any alternative that doesn't meet every "must" objective

— Write in balance of data in "want" boxes for each alternative.

- Avoid writing "Yes" and "No" data in "want" boxes.
  Use facts, figures, opinions, and impressions.
- Don't utilize "good/better/best" classifications—use specific information.
- Weight each alternative concerning each "want" objective, on a scale of 1 to 10—assigning 10 to the best alternative for each objective
- Multiply objective weight by alternative weight and record on grid
- Add scores for each alternative

4. ANALYZE RISK.

- Select top two alternative scores for risk analysis
- Evaluate probability and seriousness of critical risks for each alternative, from 1 to 10 ("10" = highest risk)
- Don't "double-load" decision by rewriting an objective as a risk
- Multiply probability and seriousness ratings, add totals, and compare
- Don't subtract risk scores from earlier objective/alternative scores
- Based on final comparison of the two alternatives' objectives and risk scores, make a balanced decision

On the following page is a *Decision Making Work Sheet* and grid that you may copy and use to make your decisions.

DECISION MAKING WORK SHEET

1. Write an open decision statement (i.e., "Select the best...").

2. List all important objectives.

   • Identify and separate "want" and "must" objectives.
   • Weight the "want" objectives, from 1 to 10 ("10" = highest weight).

3. Create and list the alternatives.

   • Brainstorm a list of alternatives on another sheet of paper.
   • Select three or four best alternatives for analysis.

4. Write data.

   • Write data in "must" objective boxes for each alternative first.
   • Eliminate any alternative that doesn't meet every "must" objective.
   • Then write in data for "want" objectives—use facts, figures, opinions, and impressions (not yes/no).

5. Assign weights to each alternative for each "want" objective. (Assign a "10" to the best alternative reflecting each objective, and an appropriate lower score to the other alternatives.)

6. Multiply each objective weight by each alternative weight, and record.

7. Add column scores for each alternative, and compare totals.

8. Taking the top two alternatives, identify the critical risk objectives, and assign "probability" and "seriousness" values (10–1 scale, "10" = highest risk). Multiply probability and seriousness ratings, add risk totals for each alternative, and compare.

9. Make selection based on final comparison of objective/alternative scores and risk scores.

Objectives ("musts" and "wants")	Weight	Alternative 1	Alternative 2	Alternative 3
		Data & Value	Data & Value	Data & Value

Total product scores

Alternative 1
Risk: P S
_____ ___ x ___ = ___
_____ ___ x ___ = ___
_____ ___ x ___ = ___
_____ ___ x ___ = ___
_____ ___ x ___ = ___
_____ ___ x ___ = ___

Total risk for Alt. 1 = ___

Alternative 2
Risk: P S
_____ ___ x ___ = ___
_____ ___ x ___ = ___
_____ ___ x ___ = ___
_____ ___ x ___ = ___
_____ ___ x ___ = ___
_____ ___ x ___ = ___

Total risk for Alt. 2 = ___

9
The Importance of Planning

Good planning is a nine-step process:

1. Determine your goals and set priorities

2. Write your priority goals in an objective form

3. Develop steps to reach your objectives

4. Identify critical steps in your plan

5. Anticipate potential problems

6. Evaluate the probability and seriousness of each potential problem

7. Determine likely causes of the highest priority potential problems, and write preventive and contingency actions

8. Repeat Steps 5–7 with any other critical step

9. Incorporate important preventive and major contingency actions into the original plan

In this chapter we will review each of these stages of successful planning. Then, use the *Planning Work Sheet* at the end of the chapter to practice planning on your job—or for any life-goals.

Why Plan?

In all human activity, planning is critical for several important reasons.

1. Knowing where you are going helps you get there. Alice said to the Cheshire cat in Lewis Carroll's *Through the Looking Glass:*

> "Tell me, please, which way it is I ought to go from here."
> "Where is it you want to go?" said the cat.
> "I don't care much where." said Alice.
> "Then it doesn't matter which way you go!" said the cat.

The cat was telling Alice that it doesn't make much difference what you do if you don't know where you want to go. But it makes a very great difference on the job to know where you want to go. If you are not moving toward a specific goal, then you have no way of knowing whether your work is productive or not. Successful people plan everything they do—every day. Plans make destinations clear. They tell how to get there. And they allow you to measure the success of your efforts.

2. Planning enables you to experience a daily sense of accomplishment. Your plans will guide you in choosing the work today that will lead to your goals—thus providing a continuous feeling of fulfillment. Distant, general aims alone don't have much influence on your immediate activities. But when you take a distant goal and specify its sub-goals, with a step-by-step plan to reach each sub-goal, then you'll see that some of these steps need to be worked on this week—and even today. By successfully carrying out today's steps in your plan you will immediately feel a sense of accomplishment.

3. Good planning prevents procrastination. The most important things in life—like long-term goals and objectives—do not create a sense of urgency until you begin to see how they must be reached. Because they appear so far off in the future, you may feel it is all right to put off action on them until tomorrow—especially since there are so many seemingly urgent things to do right now. So given the choice between "urgent" matters and long-term goals (no matter how important), most people go with the urgent and postpone the important. But when you bring your ultimate goals and objectives into the present by creating step-by-step plans, then you realize that acting on a "distant" goal is urgent now!

4. Planning prevents problems. Well-conceived plans help you anticipate potential problems before they happen. Problems are much less likely to happen if you take the time to analyze them by thinking them through, talking with others, and developing creative solutions.

5. The power of participation. If we have responsibility for others it makes a lot more sense to include these people in determining our goals, especially if they are going to play a part in carrying out the plan. If our employees participate in the development of goals and objectives, and even help formulate specific strategies, then they are more likely to be committed to the plan. This is especially true if our employees expect to be included in planning their goals.

Why We Don't Plan

Most people agree that good planning is important to the success of any project. And yet, all too often we don't spend sufficient time in planning. Why? There are many reasons:

- You may have to commit yourself to doing something today that you really don't want to do. And so, "No problem is so big that it can't be ignored"!

- You can seem like a "hero" by putting out fires caused through lack of planning. You may even make a career out of permitting crises that you then step into and dramatically end.

- It may simply seem easier to operate "by the seat of your pants"—and bounce along from one crisis to the next.

- It takes time to write goal statements and then develop plans and strategies—especially when you involve your employees.

- Your performance as a leader is often evaluated in terms of what you appear to be "doing," rather than on how well you plan.

- You may not know how to plan effectively.

Let's look at the steps in good planning.

1. DETERMINING YOUR GOALS AND SETTING PRIORITIES.

List important goals. The first step in real planning is to find a quiet place and "brainstorm" a list of the most important things you want to do and be. As you list your goals, don't stop to evaluate or judge them. Write down everything that occurs to you, even if it may seem "silly." If you have a burning secret desire, write it down! Focus on all areas of your life—whatever goals are important to you.

Don't worry about writing measurable objective statements at this point. As long as you know what you mean by what you write, that's fine. And this is your list. Don't show it to anybody.

For example, here is a recent list of my personal goals:

*1) Improve my relationship with my children

*2) Produce 10 employee training modules

3) Write another book

4) Gross X amount of dollars next year

5) Take a rubber-raft trip on a white water river

6) Buy a 1980 Corvette, with 4-speed, 454 cu. in. engine

7) Take a ride in a glider

8) Persuade my son and his new wife to move from Australia to the U.S.

9) Build a cider press before next fall

10) Learn Russian

*11) Give more quality time and effort to my marriage

12) Lose 15 pounds

13) Run a marathon

*14) Learn more about motivating my employees

Select your priority goals. After you have spent a few minutes freely creating your personal goal list, select the top three or four items and mark them with an asterisk or check mark (as I have). You can use the form found at the end of this chapter to create your list of what you most want to do and be.

2. WRITE YOUR PRIORITY GOALS IN AN OBJECTIVE FORM.

Now that you have brainstormed a list of the things you would like to be and do, and identified the most important ones, you are ready to write out your highest-priority goals in an objective form. An objective (or goal—we will use these two words interchangeably) is simply a statement of exactly what you want to accomplish. Such a statement should have the following three characteristics:

First, an objective statement should be specific, not general. For example, the statement, "To learn more about motivating my employees," (my objective #14) does not communicate enough information. What does the word "motivating" mean? How will I know when I have learned more about motivation? By what date do I want to have obtained this knowledge? Since my objective statement doesn't give enough specific information about my goal, it will be hard to actually know when I am successful—or even whether I am unsuccessful. Thus, in my objective statement I need to:

- Specify behaviors. Decide what actions I am going to take—what I will do—to learn more about motivation. For example:
  - Attend a workshop at the University on "Motivating Today's Employees" by January of this year.
  - Give each of my employees honest positive feedback on three different occasions by the end of the month.
- Identify results. For example:
  - My employees will have an average attendance rate not less that 98% during the next year.

— The employees in my section will score in the 90th percentile on the attitude survey.

Second, a good objective statement also should be measurable—*quantifiable*. "To learn more about conducting a performance appraisal session with my employees" sounds fine. But I really won't know when I have satisfactorily achieved this goal because I haven't specified my standard—or measure—of achievement. If I rewrite this objective as, "To be able to conduct a performance appraisal session with my employees by January 1 of next year," my goal is measurable, in two ways. First, I have used a word that specifies behavior ("conduct," rather than "learning"). And second, I have committed myself to a specific time period. With my goal statement thus reexpressed in measurable terms, I can figure out when I have achieved it.

Third, an objective statement should be *achievable*. There is little point in setting yourself up for failure. A good goal statement will extend and improve you, not break you.

You can develop several different types of job objectives:

- First, regular or *routine* objectives that simply specify the things you normally do on your job.
- Second, *problem-solving* objectives that you write to resolve a specific problem.
- Third, *innovative* objectives, written to facilitate new or creative ideas.
- Finally, *personal* objectives—which you write about you.

Most of your growth on the job is connected with the last three kinds of objectives. Thus, it is better for both you and your organization if you concentrate your effort in these three areas rather than on routine objectives.

Before you start to spend time working on your job-related objectives, it is best to sit down with your boss and ask how he or she feels about your priorities. Examine which of the objectives you have written are "must do," "ought to do," and "nice to do." Since your performance will be appraised on what you do, it only makes sense to complete job objectives that meet with your boss's approval.

Put your energies into only two or three objectives at any one time. Your chances of success are much better if you concentrate on a few important objectives rather than all of them at once. (Less important objectives can usually be addressed in the future.)

3. DEVELOPING STEPS TO REACH YOUR OBJECTIVE.

After you have determined which objectives you want to carry out, you can then develop the steps you will take to achieve them. As you identify the steps in your plan, set completion dates for each step. (But do not assign a final number to your steps at this point. You may need to add more steps later.)

As an example, I know a person—let's call her Elizabeth—whose objective list included becoming a manager in her organization within two years. The initial steps of her plan looked something like this:

1. DETERMINE GOALS AND SET PRIORITIES
   "I want to be a manager."

2. OBJECTIVE
   "To become a manager in my organization within two years"

3. STEPS OF PLAN WITH COMPLETION DATES
   — Meet with boss to discuss my goal.   Sept. 15
   — Write three key objectives in my present job,
     and discuss with boss.   Sept. 30
   — Analyze my leadership skills; determine my
     strengths and where I need improvement.   Oct. 15
   — Sign up for at least one supervisory workshop
     each year at the university's Management
     Center.   Dec. 1

— Attend night classes and get the 24 credits I
need to finish college, starting this semester.   Jan. 15

— Determine which management positions
might open up within two years.   Mar. 1

This is where most people stop their planning process. But wisely, Elizabeth realized that she needed to also look carefully at the steps in her plan, noting any that could cause difficulties—let's call them "critical steps."

4. IDENTIFY CRITICAL STEPS.

From past experience you sometimes know that a particular step means trouble! (Maybe you took that step before and it led to a disaster.) If a step is completely new to you, look out. "Murphy's Law"— "What can go wrong, will go wrong," may get you! Major steps, with lots of parts and pieces, are especially vulnerable, particularly if you have no experience with the step. You have also probably noted that problems can result when people have to communicate over distances by phone or letter, and also when there are a number of people involved. If a step means operating close to the limits of your space, time, or money, you probably have trouble brewing. For example, if your plan requires that you order a new item that is exactly 3 feet wide and your door is 3 ½ feet, you better get an ax! Or if someone tells you the item you ordered will be here Wednesday, and you have to have it Thursday, you might be wise to assume that it won't arrive until Friday. If a step in your plan "will only cost $99.95," and you have exactly $100.00, then you pretty well know what's going to happen!

All this potential problem analysis may sound negative. But the good news is that if you anticipate potential problems before you carry out your plan, you can often develop solutions that will greatly increase the chances that you will achieve your goal.

In the example of Elizabeth, she selected as a critical step in her plan, "Attend night classes and get the 24 credits I need to finish college." She viewed this step as a potential problem because it was new for her (she had never attended college at night). It was also a very important one. She worked for a boss who had once said to her, "Your chances of being selected as a manager in this organization are a lot better if you have a college degree."

5. ANTICIPATE POTENTIAL PROBLEMS.

Having identified the steps that may cause problems (critical steps), select one, and list the potential problems. In Elizabeth's case, she wrote down the following potential problems with her night classes step:

4. CRITICAL STEP
"Attend night classes and get the 24 credits I need to finish college, starting this semester."

5. POTENTIAL PROBLEMS
A. Night school will be very hard on my family.
B. I'll get bored and stop attending.
C. It may take longer than two years to get my degree.

6. EVALUATE PROBABILITY AND SERIOUSNESS OF POTENTIAL PROBLEMS.

The next step is to evaluate the probability and seriousness of each potential problem. That is, figure out what the probability is that the problem will occur, and then how seriously it will affect the success of your plan if it does occur. To rate probability and seriousness, use H for high, M for medium, and L for low.

In Elizabeth's case, she felt that night school would be a hardship for her family—not only in terms of cost, but also time. Attending classes would take much time away from home, and the courses also would require a great deal of time for homework.

She felt that the chances of her getting bored with school, and therefore dropping out, were very low. If this did happen, however, it would have a serious impact on her plan. Her boss would see her as a failure in something he considered very important (earning a college degree). But she thought she could finish the degree program within the two-year time limit. If she didn't, she would be so close to finishing that her boss would still support her efforts. Her analysis now looked like this:

5. POTENTIAL PROBLEMS:	6. EVALUATE POTENTIAL PROBLEMS AS TO THEIR PROBABILITY (P) AND SERIOUSNESS (S) (High, Medium, Low)

	P	S
A. Night school will be very hard on my family.	H	H
B. I'll get bored and stop attending.	L	H
C. It may take longer than two years to get my degree.	L	M

7. DETERMINE LIKELY CAUSES OF THE HIGHEST PRIORITY POTENTIAL PROBLEMS, AND WRITE PREVENTION AND CONTINGENCY ACTIONS.

Next you need to analyze your greatest potential problems by finding their likely causes, and planning preventive and contingency actions. In solving problems, you act on causes. And to prevent or prepare for potential problems, you look for likely causes. After you have identified the likely causes, ask, "What can be done to reduce the probability that this event (or likely cause) will happen?" In other words, what preventive action can you include in your plans? You also must consider: "If the worst comes to pass and the problem does occur, what can I do now to reduce the seriousness of the consequences?" In other words, what contingency action can you include in your plans from the start?

For Elizabeth, the potential problem "Night school will be very hard on my family" has a high probability of happening, and when it happens it will be high in seriousness. Thus she selected this problem for further analysis.

7. ANALYZE THE HIGHEST PRIORITY POTENTIAL PROBLEM.
"Night school will be very hard on my family."

LIKELY CAUSES	PREVENTIVE ACTION	CONTINGENCY ACTION
2 nights per week away from family	See if local educational TV station has college courses I can take at home	Enroll Bill (husband) in one or more courses with me
Shortage of money	See if organization will pay for all or part; enroll in state-supported school rather than private college	Borrow from relatives
Lack of study time	Buy course books now and start studying in advance; take courses that are easier for me	Get family to help me in studying
Family not aware of hardships	Involve family in pre-planning; have Bill talk to Joe who is also attending night school	(No action)

8. REPEAT STEPS 5–7 WITH ANY OTHER CRITICAL STEPS.

Elizabeth would then select other critical steps and repeat steps 5–7 by:

- Listing any potential problems concerning each critical step.
- Evaluating each potential problem on its probability of happening and seriousness if it happens.
- Analyzing each major potential problem for likely causes, preventive action, and contingency action.

9. INCORPORATE IMPORTANT PREVENTIVE AND MAJOR CONTINGENCY ACTIONS INTO THE ORIGINAL PLAN.

The last—and highly important—step in planning is to build your preventive and contingency actions into your plan at the appropriate points.

In our example, Elizabeth's plan will now look like this:

9. INCORPORATE IMPORTANT PREVENTIVE AND MAJOR CONTINGENCY ACTIONS INTO THE ORIGINAL PLAN
    A. Have a family meeting to discuss educational plans.   Sept. 1
    B. Meet with boss to discuss promotional goal, and determine whether the organization will assist with tuition.   Sept. 15
    C. Write three key development objectives in my present job and discuss with boss.   Sept. 30
    D. Meet with college department chairperson and identify required and elective courses. Consider elective courses that Bill would enjoy taking. Also determine at this meeting if there are college courses I can take at home.   Oct. 15
    E. Analyze my leadership skills; determine my strengths and where I need improvement.   Nov. 15
    F. Etc.

By using this planning process Elizabeth has greatly increased the probability of reaching her goal. Also note that some of her completion dates have changed to include her new activities. At this point (after incorporating the preventive/contingency actions concerning any other high-priority problem), Elizabeth can now review her plans to make certain she really can meet her initial objective of being promoted to supervisor within two years.

Many of us spend a great deal of time dealing with a variety of problems, but do very little planning. We can become so busy running from crisis to crisis that we don't take the time to plan for success—in or outside our jobs.

But when you commit yourself to identifying your goals, and follow a proven step-by-step plan to achieve them, you will find you are not sidetracked by problems. You will surely increase your level of achievement. And when you utilize these planning strategies with your employees, they too will get more productive results.

DEVELOPING OBJECTIVES WITH EMPLOYEES

We have now seen what makes up a good objective (specific/measurable/obtainable), and noted four classes of objectives (regular, problem solving, innovative, and personal). We also have examined a step-by-step planning method to use in reaching your objectives.

At this point you will need to know how to sit down with your employees and plan *with* them. Therefore, let's look at a seven-step process that has helped effective leaders conduct objective planning sessions with their employees. There seven steps are as follows:

1. Prepare for the joint meeting

2. Open the meeting

3. Discuss employee's tentative objectives and determine the measurability of each

4. Offer additional objectives if appropriate

5. Determine priorities of objectives

6. Review employee's strategies and plans to achieve key objectives, and offer ideas

7. Set follow-up dates for review session, and conclude meeting

The above steps involve specific things to do. So let's look at each step in more detail.

1. Prepare for the joint meeting

If this is the first time you have developed mutual objectives with the employee, you need to take the "mystery" out of the process by letting him or her know exactly what the meeting will be about. So meet briefly with the employee before the interview and discuss:

- the purpose of the upcoming meeting
- how the *Planning Work Sheet* is to be filled out
- any appropriate organization/department/section goals he or she needs to know before completing his or her work sheets
- when and where the meeting will take place

After this preliminary meeting with the employee, spend some time thinking of several key objectives you would like to see the employee achieve during the upcoming year. Then, using the *Planning Work Sheet,* write out the objectives as well as tentative plans and methods for how the employee will achieve them. You can share these plans with the employee in the upcoming meeting, if needed. Be sure to locate a meeting place that is private and where you can control interruptions. If it is impossible to hold your telephone calls for an hour meeting, then go elsewhere. Reserve the conference room, or find someone who is on vacation and use his or her office. You can even tell your boss what you will be doing, and ask not to be interrupted (if possible!). Whatever you do, treat this meeting as critically important, and do not allow interruptions.

2. Open the meeting.

When the employee first walks into your office or conference room, explain that you wish to help him or her

    a. better understand the organization's and department's goals and objectives,

    b. improve objectives and plans, and

    c. explore potential problems that may exist with the plans.

Next, help reduce any anxiety the employee may be feeling by telling him or her the meeting agenda. For example, you might say something like:

> "Bill, I see my role in today's meeting as being a resource for you. I may have some information you need on our department's goals, some ideas or suggestions to help improve your plans, and even some ideas about anticipating potential problems. What I'd like to do is to discuss your objectives and make sure that they are measurable statements—then offer any additional specific objectives if appropriate. I'll also try to help you set some priorities so you know where you need to spend your time; review your strategies and plans and offer ideas if needed; and then set up specific follow-up dates. This is your meeting, Bill, and I am here to help you any way I can."

Use your own words to explain generally to your employee what is going to happen, and your role in the meeting.

3. Discuss employee's tentative objectives, and determine the measurability of each.

In Step 3, ask the employee to relate the objectives he or she wrote. Here, review only the objective statements at the top of the *Planning Work Sheet,* since the specific plans and methods will be discussed later after setting priorities. As the employee reads his or her first objective, make sure that it is specific, measurable, and has target dates.

As the leader you can help the employee in identifying his or her ideas for improving objectives by asking questions such as:

- "How will you know when you are successful?"
- "What will you be able to do (or avoid doing) when you have achieved your objective?"
- "What conditions will exist when you finish?"
- "What tangible results will be achieved?"
- "What are you going to do to make this happen?"

During the discussion of the employee's objectives it is not necessary to determine whether the objectives are feasible or appropriate. You can discuss feasibility in Step 6 when you review the employee's plans. And you can deal naturally with the question of appropriateness in Step 5 when you and the employee set priorities. Remember, what looks initially like an impossible objective may turn out to be possible after reviewing the employee's strategies and plans.

4. Offer additional objectives if appropriate.

After reviewing each of the employee's objectives in Step 3, you may have additional organizational, departmental, or sectional objectives that he or she hasn't addressed. So here is where you can offer additional topics that you feel are important. Since you took the time to write out several objectives before the meeting, you will be ready at this point to make any needed suggestions.

5. Determine priorities of objectives.

Ask the employee to arrange, in order of priority, the objectives that were discussed in both Step 3 (his or her objectives) and Step 4 (your objectives). Then, two or three key objectives should be selected for the immediate future. Objectives that are not selected as first priorities can be deferred to quarterly follow-up meetings, and implemented as the initial objectives are achieved. You deliberately should restrict the number of objectives initially selected for two reasons.

employee's chances of success are better if his or her efforts are concentrated on only a few key objectives. Second, you can improve your chances of following up the employee's progress if you have a reasonable number of objectives to monitor.

6. Review employee's strategies and plans to achieve key objectives, and offer ideas.

As the employee discusses his or her plans and methods you can do several things. First, if the employee has a good plan, be sure to say so. Second, ask what you can do to help the employee reach his or her objectives, and feel free to offer your suggestions for how the plans could be further improved. Third, with each objective ask the key question, "If we do this, what could go wrong?" to elicit any potential problems. Then offer suggestions or ideas for preventive or contingency solutions, and include these ideas in the original plan. Finally, review the target dates for the objective and action steps, and adjust them to make them more realistic if indicated.

7. Set follow-up dates for review session, and conclude meeting.

Tell your employee that you will be available to discuss his or her plans whenever needed. But to ensure that you will really follow up with the employee's progress toward his or her objective, set specific dates in the employee's presence, and write them in your calendar. Normally one follow-up meeting each quarter will be sufficient, with additional meetings scheduled as needed.

In concluding the meeting, ask the employee to provide you with a copy of the objectives *Work Sheets* after the meeting. Then spell out your positive expectation by saying: "I know you can do it!" Finally, express your appreciation for the time and effort that he or she spent preparing for this meeting.

On the following page is a *Leader's Checklist* of the key steps in writing objectives with your employees. Following that is a *Planning Work Sheet* that you may copy and use for each of your key objectives. Remember to write your objectives in specific and measurable terms so that you and others will know when you have reached them. You also can make copies of this *Work Sheet* to give to your employees for use in writing their objectives.

LEADER'S CHECKLIST FOR DEVELOPING OBJECTIVES WITH EMPLOYEES

1. PREPARE FOR THE JOINT MEETING.

- Tentatively complete the *Planning Work Sheet* on key objectives for this employee
- Meet in advance and:
  - — discuss purpose of upcoming meeting
  - — give employee a copy of the *Planning Work Sheet*
  - — present any appropriate organizational, department, or section objectives
  - — state when and where the meeting will take place
- Plan minimum of one hour for meeting, and ensure:
  - — privacy
  - — no interruptions

2. OPEN THE MEETING.

- Explain your role as a resource for:
  - — organizational goals and objectives
  - — your department or section goals
  - — ideas and suggestions
  - — analysis of potential problems
- Outline the meeting agenda

3. DISCUSS EMPLOYEE'S TENTATIVE OBJECTIVES, AND DETERMINE THE MEASURABILITY OF EACH.

- Ask employee to relate his or her objective or goal statements (do not discuss specific plans at this time)
- Ensure that each objective is specific, measurable and has a target date

4. OFFER ADDITIONAL OBJECTIVES IF APPROPRIATE.

- Offer additional objective(s) only if necessary

5. DETERMINE PRIORITIES OF OBJECTIVES.

- Ask employee to prioritize all of the objectives
- Discuss the employee's priorities and reach a consensus, if possible
- Limit the number of objectives to two or three for the initial time period

6. REVIEW EMPLOYEE'S STRATEGIES AND PLANS TO ACHIEVE KEY OBJECTIVES, AND OFFER IDEAS.

- Provide specific positive feedback to the employee about any of his or her significant plans or strategies
- Ask what you can do to help the employee reach his or her objectives
- Offer your ideas and suggestions to improve the employee's list of activities
- Analyze potential problems by asking "What could go wrong?"
- Develop contingency or preventive actions for potential problems, and incorporate into plans
- In light of planning analysis above, examine original target dates in each objective and adjust if needed

7. SET FOLLOW-UP DATES FOR REVIEW SESSIONS, AND CONCLUDE MEETING.

- Tell employee that you are available to discuss his or her progress whenever needed
- Inform employee that there will be scheduled follow-up meetings (e.g., quarterly)
- Write specific dates in your calendar (in the employee's presence) for the first follow-up meeting (approx. 3 months)
- Ask employee to provide you with a final copy of the *Planning Work Sheet* after the meeting
- Spell out your positive expectations
- Express your appreciation

PLANNING WORK SHEET

1. DETERMINE YOUR GOALS AND SET PRIORITIES.

Don't stop to judge or evaluate your goals as you write them
down. Just list those things you want to do, be, or become,
as they occur to you. Consider all areas of your life: business,
family, education, hobbies, religion, etc.

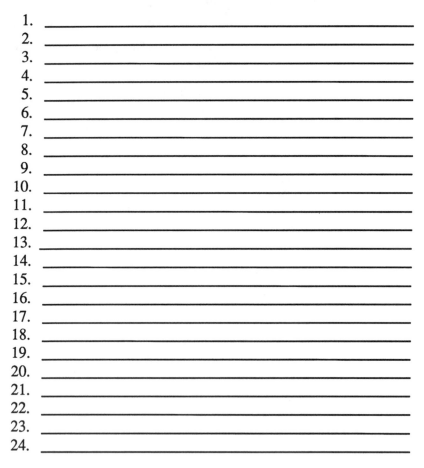

1. _____
2. _____
3. _____
4. _____
5. _____
6. _____
7. _____
8. _____
9. _____
10. _____
11. _____
12. _____
13. _____
14. _____
15. _____
16. _____
17. _____
18. _____
19. _____
20. _____
21. _____
22. _____
23. _____
24. _____

Now, put a check mark or asterisk beside your top three goals at
this time in your life.

2. WRITE YOUR PRIORITY GOALS IN OBJECTIVE FORM.

After writing your goals (brainstorming without making judgments), and identifying those with the highest priority, select your most important goal and write it in specific, measurable terms, with a deadline (see text). This objective statement should be written below.

OBJECTIVE: _____

_____

_____

3. DEVELOP STEPS TO REACH YOUR OBJECTIVE.

STEPS OF PLAN: Check critical steps
                                        (see Step 4 on the
                                        next page)

1. _____   _____
2. _____   _____
3. _____   _____
4. _____   _____
5. _____   _____
6. _____   _____
7. _____   _____
8. _____   _____
9. _____   _____
10. _____   _____
11. _____   _____
12. _____   _____
13. _____   _____
14. _____   _____
15. _____   _____
16. _____   _____
17. _____   _____
18. _____   _____
19. _____   _____
20. _____   _____

4. IDENTIFY CRITICAL STEPS IN YOUR PLAN.

Analyze the steps that have the highest risk of encountering problems. These are critical steps. Mark critical steps with an asterisk or check mark (list on previous page) and then write one of them at the top below. (The following analysis will be repeated later for the other critical steps.)

5. ANTICIPATE POTENTIAL PROBLEMS.

Answer the question, "What can go wrong with this step?"

6. EVALUATE PROBABILITY AND SERIOUSNESS OF POTENTIAL PROBLEMS.

Use H = High, M = Medium, L = Low.

CRITICAL STEP: _____

POTENTIAL PROBLEMS WITH THIS STEP:	Probability	Seriousness (High, Medium or Low)
_____	_____	_____
_____	_____	_____
_____	_____	_____
_____	_____	_____
_____	_____	_____
_____	_____	_____
_____	_____	_____

7. **DETERMINE LIKELY CAUSES OF THE HIGHEST PRIORITY POTENTIAL PROBLEMS AND WRITE PREVENTIVE AND CONTINGENCY ACTIONS.**

LIKELY CAUSES	PREVENTIVE ACTION	CONTINGENCY ACTION

8. **REPEAT STEPS 5–7 WITH ANY OTHER CRITICAL STEP(S)** using copies of this *Work Sheet*.

9. INCORPORATE IMPORTANT PREVENTIVE AND MAJOR CONTINGENCY ACTIONS INTO THE ORIGINAL PLAN.

Write a new plan that incorporates important preventive and contingency actions (from Step 7 and 8) as new steps in your original list of steps on page 198. Write all steps in chronological order, and number the steps. Finally, write a completion date for each step.

Step Number	Step	Completion Date
____	_____	____
____	_____	____
____	_____	____
____	_____	____
____	_____	____
____	_____	____
____	_____	____
____	_____	____
____	_____	____
____	_____	____
____	_____	____
____	_____	____
____	_____	____
____	_____	____
____	_____	____
____	_____	____
____	_____	____
____	_____	____
____	_____	____
____	_____	____
____	_____	____
____	_____	____

10
Managing Your Time

Remember when we were young, and those lazy summer days stretched on and on? Remember when the closer it got to summer vacation, the longer it took to arrive? Remember when the time from one holiday to the next seemed endless?

And now, why do our days seem hurried, almost mysteriously shortened? What happened? What happened to time?

Certainly our perception of time is dependent on what we're doing. We all know how waiting for something we want to happen seems like forever, and how a disagreeable task seems to take so long.

But that's only part of the answer. Our perception of time also is affected by the number of new events we're conscious of in a given period of time. For example, a drive from point A to point B on an unfamiliar road may seem to take forever. But if we travel that same distance on a familiar road, the trip seems shorter.

Similarly, when we engage in familiar, habitual tasks, we often wonder at the end of the day where the time has gone. The danger here is that we may not be aware of the way we have managed (or haven't managed) much of this routine time.

Most of us want to become increasingly effective in what we do. But the desire to improve is not all that is necessary. We also need to become aware of how we have been managing our time, so that we can understand what positive change can be made, and why.

Time management is actually a matter of asking yourself some personal questions. The first is: "What are the things that are truly important to me?" Second, "How much of my time am I giving to these things?" And third, "What takes up my time while contributing very little to my goal—or to the quality of my life?"

Time management also means accepting responsibility. It's easy to say, "I have trouble managing my time because . . .

- Other people always interrupt me.
- There is too much paperwork.

- Others misfile reports.
- My boss changes his or her priorities.
- Others won't cooperate with me.
- There are too many emergency project requests.
- The computer is always down.
- It always seems like I have to wait for others.
- My employees require too much of my time."

Agreed—many of these problems do occur. But they occur to everybody! And you know that some people, facing these same problems, are much more productive than others.

Good time managers will surely appreciate Reinhold Niebuhr's prayer: ". . .give us grace to accept with serenity the things that cannot be changed, courage to change the things which should be changed, and the wisdom to distinguish the one from the other." Effective leaders have learned to accept the things they can't change, and to take responsibility for the things they can. And they recognize the difference.

If you can exert some control in your life, to make certain decisions, and to accept part of the responsibility for what you do or don't do—then you can do something about your life. And it's your choice!

Awareness of time

Given that you have a positive attitude, that you want to be increasingly effective, and that you are willing to accept responsibility for change, what's next? What are some things you can do to manage your time more productively?

First, look closely at what you've been doing with your time. Peter Drucker has said, "Memory is treacherous; don't trust it." That is, what you think you did and what you've really done are often two different things. So you must have some way of obtaining accurate data about past actions to use in decisions for the future. The best method is to use a "Time Log" to record accurately where you are spending your time.

Reproduce copies of the Time Log below, and use it to record your daily time expenditure. Record everything you do. Write down when someone interrupts you, and when you interrupt yourself. Note telephone calls, incoming and outgoing; visitors; trips to the water fountain; a coffee break. Write it all down. To obtain enough data for a complete analysis of your time, you should plan to record a minimum of three full days, both at work and at home.

TIME LOG

NAME: _____ DATE: _____

Time	Activity	Time Consumed
____	_____	____
____	_____	____
____	_____	____
____	_____	____
____	_____	____
____	_____	____
____	_____	____
____	_____	____
____	_____	____
____	_____	____
____	_____	____
____	_____	____
____	_____	____
____	_____	____
____	_____	____
____	_____	____
____	_____	____
____	_____	____
____	_____	____

When you have finished collecting information on how you actually spend your time, add up your time in categories. This will be a major help to figure out whether the way you spend your time is really how you want to spend it. Using the following chart, categorize and record each day's information from your Time Log sheets.

WORK:	Day 1	Day 2	Day 3	Day 4	Day 5	Total	%
Unscheduled visitors (pleasure)	___	___	___	___	___	___	___
Unscheduled visitors (business)	___	___	___	___	___	___	___
Scheduled visitors (pleasure)	___	___	___	___	___	___	___
Scheduled visitors (business)	___	___	___	___	___	___	___
Visitors subtotal						___	___
Outgoing telephone (pleasure)	___	___	___	___	___	___	___
Outgoing telephone (business)	___	___	___	___	___	___	___
Incoming telephone (pleasure)	___	___	___	___	___	___	___
Incoming telephone (business)	___	___	___	___	___	___	___
Telephone subtotal						___	___

WORK: (continued)	Day 1	Day 2	Day 3	Day 4	Day 5	Total	%
Boss time							
Subordinate time							
Group meeting							
Waiting							
Breaks & lunch							
Reading							
Writing							
Faxing							
Planning							
Physical work							
Miscellaneous							

Total of all work categories

HOME:	Day 1	Day 2	Day 3	Day 4	Day 5	Total	%
Yourself							
Spouse							
Children							
Friends							
Chores							
Eating							
Sleeping							
Civic							
Business							
Recreation							
Miscellaneous							

Total of all home categories

Grand Total

After categorizing and recording your Time Log information, decide which time expenditures you wish to change. To do this, you'll need to ask some tough questions, including:

1. Did I use any time to plan for the future?

2. Have I recorded activity—or "results"? (Activity = what I did. Results = what I accomplished.)

3. What was the longest period of time spent on one thing without interruption?

4. Which interruptions were most costly?

5. What can be done to eliminate or control these interruptions?

— Which telephone calls were unnecessary?

— Which phone calls could have been shorter yet equally (or more) effective?

— Which visits were unnecessary?

— Which visits could have been shorter yet equally (or more) effective?

6. How much time did you spend in meetings?

7. Did I find myself jumping from task to task without completing the previous one?

8. Did crisis work push more important things aside?

9. Did I notice a self-correcting tendency occurring as I recorded actions throughout the week?

10. How much quality employee development time did I spend?

When you have answered these questions, you are in a much better position to decide what you must change to save time in your work and personal life. Of course you may discover that what you are doing is exactly what you want to do; if so, your final decision will be to do nothing. In either case, the information will help you make the right decision.

And when you make changes, be aware of two points:

1. Increasing the amount of time spent on one activity will require that you take time from another activity.

2. Changes can sometimes cause problems that, in turn, take even more time to fix.

What is Urgent?

Dr. Charles Hummel once wrote an article entitled, "The Tyranny of the Urgent." In it he distinguished things that are truly important from those that seem "urgent." When important things and urgent things occur simultaneously, which usually wins our attention? Let me give you an example. Many years ago, I made a decision to leave the organization I worked for in St. Paul and move my family back to my home state of Virginia. I planned to be my own boss as an independent training consultant. After a couple of grim years, I finally achieved my bottom line financial goal—i.e., we weren't starving!

At the time, my office was in our converted garage. Because we had many children, I had a business telephone line and a family line.

One Friday evening at 5:30 we were sitting down for supper when the business line rang. I asked the children to quiet down, and answered the phone. "International Training Consultants. Dick Leatherman speaking. How can I help you?" I said.

The caller was the program director of a local university's management center. He was extremely agitated—so much so I could hardly understand him. Because I was also getting some noise in the kitchen, I put him on hold and went down to the garage to continue the call. "What's wrong?" I asked.

His story was a program director's nightmare. He was at the end of a weeklong seminar for about a hundred purchasing agents from up and down the Eastern seaboard. The keynote speaker for Saturday morning was the dean of one of the country's leading law schools. But because the dean had the flu, he wouldn't be there in the morning.

So the program director pleaded, "Dick, will you be our keynote speaker tomorrow morning? We don't care what you do. Just come in and do something!" Let me tell you, that request made me feel good. He had called me first!

But let's put him on hold for a minute so I can tell you about several things I had already scheduled for the Saturday in question.

First, because my office was at home we had some pretty strict rules about the children bothering me when I was working. A week before the program director's call, I had been working in my office when Matthew Leatherman (he was about seven years old at the time) careened in with a big emergency. Well, he wasn't broken or bleeding, and the interruption irritated me. As a result I wasn't very nice to him. And as he sulked out of my office, he said under his breath (but just loud enough for me to hear him), "Daddy doesn't have time for me anymore since he has his own business." And Matthew was right. I wasn't spending as much time with him as I once did. So I said, "Hold it, bud. You're right. I don't spend as much time with you as I used too. But I'll tell you what—let's you and me have a turtle day next Saturday morning. How about it?" "Oh, yes!" he exclaimed, and I got a big hug.

Do you know what a "turtle day" is? It's when you take a seven-year old boy out to look for turtles. The fact that you probably won't find any is not the point. It's what you can talk about while you look! One-on-one private time between a daddy and his son. That's the point!

And there was another important thing I had scheduled for that Saturday. Laurie, my 16-year old (going on 21), had asked me the preceding Wednesday if I would teach her how to drive. I said, "Hey, Honey, my tax dollars help pay for you to get professional driving in-struction at your high school! Besides, you don't want to learn my bad driving habits." (I'm a lousy driver.)

"But Daddy, " she replied, "I've never driven a car, and I get my 'behind-the-wheel' instructions next week. The other kids will be in the car too, and I don't want to make a fool of myself in front of them!" "Oh, I see," I said. "I'll tell you what—let's spend some time next Saturday at the shopping center parking lot, and you can scare me to death!" "Fantastic!" she said. And I got a big hug for that, too.

The last thing I had scheduled for that Saturday was time with my youngest daughter, Leanne. Her "Uncle Frank" had made her a giant doll house. It was a marvel to see! It was carpeted, and it had real windows. It also had a low-voltage lighting system with a miniature chandelier hanging in the dining room.

Well, Leanne's house had an attic fire. Somehow the low-voltage wiring had shorted out, and the transformer had burned up. She had been "reminding" me to fix it for a couple of months. And the Tuesday before the Saturday in question, she had asked, "Please, please, please," (or were there four "pleases?") "fix my doll house?" I said, "Tell you what I'm going to do. I'll put the transformer in your doll house this coming Saturday. At the same time, I'll teach you how to solder wires." I got another big hug for that!

Remember, we still have the program director on "hold." What do you think I told him when he frantically said that Friday evening, "Dick, we don't care what you do. Just come in and do something!" Yes—I said "Okay." Then I walked up to the kitchen and said, "Guess what, gang? Daddy has a seminar at the Hyatt House tomorrow morning!" There was dead silence. Then my oldest daughter said, "Daddy!" and walked out of the room. Matthew said, "But . . . but . . . what about turtle day?" And Leanne, with all the faith and trust of a young child in her father, said, "That's OK, Daddy. I know you'll fix my doll house someday."

I did eventually fix the doll house, go turtle hunting with Matthew, and give Laurie some hints on driving. But not that day—when I let the "urgent" win out over those things that were truly important to me.

Two lessons can be learned from my experience. First, there is no end to it: the "tyranny of the urgent" is a battle we all will fight day after day. Do you imagine this was the last time I let a crisis get in the way of something that was really important? The thing we must try to do at home and on the job is to choose well when the urgent tries to displace the truly important.

Secondly, as Peter Drucker has said, "Learn to say 'no' nicely if you can, but nastily if you must. But learn to say 'no' so that you have time for the really important things in your life."

If saying "no" is difficult for you, recognize that you can't say "yes" to everything. In other words, you have a right to say "no." A simple, "No thank you" is often sufficient and appropriate for those situations where a personal relationship with the other person is not important to you. And sometimes you must say "no" more than once. If the relationship with the other person is important to you, first acknowledge the request, then say "no," and last add an explanation.

But how do you know when to say "no"? By realizing what is important to you. And how do you ensure that important things are not pushed aside by "urgent" things?

By planning! Planning allows you to identify important goals, and put them into action. The resulting activities generated by this analysis then become a part of your daily planning.

DAILY PLANNING

Daily planning is making a "to-do" list for each day. This list should include the priority items that should be done immediately, as well as things that you can do today to help carry out your long range goals. It doesn't have to be anything fancy—just a small piece of paper you carry in your pocket or purse to jot down the things you have planned for that (or the next) day. It doesn't make any difference when you do it, whether the first thing in the morning, or at the end of the day. Just so you do it daily!

But keeping a to-do list daily may involve a significant amount of time. For example, even if you spend only 10 minutes a day making your list, that adds up to 2400 minutes—or 40 hours—a year! So there is a cost for doing a daily to-do list. And thus there must be a compelling reason to lead you to do such daily planning.

In fact, there are many good reasons why effective people plan daily. First, when you visibly identify all the things you feel you need to do today, you can establish your priorities by seeing what's important, and what's only urgent.

Daily planning also helps your boss set priorities with you. For example, if your boss constantly interrupts you with new crisis requests, it's strategically helpful to hold up a daily to-do list and say, "OK, boss, where does that fit on my list?"

Third, a to-do list acts as a memory aid. I, for one, have reached an age where, if I don't write it down, there is only a very small chance I'll remember what it was that I said I absolutely wouldn't forget!

I use a daily to-do list for yet another reason. It tells me what to do next after finishing a task. I am a very task-oriented person. While I'm working on a task I'm usually not thinking of other things that need to be done. Then when I finish a job, because I can't think of what I wanted to do next, I may simply take a break. But if I have a to-do list in front of me, I can see exactly what I need to do next.

Others who keep daily to-do lists report that it simply feels good to scratch tasks off their list as they are completed. In other words, you have set up a way of giving yourself immediate positive feedback as you complete each task. Finally, I save my lists for a month or so and review them to see if I can discover any way that I can further improve my time management. For example, if I haven't completed a task that I had planned to do that day, I immediately rewrite that task on the next day's list. And if I see that I rewrote a particular task more than once, I realize that I may be procrastinating.

If you don't now use a daily to-do list, try it! It will be time well invested. Or simply commit yourself to keeping a list for 20 working days. When you see that it pays off, you will continue to use such a list, without difficulty—because you've gotten into the to-do habit.

On the next page is an example of a to-do list. Make as many copies as needed, and then stack the sheets and staple them at the top to make your to-do pads.

MANAGING YOUR TIME

Tasks to Do	Priority	Time

MANAGING YOUR TIME

Tasks to Do	Priority	Time

MANAGING YOUR TIME

Tasks to Do	Priority	Time

MANAGING YOUR TIME

Tasks to Do	Priority	Time

SUMMARY

We have presented several concrete strategies for managing your time well:

- Time logs
- Prioritizing "important" things over "urgent" ones
- Daily planning with "to-do" lists
- Creating a plan for the future

Using these techniques will allow you to do key tasks on schedule—and have more time for creative thinking, for your boss, for your employees, and for yourself. To become a better manager of your time, you need to spend it on those things that are really important. In short, you need to take control of your life!

11
Managing and
Conducting Meetings

"You mean you expect me to stand up in front of a group and lead a meeting?" You bet! Good meeting leaders are not born knowing how to lead meetings well. They learn! And they usually learn the hard way. For example, one well-known research study of five organizations found that they ranked ineffective meetings as one of their top five time-wasters.

But you don't have to learn how to conduct successful meetings the hard way! You can learn by studying topics such as meeting preparation, facilitation skills, and meeting follow up. And it's much easier to learn how to manage and conduct meetings if we break down this activity into its steps, and examine each one. There are six key steps:

1. Prepare for the Meeting

2. Open the Meeting

3. Use the Appropriate Process

4. Obtain Acceptance

5. Close the Meeting

6. Follow Up

Let's look at each of these steps in detail.

1. PREPARE FOR THE MEETING.

Leaders who prepare for their meetings conduct better meetings. It's as simple as that. You will find in this chapter the proper method of preparing for any meeting. But note: unless you are willing to invest time in doing so, your meetings will be less effective than they can be. So it's up to you. If you want real results in your meetings—and your employees to feel good about them—then you must prepare. Here's how.

Start early

Don't leave your preparation for important meetings to the last minute. Waiting too long to start the preparation process drastically reduces what you can accomplish. You may find that you need a couple of overhead transparencies, but don't have time to get them made. Or a key member can't come because he or she didn't have enough advance notice. Or you realize you should have a written agenda to hand out, but don't have time to have it typed, much less copied. These—and many other—problems can occur if you wait until too late to prepare for your meeting. But by taking a few minutes to think through the things that need to be done, you can usually determine how much time you need to prepare. Included at the end of this chapter is a *Meeting Preparation Checklist* that you can copy and use to help yourself prepare for your meeting with plenty of time to do what needs to be done.

Communicate

Let those who are to attend the meeting know, in writing, the "who, what, when, where and why" of the meeting. If this is not a regularly scheduled meeting, it is especially important to confirm in writing (or orally for small groups) the meeting time and place. For all meetings, routine as well as special, make sure that the members receive the meeting objectives and agenda in advance. In general, the more details the members have about the meeting ahead of time, the better prepared they will be for it.

Meeting objective. Some meetings really get crazy because the leader didn't truly think through in advance what was supposed to be accomplished—and no one else knew either! If you don't know where you are going in a meeting, how will it achieve its goal? So one of your key tasks in preparing for a meeting is to think through why you need the meeting. What do you want the members to do in the meeting—and do as a result of it? What do you want them to learn? To consider? To decide? To act on? What do you want to achieve in the meeting? What should happen when the meeting is over? Answering these questions will result in clear objectives for your meeting. If you don't know the answers, you should think about not having the meeting—and save everybody a lot of time!

A meeting objective is simply a description of what you, or the members, want to accomplish as a result of the meeting. For example, you could hold a meeting to provide—or obtain—information, identify problems, determine the cause of a specific problem, make a decision, create a plan, or train employees. In other words, an objective expresses the purpose of your meeting—and describes the desired outcome.

Meeting agenda. The agenda lists the topics that will be covered to achieve the meeting objective(s). It describes what you will do in the meeting—the activities that will take place to accomplish the desired results. For example, if the objective of the meeting is to make a group decision, the announced agenda of topics/activities might look like this:

A meeting will be held on January 5 at 8:30 AM in meeting room "B" to select our priority problem areas for analysis.

Objective:
> The group will select, by consensus, our three most important problems.

Agenda:

1. Discuss the need for a decision.

2. Determine the factors we should consider in making the decision.

3. Brainstorm a list of problem areas.

4. Make a final decision, using a consensus process.

5. Assign responsibilities to specific individuals to carry out our decision.

Prepare your content

After you have written down your meeting objective(s) and established the agenda, you are ready to examine your role in the meeting. First, consider what you need to do in the meeting, and second, what you need to do to prepare for your part in it. For example, if you were in charge of the meeting described above, you would probably want to talk to your boss to see what problems he or she sees in your section. You will also need to spend time thinking about the major problems as you see them. Then make a list of these problems in case some of them are not brought up for discussion by others in the meeting.

Or you may want to prepare handouts, have reference material available, or even invite a subject matter expert to sit in on the meeting. The key is that whatever needs to be done will take time. And the time to begin is usually well before the day of the meeting. Next, consider what you want the members to do in the meeting. Then determine if any of them need to do something in preparation for it. Certain individuals may need to know in advance that they will be asked to offer their expertise, or to bring their records and files for reference. Or you may wish to assign specific meeting roles to key members, such as "Recorder," "Facilitator/Observer," or "Leader." Then communicate with these members before the meeting so that they will have time to prepare for their part in it.

Assign meeting roles

One of the best ways to manage and conduct successful meetings is to assign specific meeting roles to the members in advance. This will not only get your people more involved in the meetings; it will also create more productive meetings. So let's look first at your role in the meeting—and then at four other roles that you can assign to your employees.

Your Role (the boss). I've stayed away from using the term "boss" throughout most of this book. In this chapter, however, I don't see any way of avoiding this term in order to distinguish you as the formal leader (supervisor, manager, or executive) from the meeting leader. The "boss" and the group leader might be the same person: but they don't have to be. As the boss, you don't always have to lead your meetings—you can delegate that responsibility to one of your key employees! You might even choose not to be present at the meeting! Many organizations today elect to have their employees meet without their boss in order to solve production problems, increase quality, or help their non-exempt employees become more involved in and challenged by their work.

Of course, even if you don't attend your employees' meetings, you are still in the communication loop. You will be asked to offer your input, obtain resources for the team members, and make decisions. And don't worry about "giving away your power" by delegating responsibility and authority to your people to hold their own meetings. You will be surprised at how new (and more important) tasks will arise to fill the time made available for you by appropriate delegation of meeting responsibility. You will also find that your people will become much more excited about their jobs; and that you will be amazed at the ideas they come up with—if you just turn them loose! Someone once said that a boss's job is to give employees what they need to do their jobs—supplies, tools, training, authority, and responsibility—and then to stand out of the way!

Of course, the first time you elect not to attend an employees' meeting, you will need to provide them with helpful, clear guidance on how to conduct their meetings. Ask them to assign meeting roles, to use an easel, and utilize the best process for the task at hand. Also tell them that you need to be informed of the meeting results—and that you will help them in any way you can.

If your anxiety over allowing your employees to hold meetings without you is too strong, then try attending a meeting as a participant, and ask one of your employees to be the meeting leader. This will satisfy your need to keep some control, and also give increased responsibility to your people. And you will probably find that your biggest problem is keeping your mouth shut and letting your employees run the meeting.

Meeting Leader. Whether you choose to lead the meeting yourself or to delegate this responsibility to someone else, someone needs to take the leadership role. So let's look at what a good Meeting Leader does.

First, effective Meeting Leaders should establish and send out the meeting agenda, prepare needed handouts, arrive early, start on time, and end on time, and use an easel to keep the meeting on track.

Second, Leaders need to be able to handle problem participants. Here are some common problems the Leader may encounter with his or her group—with suggested solutions.

1.   One team member monopolizes the conversation

Possible cause:	*Solution:*
You—the boss—talk too much.	Ask a peer (another supervisor, manager, or executive) to attend your meetings to give you feedback.
The member has expertise in the subjects being discussed.	Ask member to submit a position paper to all of the group members prior to the meeting.
The member doesn't know he or she has a problem.	Ask member for permission to conduct a frequency count of the number of times he or she speaks.
The Leader doesn't exert control because he or she isn't the boss (but is an assigned leader).	Tell the Leader that he or she has management's full support, and needs to control a monopolizing speaker.

Tell the group members that others are going to have a chance to serve as leader, and that they should treat the present leader the way they would want to be treated.

Provide the members with training on group roles and rules.

The Leader doesn't know how to manage the situation tactfully.

Teach the leader how to:
— interrupt tactfully and shift the discussion to others by using a question.
— express his or her concern to the employee privately, describe the negative results of mono-polizing, and ask for cooperation.

2. A member does not participate.

Possible cause:

Solution:

The member is shy.

Assign him or her the role of Recorder (see page 214).

Involve the member in the discus-sion by asking him or her questions.

Give positive reinforcement for any contribution.

The member is bored.

Assign him or her the role of Recorder, Facilitator/Observer (see page 214), or Meeting Leader.

Get him or her more involved by assigning tasks for later completion.

The member is angry.

In private discussion, determine the cause of his or her anger. Attempt to identify solutions to resolve the problem, and counsel if needed.

3.   A member is continually tardy or absent.

Possible cause: *Solution:*

The member has a bad   Stress the importance of being
habit of lateness/absenteeism. present and on time (tardiness
                                and absence are not fair to the
                                group).

                                Require performance by taking
                                disciplinary action.

There is a work environment   Change the employee's environ-
problem.   ment so that he or she can attend
                                the meetings and be on time.

The member doesn't know   Communicate your expectations.
what is expected of him
or her.

4.   A member carries on distracting side discussions (talks to
     individuals next to him or her).

Possible cause: *Solution:*

The member doesn't   Look at the talkers.
realize he or she is
causing a problem.   Say to the group as a whole (not
                               looking at the talkers), "One at
                               a time, please."

                               Ask the group if everyone can
                               hear the speaker.

                               Ask an adjacent member a ques-
                               tion so as to interrupt the side
                               discussion.

                               Walk over and stand near the
                               talkers.

Ask talkers if they would like to share their ideas.

Stop and wait (but not until the other techniques have proved ineffective).

The member has a bad habit of carrying on side discussions.	Use the above strategies. If unsuccessful, counsel the member in private.
Two close friends are sitting together.	Use the above strategies. If unsuccessful, place desk name tags in advance in order to separate "friends."

5. A member sidetracks the discussion (leads the group away from the subject).

Possible cause: *Solution:*

The member doesn't know what the discussion is about.

Use visual aids (begin writing on easel, turn on the overhead projector, etc.).

Ask the member how his or her comments relate to the meeting objective.

Direct a question to the group that brings the discussion back to the subject.

The above problems and related causes include most of the difficulties a Leader will encounter in conducting a meeting. Leaders also need to be familiar with and comfortable using a variety of meeting processes like problem-solving, decision-making, and planning. (These group processes and others will be discussed later in this chapter.) Finally, astute Leaders are not bothered by conflict. They know that disagreements are expected, are healthy—and can be managed.

Recorder. The Recorder is responsible for recording: who attended (and did not attend) the meeting, the topics that were discussed, the key points that were made (not every word that was spoken), and who made them, and who agreed to do what (and when) as a result of the meeting. At the end of the meeting, the Recorder should also summarize the topics and task assignments, copy all easel paper and boarded items (after the meeting), and follow up by promptly sending out minutes of the meeting to all group members. The Recorder should also keep files on all meetings.

Facilitator/Observer ("F/O"). Next to the Leader, the Facilitator/Observer often plays the most crucial role in a meeting. Members who take on this role must be insightful, knowledgeable, tactful, and courageous. They must be insightful in order to keep their focus on the *processes* taking place in the meeting, not the topics or content of the discussion. They must therefore be knowledgeable about group meeting processes. They must be tactful when providing feedback in a non-judgmental way to members about their performance. And they must be courageous in order to provide you, the boss, with feedback when you as the group Leader make mistakes or talk too much as a group member.

Facilitators/Observers need to make an agreement with you, the boss, and the members as to what they will and will not do in the meeting. For example, should the F/O interrupt discussion when it is off track—or wait until the meeting is over? Should he or she suggest an appropriate process for a topic that is going to be discussed? What will be the specific nature of the F/O's involvement in the meeting? Questions such as these need to be answered prior to the meeting.

Most groups—and Leaders—want their F/O's to be active in the meeting as a facilitator. In other words, if the group gets off course, the F/O lets them know it. And when the group is uncertain about which process to use, the F/O makes suggestions. However, most groups agree that the F/O's feedback should be directed to the *group,* not to individuals, and that personal feedback to you as Leader should be given privately. And the majority of groups want their F/O's to focus upon how the group is functioning, not on the content of the meeting. Thus, the F/O normally does not get involved in the topics under discussion.

Because of their great influence, F/Os also need to refrain from sending nonverbal signals as they observe the meeting. Utterances (saying "Uh, oh!") or facial contortions (rolling the eyes upward, snorting, or laughing) indicating displeasure, or any other kind of gesture or sound can affect the conduct of the meeting. The basic role of the F/O is to observe, and to facilitate only as agreed.

Some typical F/O questions are:

- "I have noticed that during the past hour only three of you have been involved in the discussion. Would it be possible to obtain input and involvement from everyone?"
- "It seems like we have gotten off the subject. How does the present discussion relate to our stated objective (or agenda)?"
- "Before we jump to conclusions and take action, do you think we have identified the real cause of the problem?"
- "Rather than settling on that solution now, should we consider other alternatives also?"
- "Have we looked at the risks in our plan? In other words, if we adopt it, what could go wrong?"

Members. The group members also have specific responsibilities in the meeting. For instance, they need to schedule their work so that they can attend all meetings, and arrive on time. They must cooperate with the other members of the group, i.e., they should listen to one another, avoid interrupting others, and refrain from putting down another member's ideas.

Members also must accept the responsibility of being involved. Although the problem of a bored member needs to be addressed by the Leader, it is that member's responsibility not to become bored in the first place! On the other hand, too much involvement by one member should also be avoided. Members need to be very sensitive to "air time" and not monopolize the discussion.

Members also should be honest with one another. They need to take the responsibility to say what they really think and feel. And if you, the boss, are present, you need to strongly encourage the members to "tell it like it is."

Finally, every group member should seek to become proficient in performing all four group roles—Leader, Observer/Facilitator, Recorder, and Member.

Equipment, Materials, and Facility

Before the meeting starts, check out all equipment, materials, and the facility. If you plan to show a videotape, does the player work? Does the overhead projector function properly, and is there an extra bulb? Is the overhead projector screen in the room and is it properly positioned? Do you need an extension cord?

If you plan to use a flip chart, is there extra paper? Do you have magic markers and are they usable? Do you need masking tape to hang up completed charts?

Is the room set up the way you want it? If your meeting objective involves making a group decision, is the room arranged so the members can talk facing each other? Are there enough chairs?

If I could give you one special piece of advice, it would be to arrive at the meeting room early. I have walked into a meeting room and discovered that the tables and chairs were missing! I have found projectors gone, video equipment borrowed, and the electrical power off at the outlets. Things that "can go wrong will go wrong," and tackling trouble takes time.

You should also learn how to effectively use the overhead projector and easel flip charts before the meeting begins. Many leaders think, "What do I need to learn about overheads and flip charts? I've been using them for years." Maybe you have. But the chances are that in reading the following information you will learn something new about how to use these two meeting tools more effectively.

Using Transparencies. Overhead transparencies are terrific; I freely admit my bias! My old outfit (the 3-M company) invented the overhead projector, and I have used it for over 30 years.

Transparencies are extremely useful both for you and for your members. High quality transparencies can be used to create a visible outline for all to follow. In addition they make it much easier for you to maintain eye contact with the group as you present program material. Also, they greatly increase the amount of information that you can present within any given period of time.

But the most important reasons for using transparencies concern the members, not you. Transparencies: (1) improve participant retention of the program's concepts and major points, (2) make it easier for the participants to remember group instructions, and (3) significantly reduce misunderstanding. The basics of using an overhead projector and transparencies are:

1. The "reveal technique" should be used in presenting a transparency. First, place a sheet of 8 ½" x 11" paper under the transparency before turning on the projector light. Then, holding the transparency frame with one hand and pulling the paper out with the other hand, reveal one point at a time. Reveal complete thoughts or paragraphs at once, not one line at a time.

2. Keep the projector light off unless an overhead transparency is on the projector. Turn off the projector between transparencies since the white glare on the screen, when there is no transparency on the projector, can be quite distracting.

3. Leave the room lights on when using the overhead. Most overhead projectors are deliberately designed so that you can keep the room lighted as you present transparencies. This helps you maintain eye contact with the group, and also allows the group members to see and interact with each other.

4. Read the information directly from the transparency as you reveal it. Do not turn your back to the group and read from the screen—except on the rare occasion when you wish to specially emphasize a specific point (e.g., using a pointer). This allows you to maintain much better eye contact with your group.

5. Use a pencil, pen or small pointer when you want to indicate particular items on a transparency. Avoid using your finger as it looks strange when enlarged many times on the screen!

6. You can write reminder notes on the white frame margins of your transparencies. A fine point, permanent transparency pen will write on the white plastic or paper frames. Caution: do not write on the transparency itself with a permanent pen. Use only an erasable pen when writing on the transparency film.

7. Read each word of the transparency—or paraphrase the key point(s)—as shown on the screen. Do not turn on the projector light and stand there silently while your group reads the transparency.

8. Focus and adjust the projector and screen before the session begins.

9. For best participant viewing, if you are right-handed, position the overhead screen in the right-hand corner of the room (as you face the participants), and place the projector in the front center of the room at an angle so that the light is centered on the screen. Reverse if you are left-handed.

Transparency Construction. Making transparencies can be fun! All the needed materials are available locally in a wide selection of films and colors. First, there are two main categories of film—dry copy and infrared. Dry copy film makes transparencies using a regular electrostatic plain-paper copier. An image is created on the transparency film in the same way you would make a regular plain-paper copy. The film is loaded in the paper holder of the copy machine, a black-and-white original is placed under the mat, and the result is a printed film.

This method will produce a black image on either a clear, or colored (red, blue, green, or yellow), background. Because the transparency film has a slightly "greasy" finish, the transparency images are not as sharp as those on infrared film. And because the plain-paper copier will produce only a black image, many users prefer the infrared method.

Several companies produce an infrared, desktop transparency machine. But if you can "beg, borrow, or buy" an old, used 3-M Thermofax infrared desktop copier, do so! If you happen to own one, dig it out. Because of the unappealing yellowish paper copies they made, these once-popular copiers were relegated to back closets. But they can be used to make outstanding transparencies with either a black image on a clear or colored background, or a colored image on clear background. Several companies offer locally-distributed film that can be used with this copier. It will produce red, green, blue, and violet images on a clear background, or black images on red, blue, green, yellow, or clear background—all from a black-and-white paper master. These color and image combinations will add great variety to your transparencies.

Felt-tip, permanent pens for use on transparencies can be purchased in a variety of colors and tip widths. These may be used to highlight key points, or to box in an important paragraph. But make sure that your pens are of the "permanent" type. Temporary, water-soluble pens will smear badly, destroying the appearance of a finished transparency.

Paper masters can be produced by any typesetter at most well-equipped print shops. The only problem is cost—typeset work is expensive. But if you have the budget and the time, it is much easier to have a typesetter lay out and set your masters than to try to make them yourself. Just hand print or type your transparency information on an 8 ½" x 11" sheet of paper, and take it to a print shop to be typeset. Be sure also to take with you a transparency frame of the size you plan to use so that the type can be set clearly within the margins of the frame. (The inside dimensions, or aperture, of a transparency frame can vary widely.) Computer desktop publishing systems can also be used to create excellent paper masters for transparency production. However, the need for large, smooth-edge letters will usually require a laser printer.

And do frame your transparencies. Frames make handling your transparencies easier, and also allow you space to write "cheat notes" on the margins.

Finally, note the two major pitfalls with designing transparencies: 1) trying to put too much on one transparency, and, 2) using print that is too small to be read by the participants. Too much information is confusing. And the tiny print is frustrating to read, especially for those seated toward the back of the room. So keep your transparencies simple. Usually, "6 x 6" is a good rule of thumb—i.e., a maximum of six words across and six lines down will keep your transparencies from being too "busy." A transparency is used to make key points, or to present a *brief* outline, and should not be overdone.

Overhead Projector. Having used overhead projectors for many years, I have had experience with many types and styles. First, my preference is always for a projector that has a built-in bulb-switching mechanism. Your bulb *will* burn out—and usually at exactly the wrong time! Projector bulbs get extremely hot, and it is very difficult to replace a burned-out bulb in the middle of a meeting. Therefore, some brands have a lever on the back of the projector that allows you to quickly—and painlessly—replace the bulb simply by sliding a new one into the socket.

I also suggest using a projector that has a polarized, frosted glass tabletop, since this will keep the light spill from glaring in your eyes throughout a long meeting.

Finally, a projector that has an on-and-off "bar" across the front is helpful. This type of switch is easier to find, and it also lends itself to the quick on-and-off switching technique required when properly using overhead transparencies.

Flip Charts. To manage your meeting effectively, a flip chart is almost a "must"! Recording your group's thoughts and suggestions on easel paper during the meeting will help keep them focused on the topic at hand. A flip chart makes it easier to review key points at any time; and it permits recorded ideas to trigger new thoughts as the meeting progresses. Also, a flip chart enables a group to use problem-solving processes in a logical, step-by-step way. And it will give you more control and, thus, better management, of the meeting. One problem in using a flip chart to record discussions is that it can slow down the meeting, since your members can obviously talk faster than you can write. While brainstorming a list of ideas, for instance, you will need to write them down and allow them to trigger new ideas. And you may get writer's cramp with the fast flow of thoughts! But you will find that your group will pace their suggestions to give you time to write.

Here are several logistical suggestions for using flip charts.

- Use dark colors when writing on easel paper. Black, dark brown, or dark blue markers are the most legible. Avoid using lighter colors like yellow, orange or green. Surprisingly, red is also a difficult color to read, and should be used only for high-lighting words for emphasis.

- Print—don't use script. Block letter printing is much easier to read from the back of the room.

- If possible, obtain easel paper with light, pre-printed "grid" lines. This will help make your printing more legible—and will look more professional.

- Use low-tack masking tape, or easel paper with a self-stick strip on the back, for taping paper to the wall, since some types of adhesive tape will pull paint off the wall when removed.

- In order to ensure that you don't forget certain points during your presentation, you can write your notes lightly in pencil on the edge of the easel paper. This will not be noticeable to the group, and will remind you of thoughts you intend to write on the easel paper.

2. OPEN THE MEETING.

It's time to begin the meeting—and you are its Leader.

Start the meeting on time! Don't punish the early arrivals and reward latecomers. If you delay starting the meeting, several things are going to happen—none of them desirable. First, you will develop a reputation for starting meetings late, and (guess what!) your members will begin arriving late. Second, some people may strongly feel that you are wasting their time by not starting on time. And third, you are going to end up in trouble meeting your time schedule.

The agenda should be recorded on the easel paper ahead of time and posted on the wall. If you haven't already assigned the roles of Recorder and Facilitator/Observer to key members, now is the time to do so. You as the Leader, the Recorder, and the Observer/Facilitator should know the processes that will be used. And if you plan to have one of your group members serve as the meeting Leader, he or she should know this well in advance to allow him or her time to prepare. Then begin the meeting by reviewing the meeting objective(s) and agenda, and move to the first order of business.

3. USE THE APPROPRIATE PROCESS.

You need to select the appropriate process for the work the group is going to do. There are four types of meeting process tools you may select from.

A. Problem Identification. Some meeting processes are used to gather and arrange data in a systematic way in order to identify problems. Note that these processes don't solve the problems—they provide information that tells what, where, and how serious they are. In other words, they help you and your employees pinpoint and describe problems, and set priorities. They can also provide information for management to use in justifying funds needed to fix a particular problem.

Such processes include:

Situation Analysis. This tool—sometimes called a "Cause-Effect Diagram"—has replaced the earlier "fish-bone" technique. It is used by teams to identify each of the causes and effects of a particular problem. It also provides a simple way of setting priorities on the problem's causes. (See Chapter 7.)

Pareto Chart. This is nothing more than a bar chart that is used to show the frequency of occurrence of a particular set of problems. For example:

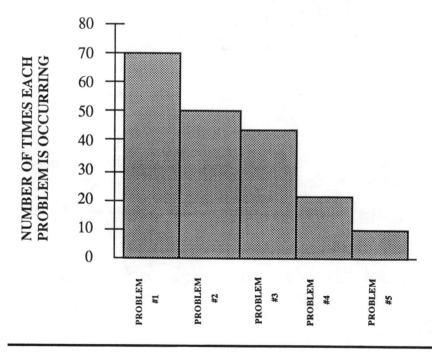

Histogram. This is a bar chart that usually plots problem-frequency against some form of measurement, in contrast to the Pareto Chart that plots frequency against identified categories. For instance:

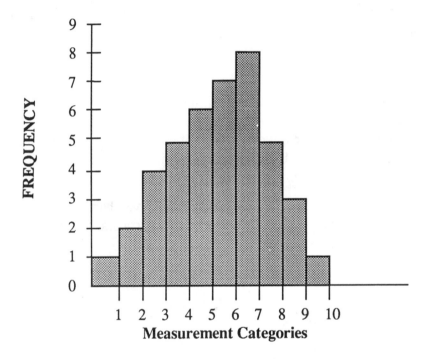

Correlation Analysis. A correlation analysis is used to examine the relationship between two different things. For example:

- Does it really rain every time you go to the beach? Simply correlate a number of consecutive trips to the beach and rainy weather (probably not much correlation).

- Do children who are read to become avid adult readers? Correlate children who are read to with number of books they read per year as an adult (likely a good correlation).

- Does teller training make a difference? Correlate customer complaints, or any other measure, with tellers who have received training and those who have not (probably a medium correlation).

Note that most problem identification groups need to be able to use basic statistics to analyze their data. They must understand such measures as Mean (an average), Median (the middle number), Mode (the most often appearing number), and Standard Distribution (the old "Bell-Shaped Curve"), and be able to calculate Standard Deviations and Chi-Squares.

B. Causal Analysis. Causal analysis is used to discover the cause of a specific problem. A group can use this method to analyze data to determine where the problem occurred (versus where it did not occur), and when it happened (vs. when it didn't). After answering these questions, a team can often identify the most probable cause of the problem. (See Chapter 7.)

C. Decision Making. Two major processes are used by teams to make decisions.

Evaluation of Alternatives. This tool is used to identify the best of several alternative solutions. Selecting the best computer or choosing the best way to do a task are examples of decisions that can be made through evaluation of the merits of each alternative. (See Chapter 8.)

Force Field Analysis. This process helps make a decision when there are only two alternatives—e.g., to buy a computer or not, or to change the way to do a task or not. Thus it is an especially good tool to use when there are two sides, pro and con, to an issue. (See Chapter 16.)

D. Planning. A planning process is used by a team to do just that—plan. A goal statement is written, and then the team helps to develop appropriate steps in the plan. Next, a technique called "Potential Problem Avoidance" is used to examine problems that might occur when the plan is implemented. (See Chapter 9.)

4. OBTAIN ACCEPTANCE.

Involvement. Involvement is usually the best way to obtain acceptance. Encourage the team members to offer ideas or suggestions. As the boss, you should not offer to do everything yourself. Delegate assignments to others. Assign the key roles of Facilitator/ Observer and Recorder, and even that of Leader.

Consensus Management. Another way to obtain involvement and, thus, acceptance is to use a tool called Consensus Management. It is a technique often used in conjunction with other processes to help teams make better group decisions. It produces more agreement among team members than traditional voting does—which usually end up with "winners" and "losers." In Consensus Management everyone "wins," resulting in greater acceptance of the group's decision. Consensus Management also generates more creative ideas than does a traditional voting process.

Consensus Management is employed at any point where a traditional vote would be taken. It is used to identify which problem(s) a group wants to address, or which topic(s) to consider at a future meeting; to analyze a list of alternative solutions to a problem, to select those the group wants to explore further, and to choose the best solution; or to determine which steps to use in a plan.

Since Consensus Management is so critical to the functioning of an effective team, let's look in detail at how it works.

1. Write the question to be considered on easel paper.

2. Brainstorm a list of ideas relating to the question (topics, suggestions, alternatives, etc.). When the group brainstorms, don't stop to evaluate each idea—simply write exactly what each person says on the easel paper. Try to obtain everyone's suggestions—but do not allow discussion at this time.

3. When all the members have had an opportunity to present their ideas, ask if any of them can be combined or eliminated.

4. Then ask each person to explain *briefly* the reasons for his or her suggestion. (Try to limit these presentations to not more then 2 minutes per person.)

5. Next, ask each member to select and write down his or her first three choices, in order of preference, from the ideas listed.

6. The members now assign 3 points to their first choice, 2 points to their second, and only 1 point to their third.

7. The leader then calls on each person in turn, recording on the easel paper list his or her point-value rating.

8. Finally, the leader adds up the total score for each item and announces the group's selection.

If the list of items happens to be long (15 or more), it is preferable to have the members select their top four, or even five, and assign 4 or 5 points to their first choice, and so on. This decision process is usually superior to traditional voting methods because, among other reasons, it better reflects the relative strength of the group's preferences for the particular ideas that have been generated.

5. CLOSE THE MEETING.

One of the Leader's jobs is to keep track of time. If a meeting is scheduled to end at ten o'clock, then unless there is a major reason not to do so, the Leader should end the meeting at ten by announcing, "We are out of time." The members will have other appointments, places to go, and job tasks to finish. If someone still has an issue to discuss, the Leader should suggest that it be covered at the next meeting (and ask the Recorder to make a note of it). Or, the Leader may invite those who are interested to stay for a short time after the meeting.

The Leader must also make certain to leave enough time to:

- Ask the Observer/Facilitator for his or her comments on the group's process.

- Ask the Recorder to summarize the meeting, and review any tasks that need to be assigned.
- Ask for volunteers or assign people to complete these tasks.
- Announce the time and place of the next meeting.

6. FOLLOW UP.

In following up, you as the Leader, must check that the people who were assigned tasks are completing them on schedule. In addition, be sure that you complete any tasks that you agreed to do!

Finally, privately thank the group members who served as Observer/Facilitator, Recorder—and Leader, if assigned—for their work in making the meeting a success.

Using the ideas and strategies presented in this chapter won't, of course, solve every meeting problem. But they will help you resolve most of them. And they will help you plan and organize your meetings so that you can conduct and manage them with significantly greater productivity and success.

MEETING PREPARATION CHECKLIST

Meeting Date _____ Location _____

Time: Start _____ End _____ Lunch _____

Meeting Objective(s) — Describe what you, or the members, want to accomplish as a result of the meeting.

_____
_____
_____
_____
_____

Topics

_____
_____
_____
_____
_____
_____
_____
_____
_____
_____

Who should attend?

_____   _____
_____   _____
_____   _____
_____   _____
_____   _____
_____   _____

Checklist (check tasks required)	Notes (person to contact; person responsible, etc.)	Date completed
PRE-MEETING MAILINGS		
___ • Agenda	_____	_____
___ • Handouts	_____	_____
___ • Assignments	_____	_____
___ • _____	_____	_____
___ **ATTENDEES CONFIRMED**	_____	_____
SPEAKERS		
___ • Contacted	_____	_____
___ • Advance copy of outline and/or speech	_____	_____
___ • Confirmed in writing	_____	_____
___ • Advance copy of handouts	_____	_____
___ • Lodging	_____	_____
___ • _____	_____	_____
YOU		
___ • Outline of day's events	_____	_____
___ • Notes of written commentary	_____	_____
___ • Handouts	_____	_____
___ • Prizes, awards, certificates	_____	_____

____ • Transparencies _____ _____
____   — Prepared _____ _____
____   — "Write-on" _____ _____
       film
____   — Marking pen _____ _____
____ • Prepared flip _____ _____
       charts
____ • Videotape(s) _____ _____
____ • Slides _____ _____
____ • Evaluations _____ _____
       (if appropriate)
____ • _____ _____ _____

____ **LODGING FOR**
     OUT-OF-TOWN
     ATTENDEES _____ _____

     MEETING ROOM

____ • Room reserved _____ _____
____   – Room key _____ _____
____   – Appropriate
       size _____ _____
____   – Entrance in
       rear _____ _____
____   – External noise _____ _____
____   – Incoming phone
       calls held _____ _____
____   – Restroom
       location _____ _____
____ • Room layout _____ _____
       drawing for setup
       person
____ • Tables _____ _____
       – Chairs _____ _____
____ • A/V equipment _____ _____
____   – Overhead pro-
       jector & spare
       bulb _____ _____
____   – Slide projector _____ _____
____   – Large portable
       screen _____ _____

___	– Video player	_____	_____
___	– Video monitor	_____	_____
___	– Video recorder	_____	_____
___	– Public address system	_____	_____
___	* Microphone	_____	_____
___	* Volume control	_____	
___	– Flip charts	_____	_____
___	* Extra paper	_____	_____
___	* Marking pens	_____	_____
___	* Masking tape	_____	_____
___	– Chalkboard	_____	_____
___	* Cleaned	_____	_____
___	* Chalk	_____	_____
___	* Erasers	_____	_____
___•	Electrical outlets	_____	_____
___•	Room lighting	_____	_____
___•	Extension cord	_____	_____
___•	Temperature controls	_____	_____
___•	Note-taking	_____	_____
___	– Scratch paper	_____	_____
___	– Pencils	_____	_____
___•	Name tags	_____	_____
___•	Desk tags	_____	_____
___•	Direction signs	_____	_____
___•	Refreshments	_____	_____
___•	Meals	_____	_____
___	– Menu selection	_____	_____
___	– Written orders when to serve	_____	_____
___	– Cost	_____	_____
___	– Gratuities	_____	_____
___	– Billing	_____	_____
___•	_____	_____	_____
___•	_____	_____	_____

12
One-on-One Training Skills

Call it JIT (Job Instructional Training), OJT (On-the-Job-Training), or even a form of Behavior Modeling. Call it whatever you want, one-on-one training is probably the oldest kind of education today. Parents have taught their children in this way for thousands of years, and senior employees long have used it to teach new employees their craft.

The Beginning of Formalized One-on-One Training

During World War I there was a critical need for almost half a million new workers. Charles R. Allen, a Massachusetts vocational instructor, was asked to develop a process for training urgently needed shipbuilders. In 1917, Allen developed "four-step, on-the-job training" (OJT), consisting of: 1) showing, 2) telling, 3) doing, and 4) checking. This method is still used today, suggesting that either our training is terribly out-of-date—or the method is tried and true.

It's the latter! Time and again this basic system has effectively trained new employees in all kinds of organizations. The four-step process works because it is just plain common sense. In fact, you probably are using it in some way to train your people.

Six Steps in Effective One-on-One Training

I would like, however, to update Allen's process. Modern behavioral science indicates that there are really six steps for effective one-on-one training:

1. **Preparing** for the training.

2. **Asking** questions to determine the trainee's experience.

3. **Telling** the trainee about the task.

4. **Showing** the trainee how the task is done.

5. **Encouraging** the trainee to do the task.

6. **Following up** to ensure that the trainee can do the task.

1. Preparing for the training.

One of the basic problems with one-on-one training is that we often don't take the time to prepare properly for the training session. In his article on the "Tyranny of the Urgent," Charles E. Hummel said: "We live in a constant tension between those things that are urgent and those things that are important." The problem is that training preparation is important, but it often doesn't seem "urgent." And because urgent tasks must be done today, important tasks like preparation for good training frequently get postponed until later. But never forget: appropriate preparation ensures that your training is concise and realistic, and it will usually ensure a positive experience for you and your trainee.

Even though most of us conduct one-on-one training, we aren't necessarily effective trainers. A major problem resulting from lack of preparation, for instance, is that we tend to talk too much! Our tendency is to tell the employee everything we know about the task, rather than just those things the employee needs to know. Wasted time, bored trainees, and frustration for everyone result from all this talking. To be effective trainers, we need to:

    A. Analyze the job that will be taught by using task listing.

    B. Determine what we want the trainee to be able to do by using task detailing.

    C. Develop our training plans and strategies.

A. Analyzing the job, or task listing. By analyzing the job, you separate what the employee must know from what it would be nice for the employee to know. By listing the key tasks for the job, and putting those tasks in some sort of order—you then can make intelligent decisions about what should be taught, what shouldn't be taught, and what can be postponed until later. For example, if you analyzed your job as a leader, it would probably look something like this:

Task Listing

Job: Leader
A. Task Listing
1. Assigns work
2. Counsels problem employees
3. Makes decisions
4. Writes goals and objectives for section
5. Develops employees
6. Conducts yearly performance appraisals
7. Gives positive feedback to employees
8. Writes exception reports
9. Holds meetings
10. Assists in selecting new employees
11. Records daily time cards
12. Coordinates work with other sections
13. Etc.

If you were a new leader and it were my responsibility to train you, I would prepare for our training by making a list of the major activities for your new job. Chances are that you would already be familiar with some of those activities. For example, if you had worked in my department, you would already have set your goals and objectives under Task 4. Therefore, I wouldn't need to spend time to teach you this task. But Task 5, "Develops employees," is one task you would not have had a chance to learn in your previous job, so I would teach this task.

B. Determining what we want the trainee to be able to do, or task detailing. By detailing the key tasks, I fairly quickly can see those specific topics that must be covered and those that don't. For example, let's imagine that you are an absolute whiz at managing your time. Now, let's really jump off the deep end and pretend that I'm a whiz at scheduling my time. If I don't take the time to think, "I don't have to teach him how to schedule his time because he's already a whiz at it," chances are that I'll bore you silly for two hours telling you how important managing your training time is!

Task detailing can also remind me to cover a key topic in our one-on-one training sessions. It tells me exactly what you and I need to do, because each task I've detailed which you don't already know how to do automatically becomes a training objective for us.

In the example that follows, I have selected Task 5, "Develops employees," from the preceding list of tasks, and then detailed all the sub-tasks you will need to do in developing employees.

Task Detailing

Job: Leader
    A. Task Listing
        5. Develops employees
    B. Task Detailing
        1. Determines training needs of individual employees
        2. Schedules time for training
        3. Does task listing
        4. Does task detailing
        5. Develops training plans
        6. Locates or devises training aids
        7. Trains
        8. Follows up to determine whether training is successful
        9. Develops revised training plan to meet any needs that still exist
      10. Etc.

Next, I will take each of the detailed tasks that you don't already know how to do and plan how the training will be done.

C. Training plans and strategies. In this part of my preparation, I would take each topic that we'll cover and develop my training strategies or plans—those steps I must take to train you to do in each detailed task. Planning is something you probably already know a good deal about, so I won't spend time here describing planning processes (I'll practice what I preach!). But I will illustrate Step 7, "Trains," from the task detailing of "Develops employees," in order to show what I would do in this step if I were going to train you to be a new leader.

Training Plans and Strategies

Job: Leader

    A. Task Listing
       5. Develops employees

    B. Task Detailing
       7. Trains

    C. Plans (strategies)
       1. Check the library for books on one-on-one training
       2. Write out the best step-by-step training model I can find
       3. Develop a skit for me to use to demonstrate how a new employee is trained
       4. Reserve the video equipment to use while practicing
       5. Reserve the conference room
       6. Etc.

This type of preparation—task listing, task detailing, and planning—will help to provide a smooth and effective training program. And note that all this essential work has been done with paper and pencil. I haven't started the training yet!

2. Asking questions to determine the trainee's experience.

Today, most one-on-one training models include the original "Show, Tell, Do, and Check" steps of the Allen JIT model—along with additional steps such as preparation and introduction. However there still seems to be little reference to determine the employee's previous experience, as shown in Step 2 of this model.

Reasons for asking questions. In conducting training I include Step 2—determining the trainee's experience—for the following reasons:

- It demonstrates a caring attitude on the part of the trainer, since he or she expresses interest in the trainee by asking questions and listening.
- It may reduce training time by revealing what the trainee already knows.
- It can reveal previous experience that might interfere with new learning.

  For example, I remember the time my typist left on vacation and I obtained the services of my printer-composer to fill in for her. A typist uses a keyboard; so does a printer-composer. Therefore, a competent printer-composer should be able to type as well as a typist. But this proved wrong! Because the word processing programs were quite different, I can tell you from experience that the letters typed by my printer-composer were sent only out of necessity! Prior experience can often slow down new learning.

- It may disclose prior experience to which new learning can be related.

How to ask questions. The idea is not just a quick, "What have you experienced before?" and, "OK, that's not the way to do things here!" The trainer must have a sincere desire to probe for any possible past experience that can be linked to the new information.

If, for example, I were teaching an adult how to make transparencies, I might first ask: "What's been your experience with overhead transparencies—or 'viewgraphs,' as some people call them?" Either I will obtain new information, or I won't. If I do, then I can use this past experience to help explain new information.

If I don't get useful information, I will probably stop this particular line of questioning. I might ask, "What kinds of programs, if any, have you attended where viewgraphs were used?" Or, "What are some of the things you like about viewgraphs?" And, "What were some of the things you don't like about viewgraphs?"

Whatever information I obtain, I listen actively, nodding my head and saying, "I see" or, "Uh-huh" at appropriate points. In addition, I don't interrupt. And I will ask clarification questions such as, "Can you be more specific?", "Could you give me an example?", or, "How was that done?"

Types of questions. Generally, the best questions to use are "open questions" which start with "What?" or "How?" In addition, there are questions that are perceived by the employee as requests for more information—although, technically, they are "closed questions" that can be answered with "Yes" or "No". Closed questions such as "Can you be more specific?" or "Could you give me an example?" may serve the same function as open questions.

Other open questions that start with "When?" or "Where?" obtain specific details and thus are less desirable for general probing of the trainee's experience. For example, if I am asking for a trainee's experience with viewgraphs, I first inquire, "What has been your experience with viewgraphs?", rather than, "When did you encounter viewgraphs?"

The least desirable questions seem to be personal *"Why?"* questions—as in *"Why* did *you* do it that way?" A "Why" combined with "you" can produce defensive behavior, since it focuses upon personal motives. However, "Why did *they* do it that way?" does not normally challenge the trainee, since it asks for an opinion about a third party.

3. Telling the trainee about the task.

"Telling" is a step any leader should be able to do well—right? Wrong! Because it's easy to tell your employees everything they might ever want to know about a specific task (after all, you are the expert!), you may tend to talk, talk, and talk. As already discussed, part of this problem is solved by careful preparation in Step 1, when you delete every task the trainee already knows how to perform. You can also help to avoid "talking problems" by carefully asking key questions to determine the trainee's experience (Step 2 above). But Step 2 can also set the stage for the talking problem! It's as if you say, "OK, I listened to you in Step 2. Now it's my turn to talk." Never forget: talking too much can get you and the trainee into deep trouble.

So remember the answers to those questions about past experience you asked in Step 2. You wanted to find out what the trainee already knew. How is that going to help you? In three ways! You learn what the trainee:

- already knows—and doesn't need to relearn.
- doesn't know—and needs to learn.
- knows—and can be related to the new task, thus helping him or her in learning it.

Explaining the job or job task. While explaining the job or job task, provide an umbrella of knowledge by giving the trainee an overview of *what* is to be done. Then tell the *who, where,* and *when* of the job—to define the job's environment. Next, tell *why* the job should be done, providing reasons that make sense. And here, stay away from the old, "We do it because it's organizational policy." Policies are not written by a deity, but by people *for* people. If you don't know the *why,* find out! Reasons for doing a task supply the trainee with motivation to do it.

Last, provide specific information that describes *how* the task is to be done. Use sketches, pictures, and even illustrations with rough drawings as you describe how the task should be done. Deliberately structure pauses in your explanation to give the trainee an opportunity to interrupt and ask questions. If your trainee chooses not to interrupt, interrupt yourself by asking the trainee questions about what you have said. For example, you can get important feedback from your trainee by asking:

"How is this like your old job?"
"What problems do you see in doing this?"
"What questions do you have at this point?"

"Hey, stupid, do you have any questions?" Avoid the time worn, "Well, do you have any questions...?" The unspoken word the trainee hears at the end of this question is "dummy"! If I am your employee, then, of course, you as my boss, surely explained the task thoroughly and wisely—and I'm obviously not too bright if I have any questions! So I'll just nod wisely and we'll both get in trouble later. Instead, ask, "What questions do you have?" The "What" implies that questions are expected! Also ask questions about what you are going to explain next. But don't set up the trainee for failure by asking things that he or she has no way of knowing about. Instead, during this "telling" portion of training, ask questions that most people would be able to answer through common sense application.

For example, if I were teaching you the key steps for effective one-on-one training, I might ask, "OK, now that we have discussed how to tell the employee what to do, what might be the next step?" Even if you responded by saying, "Let the employee do it," I would not say, "Wrong! Wrong!" Rather, I would reply, "Great! Letting the employee do it is definitely another step in the one-on-one training process. But it's not the next step. If we tell the employee what to do, and plan to let him or her do it later, what should we do before we let the trainee do it?" Here the trainee will almost always say, "Show how", or "Demonstrate it".

It's important not to get trapped into doing all the talking, even during the "telling" portion of the training. Strike a careful balance between telling and listening. And in order to listen, encourage the trainee to ask questions, to make comments, and to respond to your questions.

Everything new is difficult. One important point: don't make comments such as, "This is really simple. You'll catch on in no time." When you say this, the message the trainee hears is, "If it's all that simple, I can't fail. So if I fail, I'm not very smart!" Even with the best of motives—trying to relax the trainee—you accomplish exactly the opposite, and the trainee's tension and anxiety increase. Remember, few things that are new are "simple." Mostly, they're difficult at first!

4. Showing the trainee how the task is done.

First, note that "showing" in Step 4 is not the same as showing a drawing or picture to illustrate what has been described in Step 3. In the Step 4 you model the job to be done. And, as you demonstrate the task, give verbal clues to the trainee. "Talk your thoughts," so that the trainee both hears and sees how it is to be done, and where, when, and why it is done.

One idea you might consider is to have the trainee talk to you through the demonstration. You perform the demonstration while the employee tells you what to do before you do it. This technique gets the trainee involved in the learning process and also tells you exactly what the trainee has—or hasn't—learned. Showing the employee how the task is done through modeling may feel a little awkward in the beginning. But making a mistake or two yourself simply makes you more human. A little humor here goes a long way, and you'll find the employee to be more relaxed when it's time for him or her to practice.

5. Encouraging the trainee to do the task.

You can read a book about riding a unicycle, watch someone ride one—and even write an article on "The Joys of Unicycle Riding." But you can't do it yourself until you actually ride that thing yourself! And your employees can't learn how to do a task by reading about it, and they can't learn skills by watching you or anybody else. They have to do the task themselves—and receive feedback on their performance. That's your job as a trainer. Watch them perform in a practice session, and then provide helpful, constructive feedback.

Feedback should be tactful. In some cases this will be the employee's first job. He or she may be nervous and unsure. It's up to you not only to look for lack of comprehension, but also for opportunities to give positive feedback on what he or she has done correctly! When lack of understanding is evident, don't use phrases such as:

"You did that wrong."
"You made an error."
"There were too many mistakes in your work."
"You'll just have to try harder in the future."
"You failed!"

Instead, direct your remarks to what was done improperly, and how it can be corrected. Always stay away from the personal attack (the "You" in the above statements).

Ask questions. One of the best ways to help trainees develop task skills is to have them tell you what they are going to do before they do it. This allows you the opportunity to correct them before they make a mistake, and helps them perform the task properly the first time. If they still start to do something incorrectly, ask them to stop, then ask questions to help them think through for themselves the correct procedure. For example, suppose you observe a troubled trainee taping a transparency, and stretching the transparent tape too tightly. "Too tight!" you tautly tell the trainee.

But a better (less tongue-twisting) approach would be to stop the trainee and ask, "What could happen to this flimsy transparency's frame if the tape is stretched too tightly?" "Oh," says the trainee. "Could it bend the frame?" "You bet! How could you make sure it's not too tight?" you ask. "Maybe if I relaxed it before I stuck it down," replies the trainee. "Excellent! Why don't you try it?" you respond. In this way, you show confidence in the trainee's own ability to figure things out. This enhances the trainee's self-image, as well as better retaining the correct way to perform the task.

6. Following up to ensure that the trainee can do the task.

Following up does not mean concluding with the familiar statement: "My door is always open. If you have any questions, don't hesitate to stop by, and I'll help you any way I can." Trainees who are apprehensive about their job and job environment may not feel comfortable enough to come to you with their questions.

Following up means *you* follow up. *You're* the one who needs to take the initiative and visit the trainee on a regular basis. So do it! Make time in your schedule to visit your trainees. Good intentions don't count much here—action does!

View this step as an interview with several objectives. First, find out what the trainee is feeling and thinking about the job. Second, determine how well the job task is being done and if there are any areas that need improvement.

In order to get information, use your old friends—questions. So ask your trainees how they feel about the task: what they like about it, what they don't like, and what concerns they may have.

Then, have the trainee complete the key tasks to ensure that he or she is performing them correctly. When you see positive performance, say so! And avoid "parental" responses such as, "I'm proud of you!" Instead, try: "That's exactly right." "Excellent!" "That's good work!"

Then carefully analyze the performance, and identify areas that need improvement.

LEADER'S CHECKLIST
ONE-ON-ONE TRAINING SKILLS

1. Prepare for training.
- Task listing
- Task detailing
- Develop training plans and strategies

2. Ask questions to determine the trainee's experience.
Examples:

"What experience have you had with jobs like this?"

"What have you done in the past that was similar to this?"

3. Tell the trainee about the task.
Examples:

"This is what you will be doing."

"While completing this task, these are the people you
will be dealing with:..."

"This is where the job will be done."

"This job should be done when..."

"The reasons for doing this job are..."

Then ask:

"What problems do you see in doing this?"

"What questions do you have at this point?"

"What concerns do you have about doing this?"

4. Show the trainee how to do the task.
Example:

"Watch me; as I do this task, I'll talk my way through it
for you."

5. Encourage the trainee to do the task.

Example:

"Now you do it as I watch. And why don't you tell me what you are going to do just before you perform each step?"

6. Follow up to ensure that the trainee can do the task.

Example:

"Why don't we get back together tomorrow and see how you are doing? I'll stop by your area right after break, say at about ten o'clock."

TRAINING WORK SHEET

☐ **1. Preparation**

   A. List task: _____

   B. Detail task: _____

   C. Plans and strategies: _____
   _____
   _____
   _____
   _____

☐ **2. Determine Trainee's Experience.** Answer the question: "What does the employee already know that will (1) aid learning and (2) hinder learning?" What information do you need in order to teach this employee the specific unit of knowledge selected from your task detailing sheet? _____
   _____
   _____
   _____
   _____

☐ **3. Explanation.** What specific unit of knowledge are you going to give this employee? (Taken from your task detailing and planning work sheets.) Briefly, what will you say? (Don't try to write out a "script." This should only be your notes.) _____
   _____
   _____
   _____
   _____

☐ **4. Demonstration.** What will you do? _____
   _____
   _____
   _____
   _____

☐ **5. Employee performs the task.** What specific parts of the task do you think the employee will be able to perform correctly?

_____

_____

_____

When the employee performs the above item successfully, what will you say?

A. Describe what you saw: _____

_____

_____

B. Tell why it was important: _____

_____

_____

C. Express your feelings: _____

_____

_____

What specific part of the task may be difficult for the employee? _____

_____

_____

_____

What will you say if the employee does this incorrectly?_____

_____

_____

_____

☐ **6. Follow up.** What does the employee need to know about complicated, preventive, or corrective tasks, and/or housekeeping, that affects the performance of the task learned? _____

_____

_____

_____

What kinds of specific follow-up action will be necessary for you to take? _____

_____

_____

13
Interviewing and Selection

It is impossible to understand interviewing and selection without dealing with some legal issues. But a word of caution. Although I feel that the legal information presented here is accurate, it is nonetheless *my understanding. I am not a lawyer!* In addition, both the laws and their enforcement are constantly changing. Therefore, I cannot assume responsibility for any legal implications arising from what is presented here, and therefore I urge you to talk with an attorney about any legal problems that the applicant may encounter.

The Cost of Poor Hiring Practices

Some of the costs of replacing employees when they don't succeed are obvious: the initial cost of recruiting, interviewing and training; your time; and then having to do it all over again if the person that is hired doesn't work out.

But ineffective interviewing and selection also involve some costs—which aren't as obvious. For example, look at your employees as an investment. As with any investment, you need to realize a return. During an employee's career in your organization, the investment, in terms of salary and benefits, can be a figure exceeding one million dollars. When we stop and realize that we literally make million-dollar investment decisions, often based on only an hour or so spent interviewing and selecting an employee, it's kind of scary.

Also note that organizations operate within a larger community. And communities are very quick to judge organizations whose hiring practices result in high turnover because people and jobs were poorly matched. When the word gets around—and it doesn't take long—it becomes harder and harder to find good candidates because you don't get good applicants!

Then consider the recent trend toward litigation and possible lawsuits for wrongful discharge. Here again, nobody wins. In most states, you can still terminate an employee who isn't a member of a minority and doesn't have a contract, written or implied, for almost any reason. But if the employee feels that hiring promises weren't honored and/or that he or she was unfairly terminated, then whether or not you "win" a resulting lawsuit, you still lose. Have you ever had to sit for hours while an employee's attorney takes your deposition? It's no fun! In addition, the morale in your section or department will—note "will," not "may"—suffer when your employee leaves, either voluntarily or involuntarily. Indeed, you will be caught either way: if you don't terminate an employee who was poorly hired, you will see morale fall. And when you do terminate him or her, morale will suffer because of the termination. It's a lose-lose situation: you lose no matter what you do. Therefore, it's tremendously important to spend the time and effort necessary to hire the right candidate in the first place. And you will greatly improve your chances of hiring the best person for the job if you prepare properly for the interview.

Note that the following information about preparing for and conducting selection interviews is presented in a logical, step-by-step order. But, as you will discover, it does not always work this neatly, particularly because some steps must be done simultaneously.

Let's look at how to do this critical part of your job by first examining 1) all the things that need to be done in *preparation* for the interview, then, 2) the *interview* itself, and finally, 3) the *selection* process.

In order to see how all the parts and pieces of planning for and conducting selection interviews go together, each step is illustrated with an example. We will take the job of office clerk as our example because you probably already know what an office clerk does, and it is an easy job to quantify.

Preparation

1. Analyze the job to be filled.

The first step in preparing for your selection interview is to take a long, hard look at the job you want to fill. To do this, you need first to list the major tasks of the job, and then to determine key knowledge, skills, and interests that the future employees will need for each task. You should also decide which tasks applicants must already be able to perform when they apply, and which they can be trained to do after they are hired. Next you will need to write out the questions you will use to determine the applicant's knowledge, skills and interests for each task. And finally you need to have a strategy to discover whether the applicant is likely to be satisfied with the job conditions—salary, benefits, working hours, etc.

List the major tasks of the job. Now let's take our example of interviewing for the office clerk's position. Here's how the task-listing of this job might look:

Interview Planning Work Sheet

Position: Office Clerk

Tasks

1. Filing
2. Typing
3. Mailing
4. Handling supplies
5. Answering phones
6. Faxing messages
7. Making copies

Determine job knowledge, skills, and interests. Now you need to examine each task to determine what an applicant should know, be able to do, or be motivated to do. For example, concerning the task of "filing" in the office clerk's position, the applicant 1) must have basic reading skills, and 2) know the rules of filing (where do you file the "The 3-M Company" folder?). From this task-detailing you will later determine how well the applicant fits the job.

Interview Planning Work Sheet

Tasks	Job knowledge, skills, and interests
1. Filing	— Knows rules of filing — Has basic reading skills
2. Typing	— Types min. 45 wpm with only 1% error rate — Likes to type — Has experience with our W.P. programs
3. Mailing	— Operates postage meter — Adds and subtracts correctly
4. Handling supplies	— Fills out purchase order requests — Can lift a max. of 25 lbs. (boxes)
5. Answering phones	— Has pleasant telephone personality — Knows telephone etiquette
6. Faxing messages	— Knows how to dial a long-distance fax number — Can position documents in machine and start/stop the operation
7. Making copies	— Turns machine on/off properly — Can load paper — Trouble-shoots machine when red light flashes

Decide whether the applicant should already have the required knowledge/skills/interests. I like to list the knowledge, skills and interests required for a specific job even though I am very willing to (or even plan to) teach the employee some tasks. For example, the office clerk's task of "making copies," is not one I would ask an applicant about; I would likely plan to teach the employee how to do this part of his or her job. But by task-detailing I am able to determine prerequisites. For example, an employee who must distinguish the flashing green light from the red on the copy machine cannot be color blind. In the work sheet example below, "R" stands for "Required" when hired, and "T" means I can "Train" the employee after hiring.

Interview Planning Work Sheet

Tasks	Job knowledge, skills, and interests	Required Can Train
1. Filing	— Knows rules of filing	R
	— Has basic reading skills	R
2. Typing	— Types min. 45 wpm with only 1% error rate	R
	— Likes to type	R
	— Has experience with our W.P. programs	T
3. Mailing	— Operates postage meter	T
	— Adds and subtracts correctly	R
4. Handling supplies	— Fills out purchase order requests	T
	— Can lift a max. of 25 lbs. (boxes)	R
5. Answering phones	— Has pleasant telephone personality	R
	— Knows telephone etiquette	R
6. Faxing messages	— Knows how to dial a long-distance fax number	T
	— Can position documents in machine and start/stop the operation	T

7. Making   — Turns machine on/off
    copies   properly   T
                — Can load paper   R
                — Trouble-shoots machine
                    when red light flashes   R

Identify prescreening questions. Now you need to determine: 1) which job knowledge, skills and interests an applicant absolutely *must* have in order to qualify for an interview; and 2) what questions you will ask the applicant on the telephone to obtain this information. The idea is to create "knockout" questions that will keep you and the applicant from needlessly wasting time in an interview. For example, if "typing" is a required skill for the job, you are probably not going to teach someone that skill after he or she is hired. So in a telephone prescreening interview you need to ask about the applicant's typing skills (if this is not already indicated on the application blank), and terminate the conversation if the applicant can't type.

Therefore, in the third column of the *Interview Planning Work Sheet,* note "P" to indicate that a prescreening question should be asked; "I" to denote that the information should be obtained during the regular interview; or "P/I" if the same question should be asked both in the prescreening phone conversation as well as during the interview itself.

"Open" questions. A critical technique required in prescreening—and later in the formal interview—is the ability to ask questions effectively. Normally you can write your key questions in advance. When you write—and later ask—questions, make them "open" rather than "closed" questions. That is, start your questions with "Who?" "What?" "Where?" "When?" "Why?" or "How?" Closed questions, in contrast, usually start with "Do you?" "Could you?" "Will you?" "Have you?" or "Can you?" and are normally answered with a "yes" or "no." Open questions, therefore, help you obtain more information than closed questions. And that is your objective—information. For example, the

question, "How do you feel about typing?" is likely to get more information than, "Do you like to type?"

"Leading" questions. Think of a movie or TV courtroom scene in which one of the attorneys jumps to his feet and shouts, "Objection! Objection your Honor! The opposing council is 'leading' the witness!" Whereupon the Judge says, "Objection sustained. Council will please rephrase the question."

I'd like you to imagine that there is a "judge" present when you are interviewing, listening to your questions. And every time you ask a question beginning with "Don't you?" "Couldn't you?" "Shouldn't you?" or "Can't you?" this judge is going to jump all over you! Questions like these—termed "leading" questions—ask the applicant to agree with your preconceived opinions, and will usually bias his or her response. For instance, the question, "Don't you think that it is very important to have good work habits?" quite clearly telegraphs the answer you seek, and can invalidate the information you obtain. So don't "lead the witness." If you really want to know what applicants think or how they feel, ask them using "open" questions.

Looking at the fourth column of our *Interview Planning Work Sheet* concerning the office clerk's position, I briefly have indicated my prescreening questions next to any "P's" in the third column ("P" = prescreening question)—using open questions wherever possible.

Interview Planning Work Sheet

Tasks	Job knowledge, skills, and interests	Required Can Train	In Prescreening In Interview P/I = in both	
1. Filing	— Knows rules of filing	R	P	"How well do you know the rules of filing?"
			I	
	— Has basic reading skills	R	P	"How well can you read?"
2. Typing	— Types min. 45 wpm with only 1% error rate	R	P	"How fast do you type?"
	— Likes to type	R	P/I	"How do you feel about typing?"
	— Has experience with our W.P. programs	T	I	
3. Mailing	— Operates postage meter	T	I	
	— Adds and subtracts correctly	R	P I	"Can you do basic math?"
4. Handling supplies	— Fills out purchase order requests	T	I	
	— Can lift a max. of 25 lbs. (boxes)	R	P	"Can you lift at least 25 lbs?
5. Answering phones	— Has pleasant telephone personality	R	P I	Listen to how he or she sounds during phone call
	— Knows telephone etiquette	R	P	Listen for key behaviors during phone call
6. Faxing messages	— Knows how to dial a long-distance fax number	T	I	
	— Can position documents in machine and start/ stop the operation	T	I	

7. Making copies	— Turns machine on/off properly	T	I	
	— Can load paper	R	I	
	— Trouble-shoots machine when red light flashes	R	P	"Are you color blind
			I	to any specific colors?"

Decide how you will determine the applicant's knowledge/skills/ interests. We can obtain information in a variety of ways. These include: asking questions in the interview, requiring the applicant to perform certain tasks, having the applicant bring in samples of relevant work, and reviewing the applicant's résumé and/or application form for specific information and questionable areas. Let's look at each of these techniques.

Asking questions. Your interview questions normally should be composed at the same time you develop your telephone prescreening questions. While writing questions to ask in the interview, follow the same guidelines that were given for writing prescreening questions: use "open" questions while avoiding "closed" and "leading" ones. Note, too, that we may want to ask the same question in the interview that we asked in the telephone prescreening call. Or, it is sometimes revealing to ask the same question in a slightly different way.

Demonstrating performance. One of the best ways to find out if applicants can do what they say they can do is to ask them to do it! It is remarkable how often interviewers ask job candidates about their skills—but don't ask them to demonstrate them. I suspect that the reason why many people in organizations today can't read (and no one knows it until a serious problem occurs) is because 1) people lacking basic reading skills are often adept at disguising this fact, and 2) they were not asked to read in the selection interview.

So, if I want to know if applicants can type, I ask them to type. If I need to know if they can use "Ohm's law," I give them voltage ($E = 10$ V) and current ($I = 2$ A) and ask them to derive resistance ($R = ?$).

If I need to know how well they can answer the phone, I have them role play with me, or, after brief preparation, answer an actual incoming phone call. If a particular job skill is important and you don't plan to teach it on the job, then figure out a way for the applicant to demonstrate his or her degree of expertise for you.

Securing samples of past work. There are times when it is appropriate and extremely helpful to ask the applicant to bring samples of past work to the interview. For example, if I were hiring someone to teach a one-day interviewing and selection workshop, I would ask for a videotape of him or her conducting an actual workshop on this subject. If I wanted to hire graphic arts people, I would certainly ask them to bring samples of their work. And if I were looking for a writer, then I'd want to see some things that he or she had written. If computer programmers were needed, I would ask them to bring hard copy samples of their work, as well as disks that I could run on my computer. So, if creative work that can be seen or heard is involved, then ask the applicant to bring samples of that work to the interview.

The résumé and application. Résumés are often written to present information in the best possible way—and this is a problem as well as an asset. You seldom see on a résumé, "I really didn't like my boss, so I quit." Or, "After I work for an organization for a year or two, I need to move on to greener pastures." Yet, these are two of the main reasons that people actually quit. Or when was the last time you read a résumé that said, "I am so desperate for work that I'll take any job. Even yours!" Therefore, interpret what you see on a résumé by realizing that the applicant has positioned the information in its best possible light.

An experienced eye can tell you a great deal. Does the work history show frequent moves? Then what does this say about the applicant's intention of staying with your organization? Are there gaps in the employment history? What questions do you need to ask about those gaps? And is the applicant's work history actually a good fit for the job you are trying to fill?

Are there any blanks in the application form? If so, why were they not filled out? What questions do you need to ask to obtain the missing information? Has the applicant been unemployed? How long? Why did he or she leave one job before finding another?

The applicant's handwriting can tell you something not only about neatness, but about carefulness. If an application is typed, do you also need to ask to see a sample of the applicant's handwriting?

Let's return again to our *Interview Planning Work Sheet* for the office clerk's job to fill in the questions, demonstrations and samples we will use where "I" (Interview) is indicated.

Interview Planning Work Sheet

Tasks	Job knowledge, skills, and interests	*R*equired Can *T*rain	In *P*rescreening In *I*nterview P/I = in both	
1. Filing	— Knows rules of filing	R	P	"How well do you know the rules of filing?"
			I	"Please put these files in order."
	— Has basic reading skills	R	P	"How well can you read?"
			I	"Please read this paragraph aloud."
2. Typing	— Types min. 45 wpm with only 1% error rate	R	P	"How fast do you type?"
			I	"Please type this letter."
	— Likes to type	R	P/I	"How do you feel about typing?"
	— Has experience with our W.P. programs	T	I	"What W.P. programs are you experienced on?"

3. Mailing	— Operates postage meter	T		I	"Have you used a postage meter?"
	— Adds and subtracts correctly	R		P	"Can you do basic math?"
				I	"Please do the necessary math on these figures."
4. Handling supplies	— Fills out purchase order requests	T		I	"Please fill out this form like this sample."
	— Can lift a max. of 25 lbs. (boxes)	R		P	"Can you lift at least 25 lbs?
5. Answering phones	— Has pleasant telephone personality	R		P	Listen to how he or she sounds during phone call
				I	Conduct a role play.
	— Knows telephone etiquette	R		P	Listen for key behaviors during phone call.
6. Faxing messages	— Knows how to dial a long-distance fax number	T		I	"What's been your experience with a fax machine?"
	— Can position documents in machine and start/ stop the operation	T		I	"Show me how you would send this fax."
7. Making copies	— Turns machine on/off properly	T		I	"What's been your experience with office copiers?"
	— Can load paper	R		I	"Please make a copy of this."
	— Trouble-shoots machine when red light flashes	R		P	"Are you color blind to any specific colors?"
				I	"What colors are these dots?"

Determine other job requirements. Before the interview, you also need to plan questions that will help you determine whether the applicant is appropriate for other aspects of the job. For instance, if the salary were advertised, then the applicant has applied for the job knowing what the position pays. But if salary has not been mentioned, you will need to decide how well the applicant's expectations match what the job pays.

One way to determine how satisfied the applicant might be with the salary requirements is to review past salaries indicated on his or her résumé, as you ask appropriate questions during the prescreening telephone interview. If prior pay is not noted in the résumé or application, you can simply ask, "What was your salary in your last (or present) position?" Or, "What kind of salary range are you looking for?"

You may also need to ask questions about the applicant's desires and expectations concerning working conditions, work hours, vacations, holidays, benefits, and insurance. If the job requires that the employee normally work alone, then you need to determine whether the applicant likes to do so. If the job hours are unusual, then you may need to ask questions to make sure that the hours will not be a hardship.

At the end of this chapter is a blank copy of the *Interview Planning Work Sheet* we have been using for illustration. You may copy and utilize it in planning and conducting your prescreening contacts and selection interviews.

2. **Review interview plan to ensure that it complies with the law and, if appropriate, your organization's Affirmative Action Program.**

There are two key areas that you should evaluate to ensure compliance with the law in your interviewing and selection practices. The first has to do with questions that should not be asked either on the application form or during the interview. The second area concerns employee ratios with regard to minority status, sex, and age. Let's look at each of these in more detail.

Questions asked. The questions on your application form, as well as those asked in interviews, must be unbiased in terms of the race/ethnicity, religion, sex, age, handicap, and national origin of applicants. Most employers today are aware that asking informational questions of job applicants in the above areas can be illegal. But we cannot assume that everyone is well familiar with the law and legal guidelines in this regard, and so we are going to examine in some detail each of these areas. It should also be noted that we are frequently unaware of what we don't know—and that it is not always obvious that asking certain questions of applicants can pose legal difficulties.

Of course, some of the questions discussed below are OK when asked *after* the candidate has been offered and has accepted employment. For instance, the personnel department will need to know the age of the new employee for retirement purposes, and family information needs to be obtained for insurance purposes. On the other hand, questions about religion are not legally proper at any time.

Race/ethnicity. If the purpose and result of an organization's hiring procedure is to deliberately hire minorities, then most questions concerning race/ethnicity are legal. But if the intent, *or effect,* of the hiring procedure is to exclude minorities, if the organization's present minority-to-nonminority ratios are suspect, or if a rejected applicant feels that he or she has been excluded due to race/ethnicity, then questions such as the following can place you in very serious trouble:

— "What is your race?"
— "Where were you born?"
— "Where did your family originally come from?"
— "Are you a naturalized citizen?"
— "How did you learn to speak Spanish?" (or any foreign language)
— "What was your wife's maiden name?"

Asking applicants for a photograph, or for a birth certificate or baptismal record as proof of age, is also illegal.

Religious preferences. As indicated, questions concerning an applicant's religion are always illegal. Simply do not ever ask questions such as the following:

— "What is your religious affiliation?"
— "What church do you go to?"
— "What religious holidays do you observe?"

Marital and family status. Questions concerning marital or family status are normally illegal—unless you ask the same question of both sexes, and you have a job-related reason for asking. Questions such as the following may result in trouble for you and your organization:

— "How does your spouse feel about your need to travel in this job?" (a potentially serious problem when asked of a female applicant)
— "Are you married?"
— "Do you plan to get married?"
— "Have you ever been divorced?"
— "What are your plans about having children?"
— "What are you going to do about your children during working hours?"

Height and weight. Unless height and/or weight information is clearly relevant to a job's requirements, questions about them are usually illegal. The issue here is: why do you, or your organization, want to know? If particular height and weight qualifications are absolutely critical to a job—and you can prove it—then the questions may be OK. Otherwise, it's none of your business. Don't ask questions such as:

— "How tall are you?"
— "How much do you weigh?"

Age. Most interviewers today do not ask an obvious age-inquiry question like "How old are you?" But I have heard disguised ("clever") questions asked to secure approximate age information-- which are not clever at all. In fact, the following questions (asked before hiring the applicant) would be very obvious to an opposing counsel in a courtroom:

— "How old is your oldest child?"
— "What year did you graduate from high school/college?"

Other questions. You should be aware that there are other questions which are inadvisable because they are potentially related to the above issues even though they may not appear to be. For example:

— "Do you have any friends or family working for us?" (A hiring preference for friends or family members of your employees could restrict opportunities for minorities.)
— "Have you ever been arrested?" "Have you ever been in jail?" (Since some minorities have higher rates of arrest or incarceration than others, these questions may discriminate.)
— "Tell me about your credit rating." "Do you own your own home?" "What kind of car do you have?" (I call these questions "stupid questions" because anyone asking them has got to be marginally intelligent and in the wrong job. Unless these socioeconomic questions are clearly job related, don't ask them because they tend to discriminate against certain minorities.)

In general, then, the rule is that if your questions do not clearly relate to specific job requirements, they are potentially illegal because they may be viewed as tending to discriminate on a basis other than job qualifications.

Are applicants appropriately representative in terms of race/ ethnicity and sex? If the effect of your hiring action is to either institute or perpetuate a policy of noncompliance with the law concerning race/ethnicity and gender, you may be in serious trouble. So you need to take the initiative, either with your personnel department or management, to ensure that you are appropriately encouraging minority applications and interviews. If you are located in an area with a 35% minority population, for example, it is reasonable that you seek to interview minority applicants reflecting at least this percentage.

3. Determine who will interview the applicants.

There are some very good reasons why you might wish to involve others in the interviewing and selection process. For example, you could include other leaders who are your peers in order to gain additional insight into an applicant's suitability for the job.

Multiple interviewers can also protect you from yourself. I remember interviewing an applicant whom I nearly hired on the spot when he informed me that he attended the same college I did. Fortunately, others were also involved in the hiring decision and helped me see my bias.

Of course, involving others will significantly increase your cost of hiring. But if we are talking about million-dollar decisions—as we are—then it can be a good idea to invest additional up-front time and money to ensure that you make the best possible selections.

If the applicants are going to be interviewed by more than one person, be sure to provide all interviewers with copies of an *Interview Planning Work Sheet* that spells out the knowledge, skills, and interests needed for each task and the questions to be asked. Decide in advance who will focus on what aspects of the job, and which questions each interviewer will ask the applicants. Then set up a schedule and notify each interviewer by interoffice mail as to who will be interviewed, when, and where.

An excellent strategy being used more and more today is to involve the potential employee's future co-workers in the interviewing and selection procedure. After all, if your employees are going to work with—and probably help train—the new person, they will feel much better about who is selected if they have had a hand in the decision. In addition, the chances are that your current employees know the work better than anyone else, and they can even assist you in developing the interview questions. Finally, new employees appreciate knowing that their co-workers were involved in choosing them.

4. Establish an interview area.

Since interviews are important, schedule them in private locations where you can control interruptions. Use a conference room, with a sign on the door stating: "Interviews in progress. Please do not interrupt." Or find the office of someone who is on vacation. You can use your office if necessary—but don't allow yourself to be interrupted! Tell people who might normally interrupt you that you will be interviewing and do not want to be interrupted. And ask that your phone calls be held.

Arrange the interview seating so that it is conducive to sharing information. In other words, avoid an "I've got all the power" arrangement if you really want information from an applicant. Meet in a neutral area if possible; again, a conference room is preferable. If you must use your office, don't sit behind your desk. Try sitting across the corner of your desk, or in front of it, using a guest chair. Whatever you do, set up the interview area so that it helps create a true conversation with the applicant, not an "interrogation."

Finally, place a small clock where you can see it while you are looking at the applicant, or where it can be seen as you look down at your notes. If you glance away from the applicant to check your watch or a clock, he or she will feel that you are pressed for time.

5. Prescreening telephone interviews.

After you have identified the job requirements, examined the résumé or application form, written prescreening questions, examined your applicants' application forms and decided what they should bring with them to the interview, you are ready to conduct brief telephone interviews. These will allow you to separate those applicants who are not suitable for the job from those you will wish to interview further.

If you determine that an applicant is a possible fit, let him or her know what must be brought to the interview (work samples, etc.). You can also advise the applicant where, when, and with whom the interview will take place.

As you schedule prescreened applicants for interviewing, plan at least 45-minute interviews with a minimum of 15 minutes between appointments. Interviews are exhausting to conduct. (Wait until you conduct ten 45-minute interviews, and see how you feel at the end of the day!) A 15-minute interval between interviews will give you time to complete your notes and reorganize before the next candidate arrives. It will also give you extra time in case you go beyond your scheduled time with an applicant.

The 45 minutes of allotted time can be flexible—depending on the level of the job being filled, as well as on the experience of the applicant. If you are conducting an interview for a job that requires extensive experience, for example, then the chances are you will need significantly more interviewing time to allow the candidate to present the needed information.

Interviewing

1. Opening.

Recently I wrote a book for employees titled, *Is Coffee Break the Best Part of Your Day?* I sent the manuscript to some possible publishers, and received three contracts. Two of the three were from large, old-line publishers. And they were not very friendly—even a little bit arrogant—like they were doing me a favor by offering to publish my book. The third publisher was quite a bit smaller. But the representative, Bob Carkhuff, was personable, flexible, and in our discussion said, "I want this book. I want to be your publisher!" Guess who I chose? Right! Not one of the big publishing houses, but the smaller one who genuinely wanted my book (HRD Press—who now has all of my business).

It's the same way with job candidates. All too often we see leaders acting like the old-line publishers I encountered: stern, distant, interrogative, superior—not very friendly! But remember, your good candidates are likely to receive a number of job offers. So if you want them to accept your offer, treat them the way you would want to be treated—with interest, respect, and friendliness. There is also a direct correlation between our candidates' willingness to openly share information and the consideration we show them. So treat all candidates the way you would want to be treated. (Who knows, it might be you—or your children—out there job hunting some day.)

Also, avoid saying, "I'm Mr...." "Ms...." or "Dr...." It will sound very formal—and unfriendly! Use your first name. If a candidate uses a title in speaking with me, I gently say, "Dick, it's *Dick* Leatherman." If the candidate continues to use the title, then that is his or her choice.

Establish trust. The greater the level of trust between you and the job candidate, the greater the quality and quantity of information you are likely to receive. And you need information in order to make a good decision. First, a trusting environment is established by following the suggestions made earlier concerning preparing for the interview: scheduling interviews at a private location where you can control interruptions, not allowing yourself to be interrupted, having your phone calls held, and arranging the seating so that the candidate is comfortable.

But trust is also established by what you say. If you will begin the interview openly by stating why it is important for both of you to be honest in the interview, it is much less likely that the candidate will say only what he or she thinks you want to hear. For example, tell your candidates at the outset that it is important for you to let them know exactly what the job is—its good points *and* its bad points; and what it *isn't*. Indicate that it's important that you level with them because if they are offered the job and accept it, they will expect it to be as you described it in the interview. If it is not, then both you and the new employee will have a serious problem.

On the other hand, if the employee provides you with "fantasy information" based on what he or she thinks you want to hear, you may have the makings of a disaster—such as a new employee who is totally unsatisfactory in performing the work. And unsatisfactory employees make for unhappy employees—and unhappy bosses.

Here is an example of what an interviewer might say to a candidate:

> "Jack, before we start the actual interview, I need to say something very important. I think that you and I should try to be as honest as possible with each other. Not that I think you would be deliberately dishonest. But there is a natural tendency for applicants to try to appear as qualified as possible in the interview—as well as for me to make this organization sound great, and the job even better. Sure, I'm proud to work here. And I know you are proud of your accomplishments. But we're both going to get in trouble if we don't level with each other. You, by telling me what you're really all about; and me, by telling you what the job actually is—warts and all! If we don't do this, you may end up with a job you can't stand—or aren't truly qualified for. And then I will end up dealing with all the problems that will cause."

If you and the candidate can both be straight with one another, then you both will win. If not, you both lose!

Ask for permission to take notes. If you do not take notes during your interviews, it will be impossible to remember what the candidates have said—even by the end of the day. Your temptation will be to use a tape recorder; or, conversely, not to take notes at all. The former will inhibit the candidate. And the latter, as indicated, will make it very difficult to remember what was said. Making handwritten notes is the best procedure. So tell the interviewee that you will be interviewing a number of people, and that, unless you take notes, it will be difficult for you to remember the important things that were said. Then ask the candidate if it will be all right for you to take notes.

But a caution here. If you try to write down everything that is said you will inhibit the conversation and slow down the free flow of information. Therefore, make brief notes and flesh them out immediately after the interview. You will then be able to maintain better eye contact and rapport with the candidate, and enhance communication. This will allow you to be aware of important visual cues that might otherwise go unnoticed.

If the candidate says something that might be viewed as negative, don't immediately write it down. The candidate may be aware that what was said was not positive, and if you quickly note it, he or she may begin to feel inhibited. So wait a moment or two before making such a note.

Describe the interview format. In general, there are two ways to proceed with your questioning. 1) The traditional method is to ask candidates prepared questions about their experience, knowledge, skills, and interests; and to describe the job. 2) The other approach is to show the candidates your list of job tasks and related knowledge/skills/interest requirements, and then ask them to describe how their experience matches each task area. Both formats have advantages—and disadvantages.

Ask—then tell. The traditional approach to interviewing holds that you should obtain information from the candidate before describing the job. This "ask—then tell" format, of course, allows you to learn about the candidate's background before he or she is fully aware of the requirements of the job. The theory is that keeping candidates "in the dark" about the specifics of the job will allow you to obtain more honest information from them—i.e., will keep them from slanting what they say toward the just-learned job requirements. And it is obviously true that human nature will lead candidates who want a job to present themselves in the best possible light in relationship to that job. (Candidates often do so even when they really don't want the job, because it feels good to be made an offer.) Using the "ask—then tell" approach, you might say:

> "Sue, here's how we'll spend our time today. First, I'd like to
> ask you some questions about your experience and interests.

Next, I'll tell you about the job—and you'll have a chance to ask questions. Finally, I'll let you know our decision within approximately a week.

"So, the first thing I'd like to ask you is...."

The disadvantage of this approach is the amount of work it requires you to do (although some see the extra effort as producing an advantage). You must design a considerable number of relevant questions ahead of time, worry about their legality, and then ask them in such a way as to elicit the information you will need later in making your selection decision. It's not an easy job.

Show—then ask. A different—and many feel, better—interview format is to begin by showing candidates your list of job tasks and required knowledge, skills, and interests (but not your prepared questions with each of these). Then ask them to describe how their experiences and abilities relate to each task item—and sit back and listen. You will need to ask a few clarifying questions, but for the most part the candidate will do the talking.

This approach has several advantages. First, it is a lot easier since you don't have to spend so much time and effort designing and asking prepared questions. Second, candidates are usually more comfortable because they will not perceive themselves being "interrogated," but are simply talking about themselves. And since they are more comfortable, you will probably get more information. Third, the information you obtain will likely be more useful. If candidates know what you want them to be able to do they are better able to tell you their relevant experiences, which provides the information you need to make your selection decision.

To use this approach, you might say:

"Dan, first I'll give you some specific information about this job. Next you will have time to tell me about yourself and how your experience fits the needs of the job. Then, I'll answer any other questions you may have. Last, I'll let you know what happens about a week after the interview.

"So, let's look at the job. Here's a list of the major tasks in this position, as well as the knowledge, skills, and interests we feel are required for it. What I'd like you to do is to take, one at a time, each task and its related knowledge, skill and interest requirements, and describe how your experience fits that part of the job. I have a copy of this list that I'll use as a reference as you talk. And I'll ask any questions I have as we go along. So why don't you take the first task, and go from there."

The main disadvantage of this approach has already been indicated: telling the candidate about the job first can result in biased information.

2. Determine the candidate's suitability for the job.

At this point (Step 2) we will follow the more traditional interview method of asking prepared, task-related questions, and then describing the job (Step 3). But keep in mind that the general format that you use—whether "ask—then tell," or "show—then ask"—is up to you.

Ask questions. Having opened the interview and described the procedure you will follow you now ask your prepared questions to determine the candidate's knowledge, skills, and interest. We have discussed in detail how to design effective questions based on your task-listing and detailing. But we also need to say a word about listening.

Listen. Practice good listening skills during the interview! Don't interrupt candidates while they are speaking. (There are exceptions, of course, even to this rule—e.g., dealing with a nonstop talker.) Normally, the more we listen the more we learn. Maintain good eye contact. And remember that you can process the information you hear more quickly than the candidate can speak. So be careful that your attention doesn't wander as the candidate talks. Instead, use the "extra time" to consider and note questions you should ask when you have an opportunity.

Sensitive topics. At certain points in the interview you may need to explore sensitive topics. Such questions will yield more useful information if they are carefully prefaced—for example, "In confidence, could you tell me more about...?" Or, "If you don't mind my asking, what can you tell me about...?" And if what you are told is confidential, treat it as such.

Don't ask questions the candidate can't answer. When trying to determine factual information, don't embarrass candidates by asking questions they may not be able to answer but feel they should. For instance, if you ask, "Exactly how many days were you absent from your job last year?" the candidate will feel that you expect him or her to have that information at his or her fingertips, as well as feel somewhat threatened by the question. It is much better to begin such factual questions with words like "Approximately," "Usually," "Normally," or "Generally," e.g., "Approximately how many days were you absent from your job last year?"

Respond. A successful interview is one in which the candidate does most of the talking and the interviewer most of the listening. But good listening is not just sitting there in frozen silence! There are many things that you can do—and say—to facilitate a natural flow of a communication.

Posture. When actively listening to someone, your posture is called "attending." You attend a person when your body communicates that you are interested in being with them and hearing what they have to say. To attend candidates in the interview, simply lean forward as they talk, and encourage them by nodding your head, etc.

Clarifying and Summarizing. Use the listening tools of clarifying and summarizing. Clarification (sometimes termed "paraphrasing") is nothing more than repeating, in your own words, what you understood the candidate to have said.

Summarizing what has just been said is also a good way to ensure that what you heard was what was really stated. Summarizing will also improve your retention. After your summary, quickly return to listening—and the candidate will often provide more information on what he or she was saying. Both of these tools—clarifying and summarizing—cause you to listen better, and allow you to check your understanding.

Repetition. A similar strategy to encourage a candidate to talk is termed "repetition." Simply repeat the last words of what the candidate has said, ending with the tone of a question in your voice. For example, suppose you are interviewing candidates for an office clerk's position. You have just asked about the candidate's experience in taking incoming telephone calls. The candidate responds by saying, "Well, several years ago when I was with the Intrusive Care organization I spent a lot of time on the phone." Then just repeat the candidate's key works in the form of a question: "So when you were with Intrusive Care, you spent a lot of time on the phone?" The candidate will usually respond by giving you additional information. In this case the candidate might add, "Yes, I was a telephone solicitor responsible for selling perpetual burial plots. It was a tough business. I really had to push for a sale!"

Verbal prompts. As you listen, verbal prompts such as,"I see," "That's interesting," "Good," "Uh, huh," or "I didn't know that" can also be used to encourage candidates to continue to talk. Often these comments elicit more information even than asking another question.

We should also note that silence is a powerful communication tool. It's all right for you not to talk! Simply wait a moment to see if the candidate wants to say more about his or her thoughts. Just don't let the silence become awkward for the candidate.

Probing questions. When you ask a prepared question, you may need to follow it up with another question in order to obtain more information. These are called "probing questions"—such as:

"Can you tell me more about that?"
"What else?"
"Why did that happen?"

"What happened next?"
"Then what?"

But when you ask probing questions, avoid using too many in a series. Like a detective, you may begin to sound "interrogative"!

"Where were you on the night of the murder?"
"What time did you leave the party?"
"What happened next?"
"Then what?"

Don't make your candidates feel like they are suspects in a murder investigation. Remember, helping the candidate feel at ease is the best way to secure information. So all of your questions should be designed to produce confidence and relaxation by showing your positive interest.

"What if" questions. Sometimes an excellent way to obtain information is to ask a hypothetical "What if" question. For instance, you might ask, "Patricia, if you were given the responsibility for running this section, what would you do?" Or: "Suppose that you got this job, Ann. What strengths would you bring to it?" Such questions offer much insight—both about the candidate's approach to situations as well as his or her ability to "think on one's feet." But keep in mind that "What if" questions are asking candidates to generalize from their own experience to a specific situation, and this can make some people nervous. So be supportive in asking "What if" questions.

Provide positive feedback. When candidates say something positive about themselves, it is important to respond in a positive manner by saying, for example, "That was quite an accomplishment." "You must have been very proud of that." or even just "Very good!" and "That's great!" So listen carefully for things the candidate is especially proud of, whether it is the way that a job was done, recognition that was received, or accomplishments in school. Providing positive feedback helps increase your rapport with the candidate, and usually helps obtain more information.

Ask for a task demonstration. As mentioned earlier, if you want to know if a candidate can perform a task properly, the best way to find out is to ask him or her to do it.

To use a humorous "parable": Suppose that I had a lifelong ambition to become a medical doctor—but my dream had not been realized. Then one day while reading a *Popular Mechanics* magazine I saw a classified ad that said, "Make big money!!! Learn to be a physician at home on your own time through our approved correspondence training program!"

So I signed up, sent in my check, and began receiving my reading assignments. As it turned out I was pretty good at learning the material, and made high grades on all my open-book exams. I found the section on "Removing the Appendix" especially fascinating, and even made an A+ on that particular lesson.

Now the question is: how would you feel about hiring me to take out your appendix? But too often we only ask candidates if they can "take out an appendix," rather than asking them to demonstrate their ability as we observe. Arranging simple hands-on task performances is not difficult to do, and is well worth the effort in what you will learn about the candidate.

Ask for samples of past work. Asking candidates to bring with them particular samples of their past work is also a concrete way to examine their ability to perform a task. (Be aware, of course, of the possibility of a candidate submitting someone else's work!) We have already given examples where work samples are appropriate and helpful.

Tactfully conclude the interview if the candidate is not suitable for the position. Even after careful prescreening of candidates you may discover in the face-to-face interview that a candidate's qualifications are inadequate. When this occurs (and it will), you should not waste your time—or the candidate's—with further interviewing. You can diplomatically end the interview by providing a brief, general description of the job, answering any questions, and then standing as you indicate that all candidates will be notified promptly by mail. Then walk toward the door and shake hands goodbye. If you do get questions from the candidate, answer them briefly—and continue to end the interview.

For example, you might say:

> "Well, Betty, in closing I really appreciate your time in meeting with me. As we stated in our ad, the job is for an office clerk. We are looking at a number of candidates and will notify each of you by mail of our decision. You should hear from us in about a week. Do you have any other questions?" (Note this is a "closed," not "open," question.)

Succinctly answer any question(s) that the candidate may have, and then stand and say:

> "Thanks again for coming in." (Walk toward the door and shake hands.) "Goodbye."

The objective in concluding the interview early is to save everyone time, and in such a way as not to insult the candidate or hurt his or her feelings. So avoid giving the candidate the feeling that he or she is being given the "bum's rush." Attempt to leave all candidates feeling that you are genuinely interested in them (which you should be), and that you have courteously answered all of their questions.

3. Describe the job—honestly.

In conducting interviews remember that your overriding objective is to obtain information—and then to tell the candidates enough about the job so that if they receive a job offer they will be able to make an informed decision about accepting the job. If you try to "sell," "persuade," or "convince" the candidate that this is the best job in the country in the best organization in the world, you may be successful in getting a short-term employee—but you might have trouble converting this person into a long-term worker!

In my experience, most leaders spend too much time in the "telling" mode. It's almost as if we say to job candidates: "OK, I've asked you all these questions; and I've listened to everything you've said. Now it's *my* turn to talk!" And we talk... and talk. But when we take the time to properly prepare, making and copying an *Interview Planning Work Sheet* (minus our prepared questions), then it is a simple matter to show and discuss with the candidate the list of job tasks and their detailing in related knowledge/skills/interests. At this time you also need to review the good—and not so good—points of the job. As we have pointed out, it's important that the candidate have a realistic view of the position so that he or she can later make an informed decision if the job is offered.

This doesn't mean, of course, that you should be negative about the job—far from it! You should begin by clearly presenting the positive features of the job. Then discuss any drawbacks. Here's a capsulated example of what I say when interviewing potential sales managers for our organization:

> "This job is exciting and challenging. The people are fun, and easy to work with. Our customers are truly wonderful. Your new boss (me) is a leader who delegates both responsibility and authority.

> "Downside? The starting salary plus commission is low—though the job does have a high future earning potential. (Then smiling.) But for a job like this, maybe you should pay us!"

4. Ask for additional questions.

Now you need to give the candidate a full, final opportunity to ask questions. In soliciting questions, avoid the wording, "Do you have any questions?" Not only is this a "closed" question (inviting only a "Yes" or "No"), but it actually makes it more difficult for the candidate to respond. Instead, say: "What questions do you have?" This assumes that the candidate does have questions and encourages him or her to ask them.

5. Close the interview.

End your interview by: 1) stating that your time is up, 2) summarizing the highlights of the interview, and 3) telling the candidate what comes next.

You might say something like this:

> "Sam, it looks like our time is just about up. I appreciate your openness in this interview. I feel that I've learned a lot about you and your work experience. In particular you like working with people, you enjoy doing paperwork, and you are efficient in managing your time. You don't care much for working evening shifts. And you feel that planning is not presently one of your strengths.

> "Now, we are interviewing a number of candidates for this position. We should be finished in about two weeks; and at that time we will notify all candidates by mail.

> "Thanks for coming in."

Do not tell any candidates at this time that they are not qualified for the job. Do it later by mail. This will eliminate unwanted and unnecessary defensiveness or "bargaining" by candidates at the close of the interview. Also remember that the person you finally choose may not accept the position, and you will need to re-evaluate the other candidates.

Selection

1. Schedule a follow-up selection meeting with all of the people involved.

It is generally true that involving more people in the actual selection process will produce a better decision. However, you must strike a balance here. If only one person is involved in the decision, it will have a high probability of being biased. But if there are too many people in the selection meeting it can become difficult to get anything done. If you used multiple interviewers, then all of these should be part of the decision process. And you may wish to invite two or three of your peers to discuss the candidates and offer their opinions. As mentioned earlier, there is also great value inviting a candidate's future co-workers to participate in the decision.

2. Use a decision-making process.

A structured decision-making procedure usually leads to a better choice. I often use the Kepner-Tregoe (KT) decision-making grid to select the best candidate for a job. It is an excellent method for sorting out data and arranging it so that it makes sense. It is also a good tool for making a final selection decision.

As explained in Chapter 8, the KT process consists of four steps: 1) write a decision statement; 2) develop and weight your objectives; 3) identify alternatives and write data; and, 4) evaluate the risks. Let's see how we would use the KT procedure to select the best candidate for our office clerk's position.

Step 1: Write a decision statement.

In most cases Step 1—creating a decision statement—is straightforward. For example, "Select best person for the office clerk's position."

Step 2: Develop and weight your objectives.

The next step is to list all the factors (KT terms them "Objectives") you should consider when you evaluate the candidate. These factors can be obtained from the *Interview Planning Work Sheet* that you completed in your initial preparation for interviewing. For example, a list of key factors for the office clerk's job might look like the following on a *Selection Work Sheet.* (An example of this *Work Sheet,* for you to copy and use, is found at the end of this chapter.)

Factors

Knows filing
Basic reading
    skills
Types 45 wpm
Operates postage
    meter
Adds and
    subtracts
Lifts 25 lbs.
Pleasant telephone
    personality
Good telephone
    etiquette
Trouble-shoots
    office equipment
Not color blind
Meets salary
    requirements
Can start work now
Good work history

Having listed the important factors in our decision, we now give them weights. Begin by noting those that are "Must" factors (labeled "M")—i.e., any requirement that a successful candidate must fulfill. For example:

Factors	*Weight*
Knows filing	
Basic reading skills	M
Types 45 wpm	M
Operates postage meter	
Adds and subtracts	M
Lifts 25 lbs.	M
Pleasant telephone personality	
Good telephone etiquette	
Trouble-shoots office equipment	
Not color blind	M
Meets salary requirements	
Can start work now	
Good work history	

Next, since some of the remaining factors are more important than others, we weight each of them using a scale of 1 (least important) to 10 (most important). If other people are involved in the selection process, ask them to help you weight these factors by assigning priority numbers.

I normally begin by choosing the most important factor on the list, and assign it 10 points. Next, I pick the least important factor, and give it 1 point. Then I assign relative weights to the other factors. As our example continues below, note that the assigned weights are ones *I* have determined. If you were doing this for an office clerk's position in your organization, of course, these weights—and the factors themselves—might be quite different.

Factors	Weight
Knows filing	10
Basic reading skills	M
Types 45 wpm	M
Operates postage meter	1
Adds and subtracts	M
Lifts 25 lbs.	M
Pleasant telephone personality	9
Good telephone etiquette	7
Trouble-shoots office equipment	2
Not color blind	M
Meets salary requirements	5
Can start work now	8
Good work history	8

Step 3: Identify alternatives and write data.

Now suppose that of the people who were interviewed for the office clerk's position, three stood out—Sam, George and Edith. (K.T. terms these finalists "Alternatives".) We will then write data about each finalist for each factor. Try to write in *specific* data—not just "Yes," "No," "Good," "Poor," etc. When you later compare your candidates with each other, the more information you have, the clearer the comparison will be.

Note in our KT grid that we have used "Yes" when marking the "Must" factors. Since these candidates are finalists, then by necessity they have all passed the "Must" requirements. (Remember that the "Must" factors were used as "knockout criteria" when the candidates were prescreened.) The question then arises as to why we would list "Must" factors at all in our decision-making grid of finalists. There are two reasons. First, this lets others know all the factors that were considered. (We already mentioned the need to keep good interview and selection records for up to two years.)

Second, sometimes you may wish to take a "Must" objective and rewrite it as a new factor. For example, suppose a candidate's ability to type *more* than the required minimum 45 wpm is a factor we would like to consider in our selection decision. We would then rewrite "Types minimum of 45 wpm" to make the new factor: "Maximum typing speed." This added factor will be assigned a weight, and then considered in the selection decision. In our example on the next page we felt that typing speeds above 45 wpm were not important in the office clerk's position, so we have not rewritten this factor. It is often wise, however, to examine each "Must" factor to see if rewriting it in a way that will distinguish your final candidates from one another would be important in your decision.

Factors	Weight	Candidates		
		Sam	George	Edith
Knows filing	10	6 yrs exp.	Never filed	Some filing exp.
Basic reading skills	M	Yes	Yes	Yes
Types 45 wpm	M	Yes	Yes	Yes
Operates postage meter	1	Never used one	Used daily in old job	Has seen it used
Adds and subtracts	M	Yes	Yes	Yes
Lifts 25 lbs.	M	Yes	Yes	Yes
Pleasant telephone personality	9	Acceptable in role play	Aggressive in role play	Very good personality on phone
Good telephone etiquette	7	Didn't know the "rules"	No mistakes	Super! One of the best we've seen
Trouble-shoots office equipment	2	Experienced trouble-shooter	Lacks even the basics of trouble-shooting	Did well after seeing the service manual
Not color blind	M	Yes	Yes	Yes
Meets salary requirements	5	Last job earned less	Last job earned more	Earned quite a bit less
Can start work now	8	Yes	Yes	4-week notice
Good work history	8	Excellent	Some gaps between jobs	Excellent

After writing down specific information for each alternatives' factor, the next step is to assign weights. In this case, we will assign a "10" automatically to the best alternative for each factor, and some number less than 10 to the other two alternatives. For example, for the factor "Knows filing," we would assign Sam a weight of 10 because Sam has had more experience than George or Edith. Then, we would give Edith a "5" because she has had some filing experience, and George would receive a "1" because he has never filed.

After all the weights have been assigned, we will then multiply each alternative weight by its original factor weight as shown in the next example.

Factors	Weight	Candidates		
		Sam	George	Edith
Knows filing	10	x 10 = 100 6 yrs exp.	x 1 = 10 Never filed	x 5 = 50 Some filing exp.
Basic reading skills	M	Yes	Yes	Yes
Types 45 wpm	M	Yes	Yes	Yes
Operates postage meter	1	x 1 = 1 Never used one	x 10 = 10 Used daily in old job	x 2 = 2 Has seen it used
Adds and subtracts	M	Yes	Yes	Yes
Lifts 25 lbs.	M	Yes	Yes	Yes
Pleasant telephone personality	9	x 6 = 54 Acceptable in role play	x 1 = 9 Aggressive in role play	x 10 = 90 Very good personality on phone
Good telephone etiquette	7	x 2 = 14 Didn't know the "rules"	x 7 = 49 No mistakes	x 10 = 70 Super! One of the best we've seen
Trouble-shoots office equipment	2	x 10 = 20 Experienced trouble-shooter	x 1 = 2 Lacks even the basics of trouble-shooting	x 8 = 16 Did well after seeing the service manual
Not color blind	M	Yes	Yes	Yes
Meets salary requirements	5	x 8 = 40 Last job earned less	x 0 = 0 Last job earned more	x 10 = 50 Earned quite a bit less
Can start work now	8	x 10 = 80 Yes	x 10 = 80 Yes	x 7 = 56 4-week notice
Good work history	8	x 10 = 80 Excellent	x 3 = 24 Some gaps between jobs	x 10 = 80 Excellent
TOTAL SCORES		389	184	414

Having multiplied each of our candidate's factor (job task) ratings by that factor's weight, and totaled the scores, we can see that Edith and Sam appear to be fairly equal candidates—and that George comes far behind. Our KT decision-making grid has helped us organize and evaluate a great amount of data on three very different individuals, and led us to quite a clear (and measured) comparative ranking of them—a much-desired finding that is difficult to achieve without a systematic decision-making procedure.

But now we need to decide between Edith and Sam. So let's look at the last step in our selection process.

Step 4: Evaluate risk.

Finally we need to ask the question: "If we hire candidate 'X,' what could go wrong?" When we have identified the possible risks for each candidate, we will evaluate each risk in terms of the *probability* of it happening, and the *seriousness* if it does—again using a scale of 1 to 10. A "1" probability rating means the event is not likely to happen, while a "1" seriousness rating means that if it does happen, it won't be very serious. A "10" probability rating indicates that the event appears certain to happen, and a "10" seriousness rating means that if it does happen it will be a disaster! When we have assigned our probability and seriousness ratings, we will multiply them to get a risk rating for each candidate. If there is more than one risk with a candidate, we will add the risk ratings for a composite score.

Since two of our office clerk candidates (Edith and Sam) are closely ranked at this point—and are far ahead of the third (George)—we will do our risk evaluation only of these two—seen on the next page. (Note that "P" = the probability or the event occurring, and that "S" = the seriousness if it does occur.)

Candidate: Sam

Risk	P		S	
Poor attendance record due to several health problems. He may develop the same attendance problems here.	3	x	7	= 21
Has been out of work for several months. He may be seeking this position only because he needs a job, rather than really wanting this one. We couldn't get a handle on this in the interview.	2	x	5	= 10
Total composite risk				31

Notice that we are analyzing the risks with each candidate separately—because different candidates will have different risks. If you find a risk that is common to more than one candidate, the chances are that you have overlooked a factor (job requirement) in your initial task-listing. For example, if past attendance is important to you, then you could have written another factor, adding "Good attendance record," given it a factor weight (say, 7), and evaluated all three of the office clerk candidates in terms of it.

Now let's look at the risks in hiring Edith. What could go wrong if we hire her for this position?

Candidate: Edith

Risk	P		S	
She made a number of errors in the typing test. She said it was because she had not had an opportunity to keep up her typing skills in her old job. There is some concern that she will not be able to improve these skills on the job.	1	x	10	= 10
Total composite risk				10

Note that you should not subtract a candidate's risk score from the factor score. Only compare your candidates' risk scores to help you make a balanced decision—e.g., Sam's risk score of 31 is well above Edith's score of 10.

So the final result of our decision-making process to select the best candidate for the office clerk's position is that Edith appears to be the strongest candidate—leading the second-ranked candidate, Sam, in both job task qualifications (414 to 389) and lack of risk (10 to 31).

3. Promptly notify all candidates of your decision.

I would like to emphasize the importance of *promptly* notifying all candidates of your hiring decision. It is completely improper—and too often done—to keep job candidates who are not selected hanging on for days—and even weeks. Candidates may well have other job offers pending that they don't want to accept until they hear from you. And regardless, they normally are quite anxious to hear whether they were selected or not. Not knowing the result of a job application can be even more stressful than learning that we have not been selected. Certainly you would feel very frustrated if you really wanted a job and the employer put off contacting you about the outcome of your application.

So it is quite unfair not to notify job candidates promptly—within a week at the most. When you don't let them know your decision, they are placed in the dilemma of whether or not to call you—a difficult decision for many candidates. If they call, they may feel they will be seen as "pushy." And if they don't call, they have no idea as to when—if ever—they will find out how well they did.

If you plan to contact unsuccessful interview candidates by phone, you may also want to write what you will say prior to calling them. If letters are to be mailed, avoid sending one that looks like a "form" letter—such as:

Dear Sir/Madam:

We regret to inform you that you were not selected for the
_____ job. Thank you for your interest in our
organization.

Sincerely yours,

Mr./Ms./Dr. _____

Also, try not to give unsuccessful candidates the impression that
there was something "wrong" with them because they were not
selected. Keep your focus on the positives—as in the following example:

Dear Sue,

Thanks for all your efforts in applying for the computer
programming position here at ITC. I know that the day you
spent in interviewing would have been strenuous for anyone.

Sue, you were asked to come in for an interview because of
your excellent qualifications. And although you were not
chosen for this position, you had many strengths. The person
we selected, however, was slightly more qualified for this particular job.

I am keeping your application on file in case we I have additional needs in the future. Thanks for your interest in our organization.

Sincerely yours,

Dick Leatherman

Whether or not you give specific information to candidates as to
why they weren't selected is up to your management or personnel
department. My preference is to provide feedback if requested. But I
also recognize that because of possible litigation concerning selection

it is often more prudent not to offer such feedback—unless it is asked for.

Finally, in a letter of notification to a candidate, the specific job applied for should be referenced, and you (or the interviewer, if it was not you) should sign it.

4. File all information on candidates who were qualified but not selected, for later use.

Remember that the candidate whom you hire may not work out; or may quit shortly after being hired. Or you may soon need to hire another person for a similar job. For these reasons and others, it is wise to keep on file information you have obtained in interviews with unsuccessful candidates. This information was very expensive to get—and keeping it could save you a great deal of time and money if it reduces your need to interview additional candidates in the near future.

In addition, if you are ever asked to justify your selection, you will have the data to establish that your decision was fair, objective, and impartial (as it should be). So keep on file the *Interview Planning Work Sheet* you used to determine the job requirements and questions to be asked. And save any work sheet you used to make your final selection (e.g., KT grid, etc.). These records—on both successful and unsuccessful candidates, will be very important and useful to your organization in case of future litigation.

Here you should note that various acts and laws relating to discriminatory practices require you to keep your interviewing and selection records and notes for specified periods of time. These time periods vary, depending on the legislation and the type of job applicant. If you keep them at least two years, you will normally be within the law. But it is best to check with an attorney to make sure you are complying with existing laws.

Summary

Much information has been presented in this chapter. But as we have seen, the processes of preparing for job interviews, prescreening the applicants, conducting interviews, selecting the best candidate, and following up require thought, time, and effort. And there are really no shortcuts. The amount of time devoted to preparing for your interviews directly affects the quality of those interviews—which in turn determines the quality of the information you have available to use in the selection process. The selection process you decide to use will determine the quality of your final candidate choice. And surrounding this entire process are legal requirements concerning discrimination.

But the benefits to your organization of making good "million dollar decisions" make all of your efforts worth the energy you put into them.

In closing, I would like to offer two basic principles that will affect the quality of what you do throughout the entire interviewing and selection process:

Treat others as you would want to be treated. There are few jobs harder than looking for a job—especially if you don't have one. So have compassion! Treat job applicants with courtesy, respect, and consideration. I firmly believe that what goes out comes back. The way you treat others is the way you in turn will be treated in life.

Spend sufficient time to prepare properly for interviews. The time you spend in preparation will: 1) save time through good prescreening of applicants; 2) help you be more comfortable in interviewing candidates, because you will know what to ask; and, 3) greatly increase your chances of hiring the best employee for the job.

INTERVIEW PLANNING WORK SHEET

POSITION: _____

PAGE ____ OF ____ PAGES

TASKS	JOB KNOWLEDGE, SKILLS, AND INTERESTS	R,T	P,I P/I	QUESTIONS, DEMON-STRATIONS, SAMPLES

"R" = *Required*, "T" = can *Train*, "P" = in *Prescreening*, "I" = in *Interview*, "P/I" = in both

INSTRUCTIONS FOR THE SELECTION WORK SHEET

1. Write a decision statement (e.g., "Select the best candidate for _____ job").

2. List all important factors (Job task requirements).

   — Identify "Must" factors (label "M").

   — Numerically weight the remaining factors from 1 to 10 ("10" = most important).

3. List candidates (finalists).

   — Select only three or four best candidates for analysis.

   — Write candidate data for "Must" factors.

   — Eliminate any candidate who doesn't meet every "Must" requirement.

   — Write candidate data for remaining factors—using specific facts, figures, opinions, and impressions (not simply "Yes," "No," "Poor," "Good," "Better," "Best," etc.).

   — Numerically rate each candidate on each factor. (Do not rate "Must" factors.) Assign a "10" to the best candidate concerning each factor, and an appropriate lower score to the other candidates.

   — Multiply each factor weight by each candidate rating, and record.

   — Add column scores for each candidate, and compare totals.

4. Taking the top candidates, evaluate the risks.

   — Assign "probability" and "seriousness" values (10 to 1 scale, "10" = highest probability, greatest seriousness).

   — Multiply probability and seriousness ratings, add resulting risk totals for each candidate, and compare.

   — Make selection based on final comparison of candidates' factor (job task) scores and risk scores.

SELECTION WORK SHEET

Decision Statement _____

Factors (Job task require- ments)	W e i g h t	Candidate 1 ‾‾‾‾‾‾ ‾‾‾‾‾‾ ‾‾‾‾‾‾ Data & Rating (10–1)	Candidate 2 ‾‾‾‾‾‾ ‾‾‾‾‾‾ ‾‾‾‾‾‾ Data & Rating (10–1)	Candidate 3 ‾‾‾‾‾‾ ‾‾‾‾‾‾ ‾‾‾‾‾‾ Data & Rating (10–1)

Total scores:

Candidate 1			Candidate 2		
Risk:	P	S	Risk:	P	S
_____	__x__	= __	_____	__x__	= __
_____	__x__	= __	_____	__x__	= __
_____	__x__	= __	_____	__x__	= __
_____	__x__	= __	_____	__x__	= __
_____	__x__	= __	_____	__x__	= __
_____	__x__	= __	_____	__x__	= __
_____	__x__	= __	_____	__x__	= __
	Total risk	= __		Total risk	= __

Note: "P" = Probability; "S" = Seriousness (10–1 scale)

14

Conducting Effective Performance Appraisals

Introduction

Background. Some years ago, I had a boss who was truly incompetent in conducting performance appraisals. To compound the problem, he had no idea that he didn't know how to handle employee appraisal meetings. The result of his brief once-a-year session was that I felt bad about him and about my organization. And most important, I felt bad about me!

But I knew that his short annual presentation of my strengths and weaknesses was a poor way to conduct a performance appraisal. Since then, I have read everything I could about performance appraisals. I have also attended many workshops on this subject, conducted appraisal sessions with numerous employees, talked to thousands of managers, supervisors, and employees, and taught hundreds of workshops on the topic.

And only now, some thirty-five years after my first unfortunate experience, do I feel comfortable—most of the time—participating in a performance appraisal session. I have learned a lot, and much of it the hard way!

What's in this chapter. First, you'll review the important factors that affect the quality of performance appraisals. Next, you will look at the reasons for conducting an appraisal session. And last, you will find a step-by-step approach to use in managing the performance appraisal interviews you conduct with your employees. This planned approach will help you conduct productive, balanced, and fair performance appraisal sessions.

This method is not a "sit-back-and-listen-as-the-boss-tells-the-employee-his-strengths-and-weaknesses" approach. It is participative. But there is a cost to you. It requires you to spend time preparing for the appraisal meeting. You will also find that your appraisal interviews will run longer—to your advantage. Furthermore, there may be more open disagreements during your meeting. But an open discussion will allow you and your employee to reach a better understanding of his or her actual performance.

Factors Affecting the Quality of Performance Appraisals

There are four factors that affect the quality of a performance appraisal interview. They are the environment in which the performance appraisals are conducted, the performance appraisal system that is used, the leader who conducts the performance appraisal, and the employee.

Environmental Issues

There are several environmental issues that affect the quality of a performance appraisal. These issues include executive management support, personnel department support, delegation of the task of conducting appraisals to the appropriate people, the number of employees who must be interviewed, whether job standards exist, the employee's job, and legal issues.

Executive management support. Do your executive managers support the idea of performance appraisals by conducting quality interviews with their department heads? Or do they talk about the need for good appraisals without doing them themselves? In any case, the "buck stops with you," since you are the leader of your employees. Whatever executive managers do or don't do, you are responsible for leading your employees in the best way possible. And that means conducting quality performance appraisals regularly with your employees.

Personnel department. Has the personnel department designed the performance appraisal system and forms that help rather than hinder the process? For example, suppose your organization expects you to present completed appraisals to your employees with little or no input from them. Though two-way communication during performance appraisal meetings is essential for interviews that produce positive results, such a system is set up to encourage only one-way communications. An effective way to solve this problem is for you to conduct informal appraisal interviews with your employees shortly before the "official" appraisal sessions. This will not only produce interviews that are fairer to your employees, but also will give you better information to use later while filling out the appraisal form.

Delegation. Another environmental factor that affects performance appraisals is delegation. In other words, are the individuals who should be conducting performance appraisals allowed to conduct them? For example, a department head had two first-line leaders and twenty-one employees reporting to him. He conducted all the performance appraisal interviews with the employees to improve communications between the employees and management. He did, however, meet individually with his two leaders and discuss their employees' performances before conducting appraisal interviews with these employees. But here we have two problems—because of poor delegation. First, the department head is attempting to do performance appraisals on too many people. And second, he is bypassing the leaders who are in a much better position to know the details of their employees' performance. The results are likely to be poor appraisals and first-line leaders who appear to their employees to have little real authority.

The number of employees who must be interviewed. The number of employees who report to you also has a great effect on the quality of performance appraisals that you conduct. If you have only six employees, you can spend more appraisal time and conduct more effective interviews, than with a group of twenty-six employees. Quality performance appraisals take time—time to prepare for them, and time to conduct them. The more employees you have reporting to you, the harder it is to find enough time to do in-depth preparation and interviews.

Job standards. Appraisals are easier to conduct if both the employee and the manager understand the job, its standards of performance, and the established goals or objectives. Sometimes we run into problems during our performance appraisal interviews because our expectations may be unclear to our employees. Most of us have heard employees legitimately say, "I didn't know that I had to do that!" We have also heard such questions as, "What is a good job?" or, "When am I not doing this job well enough?" and, "When am I devoting too much time and energy to this task?" These questions suggest that the employee doesn't know what to do during his or her appraisal period.

To avoid such problems, plan to meet individually with your employees six to twelve months ahead of time to discuss their specific job responsibilities. By using a work sheet similar to the one below you will be better prepared to discuss and obtain agreement on the employee's job tasks.

JOB ANALYSIS WORK SHEET

List the main tasks of your job.	How critical is each job task? "A"= Highest "B"= Medium "C"= Lowest	What standards are used to measure your job perfor- mance?	What problems exist that handi- caps your performance?	Authority Levels* 1 2 3

* A "#1 authority level" means that the employee has total authority to do the task. He or she doesn't have to ask permission to do the task, or even tell you that it was done—the employee simply does it be- cause it's a routine part of his or her job.

A "#2 authority level" allows the employee to do the task without first asking for permission; but he or she is expected to let you know that it was done.

A "#3 authority level" indicates that the employee needs to obtain approval from you before doing that task.

You and the employee should both complete the work sheet independently of each other, and then meet and discuss how you both see the job. You will likely be amazed at the number of times the two of you do not agree about which tasks are most important, the standards for tasks, and the authority the employee has for each task. And you will find that this meeting will help greatly to ensure that the employee's efforts are on track. As a result, your next performance appraisal meeting with this employee will be fairer and more productive.

The employee's job. The employee's job can have a great impact upon the quality of the performance appraisal. Obviously, if the employee's job is monotonous and not very motivating, the performance appraisal will be more difficult. Contrast this type of situation with an employee who has an exciting or challenging job. Interested and challenged employees normally are easier to talk with during a performance appraisal interview.

Legal issues. Changing laws may affect the ability of leaders to stay abreast of the latest requirements regarding such matters as privacy issues, Equal Employment Opportunity guidelines on promotions/transfers based on past performance appraisal data, etc. Astute leaders keep themselves informed so that what they do obeys both the intent and letter of the law.

The Performance Appraisal System

Another factor that greatly affects performance appraisals is the appraisal system. How often are appraisals scheduled? How is the appraisal form routed through the organization, and who has access to it? And what information is requested?

These and other questions address the design of the performance appraisal system. And although the organization's personnel department usually establishes the system, if it doesn't work for you there are still some important things you can do.

How often are appraisals scheduled? At a minimum, appraisals should be scheduled at least yearly for experienced employees, and every six months for newcomers. If your organization doesn't follow this schedule, you can still conduct informal appraisal sessions that do.

How is the appraisal form routed through the organization? If your boss must review and sign the form before you conduct a performance appraisal interview with your employee, then your organization's system is inappropriate. A boss who must "review the form" before you conduct an appraisal interview with your employee communicates lack of trust in your ability to complete the form properly with the employee. For effective interviews, you and the employee should complete the appraisal form together, and then send it through channels.

Who has access to the form? The question here is not just one of restricting confidential information only to those who have a legitimate need for it. It is also one of allowing the employee to have full and ready access to both the blank and the completed forms. The employee needs blank copies of the form to prepare properly for the interview. In addition, the employee should be given a copy of his or her completed appraisal form to use as a reference during the year.

What information is requested? Some appraisal forms list general duties, personality traits, and work habits, and rate you on each. Other forms are customized for your specific job, with ratings assigned for each of your major job duties. (This is by far the better type of form.) The more subjective the form, the more difficult it is for you to use it fairly and consistently. In addition, the more the form rates character and personality traits such as "attitude" instead of measurable behaviors, the more difficult it is to administer.

A good appraisal form can enhance the interview results. Yet, excellent appraisals can be conducted by skilled interviewers using poor appraisal forms. So if you have a form that measures personality traits, use it. But as a part of your preparation for the interview, consider the employee's strengths and areas of needed improvement in light of his or her job performance. Then in the interview talk about performance, not personality.

The key point is to use the system in the best way you can. Don't let the system use you!

The Leader Who Conducts the Performance Appraisal

You, the person who conducts the performance appraisal—have a profound affect on the quality of your appraisal interviews. For example, your attitude toward this part of your job, what you know about doing it, and how well you do it (your skills) all make a big difference in the effectiveness of your performance appraisal sessions.

Your attitude. Your attitude will influence how much time you spend in preparation, the priority you give to performance appraisals over crises that may occur (and usually do), the amount of time you set aside for quality interviews, and how important your employees feel the appraisal session is. If you see performance appraisal as a major part of your job, you are likely to devote significant time and thought to it.

Your knowledge. Unfortunately many leaders have learned how to conduct performance appraisal interviews from bosses who lacked knowledge of how they should be done. But there are very specific things that any leader can learn how to do to improve performance appraisal results. Later in this chapter you will see some common sense strategies that will help you to be considerably more effective.

Your skill. We can all nod intelligently as we discuss the key strategies for conducting an appraisal interview. But because we are creatures of habit, the chances are that we will not use the steps effectively—though we may want to. Thus we need to have the opportunities to develop our skill in using the new things we have learned. That is why it is essential for you to select several key ideas presented in this chapter, and use them in your next performance appraisal interviews.

The Employee

The employee is the other person involved in the performance appraisal interview. And the employee's attitude toward the interview, preparation for it, and his or her performance level all affect the outcome of the session.

The employee's attitude. The employee's attitude is vital to a successful appraisal session. If the employee is hostile or feels the appraisal session is an exercise in paperwork, then the results will be poor. If you know that an employee has a negative attitude toward the appraisal interview, it is up to you to find out why he or she feels that way, and then determine how you can help the employee see the positive benefits of a performance appraisal.

There are clear benefits for the employee. For example, interviews can be exciting opportunities for employees to spend private time with you to determine how well they are doing. This is a time to talk about what the employee has done well in the past and to discuss his or her future goals within the organization. Even poor performance can be discussed in a positive way —i.e., as areas that need improvement, not as "weaknesses."

The amount of time the employee spends preparing for the interview. We have discussed the need for the leader to properly prepare for the appraisal session. But if we want the employee to participate in a two-way discussion in the interview, then the employee must be given enough time to prepare adequately.

It is up to you as the leader to help the employee in his or her preparation. Make sure that the employee has a blank copy of the appraisal form so that he or she knows what will be asked. Encourage the employee to analyze his or her strengths, and areas needing improvement. And suggest that he or she come prepared to do most of the talking.

The employee's performance level. Statistically, if you have ten employees, one will be a superstar, eight will range from "very good" to "meets minimum acceptable standards," and one will be a problem—your cross to bear. If an employee is outstanding in all categories, an appraisal is fun to conduct! When this isn't the case, the interview is more difficult to handle.

Although the strategies presented in the next section work well with all employees, they are particularly helpful in dealing with the problem employee.

Of the four key factors affecting performance appraisal quality—the environment, system, interviewer, and employee—the ones that you can influence the most are you, the interviewer, and your employee. As a result, the balance of this chapter will examine the reasons for conducting performance appraisals, and then your attitude, knowledge, and skills in conducting appraisal interviews. You will not see different types of appraisal forms, nor discussions of various performance appraisal systems used by other organizations. The emphasis will be on you—and what you can do to become a more effective leader.

One last point before looking at the reasons for conducting appraisal interviews: your ability to conduct a successful performance appraisal is far more dependent on what has been going on all year than on what you do or don't do during the interview. In other words, if you haven't been performing your job as a leader in guiding, coaching, counseling, directing, and training throughout the year, then the most impressive interviewing skills in the world won't make your interviews successful. A performance appraisal session is not a substitute for ongoing leadership. It is the result of good leadership!

Reasons for Conducting a Performance Appraisal Interview

The reasons for conducting performance appraisal sessions affect the way we conduct appraisals. The main reason that some leaders conduct performance appraisals is because their organizations require them. I often wonder how many of us would really conduct performance appraisals on a regular basis if we weren't required to by our organizations.

We also utilize performance appraisals as an opportunity to obtain information to use in making future decisions on salaries, promotions, or demotions. And, some leaders use performance appraisal interviews to tell their employees what they have done right or wrong. This first group of reasons for doing appraisals are the traditional ones that initiated many performance appraisal systems. And they are important reasons. But there are other—sometimes even more important— reasons for conducting performance appraisal interviews.

For instance, you may want to develop subordinates through coaching and counseling by creating a mutual understanding of the employee's strengths and areas of desired improvement, and then developing action plans for implementation. Or you may want to do career counseling by determining where the employee wants to go, whether he or she can get there, and what plans you can help the employee develop to achieve these goals. In addition, you may want to conduct an appraisal interview to have an opportunity to provide recognition and motivation for an employee.

The first set of reasons above—the traditional ones—require that you, as the leader, play the role of a *judge*. And if you take on the role of a "judge," the employee will quickly assume a corresponding role. A new employee may become passive and do very little talking. And an older employee may react strongly, defending himself or herself at being judged. The focus of this type of interview is on the past: you are reflecting on what has already happened.

The second set of reasons requires that you talk with your employee as a *counselor*. When you do this, you will find that he or she will be more active and participative during the interview. This group of reasons looks at where the employee is presently and what can be done in the future.

The problem here is that it is extremely difficult to play both roles in the same interview. If you play the role of judge, and, in effect, tell the employee to "sit down, shut up, and listen while I tell you your strengths and weaknesses," then it will be very difficult for you suddenly to shift gears and say, "I'm here to help you in any way that I can."

It's not impossible to play both roles in the same interview; it's just very difficult. It is all in where you choose to put your emphasis. And for real change to occur in the employee's behavior following the interview, you must place your emphasis on coaching, counseling, guiding, leading, training and helping—not judging. It is not so much what the employee has already done, but what he or she will do in the future that is important.

Nine Key Steps in Performance Appraisal

Ninety-eight leaders in five different organizations were selected by their subordinates as very competent in conducting performance appraisals. In closed-door sessions, these leaders were extensively interviewed. It was quickly discovered that they had certain common values or guidelines, such as:

1. Talk about performance, not personality. It's what has or has not been done—not what he or she "is."

2. Offer insight into the employee's problems, not indictment. Offer understanding and help—not blame.

3. Focus on development, not discipline. Focus on the future—not the past.

4. Discuss with the employee, rather than "present." Talk with the employee—not "at" him or her.

These ninety-eight effective leaders were also asked what they did and didn't do, and specifically how they proceeded, in a performance appraisal interview. Following are the nine key steps that these leaders identified as critical for conducting an effective performance appraisal interview.

1. **Prepare for the interview**
2. **Introduce the meeting**
3. **Determine the topics the employee wants to discuss**
4. **Discuss concerns not mentioned by the employee**
5. **Develop written action plans for carrying out key solutions in a specific time period**
6. **Give specific feedback on any positive performance that has not already been discussed**
7. **Summarize the interview and discuss ratings**
8. **Set follow-up dates**
9. **Thank the employee**

Several years ago I was in Houston, Texas, leading a performance appraisal workshop. One participant sitting in the back hadn't said much, and from his attitude two things were evident. First, he didn't want to be there, and second, his boss had made him come anyway! I had just presented the nine key steps for conducting performance appraisals. This individual then said sarcastically, "Don't you think this is nothing more than a canned approach to a performance appraisal?"

But before I could say anything, a new leader in the group challenged the gentleman. What she said made a powerful impact on this individual, who from that point on became an active workshop participant. (In fact, he participated almost too much—although now positively.) She said: "A football team spends a great deal of time practicing specific plays before a big game. Does that mean it's a 'canned approach'? Or a *planned* approach?"

The following nine key steps, and sub-steps, will enable you to plan and conduct an effective performance appraisal interview. Use these steps as a guide, a road map, to help you achieve your objectives.

Although each step is important, there may be times when it is appropriate not to use a particular step, or use them in another order. For example, if, in Step 3, the employee has raised all the concerns about his or her performance that you had on your list, you will not have to use Step 4, "Discuss concerns not mentioned by the employee." Or, the model suggests that you talk about all the concerns (yours and the employees), and then develop written action plans for all the important areas that needed improvement. But on closer inspection, you can see that doesn't make sense. Far more effective would be for the employee (or you) to bring up one area of needed improvement. Then immediately develop an action plan for that first concern before moving on to another area of discussion.

Let's now look at each of the nine performance appraisal steps in more detail.

1. Prepare for the interview.

Approximately two to three weeks before the scheduled performance appraisal interview, meet with the employee and state briefly where and when the discussion will be held. At this time, give the employee a copy of the performance appraisal form and ask that it be completed before the appraisal meeting. Ask the employee to examine his or her ideas about the job and how well he or she is performing in each area. Then request that the employee consider any special problems or recommendations for discussion and develop some specific plans for further improving job performance.

Filling out the form in advance will help the employee better prepare for the performance appraisal meeting. Normally, you should not ask to see the employee's completed form before or during the actual session. It's the employee's "work sheet," and is used only as an aid for him or her to plan for the meeting.

In addition, you also should tentatively complete the performance appraisal form—in pencil. Filling out the form in advance gives you the opportunity to obtain additional data if required. List the employee's key strengths and areas of needed improvement. And for the areas where the employee needs improvement, first analyze potential causes of problems by asking:

- Is he or she aware of what was expected?
- Is he or she aware of his or her performance?
- Are there uncontrollable factors?

- Does he or she lack ability or knowledge?
- Is there lack of motivation? If so, why?

Then, develop possible solutions and action plans. The causes, solutions, and plans you identify are all tentative, because your information is not complete until you gain additional information in the interview from the employee. You also want the employee, during the interview, to develop his or her ideas and solutions in order to increase his or her acceptance.

In planning for the performance appraisal session, set aside sufficient time—normally an hour. But don't make it the last hour of the day, or the hour just before another critical appointment. And since you may need to take longer than an hour, schedule the session so that extra time is available if necessary. It is also your responsibility to ensure that you and the employee can meet together in privacy with no interruptions. If you can't control possible interruptions at your office, go somewhere else.

2. Introduce the meeting.

When the employee first enters your office (or a neutral area such as a conference room), relieve the employee's tension by greeting him or her warmly. You might help him or her feel more at ease by sitting across the corner of your desk or both of you sit in front of your desk. This will reduce the "I'm-the-Boss" problem and help the employee communicate more openly.

The objective of this interview is to assist, guide, and help the employee to develop professionally. A judgmental role, as indicated, can produce passive and/or defensive employee behavior that is not conducive to development. Thus, as the interview begins, you should stress your role as a counselor, not a judge, e.g., "During this interview, I'd like to offer any assistance I can give, and answer any questions you may have. This is your interview. I'm here to help in any way I can."

3. Determine the topics the employee wants to discuss.

In the past, most performance appraisal interviews began with the leader telling the employee what he or she did "right" and "wrong." Asking the employee for the topics that he or she wants to discuss is a radical departure from this older method. But there are four reasons why this is an excellent way to begin the interview:

a.   The employee may raise an issue already on your list. It's much easier to deal with an area of needed improvement if the employee brings it up rather than you.

b.   The employee may not be prepared to talk about a topic that you bring up, which will increase his or her tension.

c.   You may discover areas of concern that you weren't aware of.

d.   You want the employee to enter actively into a discussion, not just to listen to what you have to say.

To open this part of the interview simply ask, "What topic would you most like to discuss today?" Or, "What's first on your list for today's discussion?" Note that both questions are "neutral"—i.e., they do not initially ask for a concern or a problem, but allow the employee to respond with whatever topic he or she wishes to bring up.

When you ask a question such as those above, you will usually receive one of three possible responses from the employee:

(1)   an area of concern (i.e., something the employee feels he or she needs to improve);

(2)   an area of his or her positive performance; or,

(3)   a decision not to respond, e.g., "I don't know. What do you want to talk about?"

Let's look at each of these three possible responses.

Area of concern. If the employee brings up a performance problem or other area of concern, it is likely that the first statement made by the employee will be very general. General statements such as, "I have trouble getting along with Jane," or, "Those people over in data processing won't communicate with me!" are difficult to problem-solve. Thus you may need to ask questions to help the employee be more specific. For example, "Could you give me an example?" or "Can you be a little more specific?" will provide you with more information to use to help the employee solve the problem.

When you feel the problem is defined in specific terms, the next step is to pose questions that help the employee explore the cause of the problem. Questions such as, "What do you think is the cause of this situation?" or "What other causes do you see?" should be asked even if you think you already know the answers to the questions. You do this for three reasons:

(1) The employee will be more open to your suggested solutions if he or she believes you understand the cause(s) of the problem.

(2) Identifying the most probable cause(s) increases the chances that proposed solutions will work.

(3) The employee may be closer to the problem and thus be able to see causes that you can't see.

Last, when you are comfortable that you and the employee have identified the cause of a problem, ask further questions to obtain his or her solutions—even if you believe you know the solution. The purpose in asking for a solution, rather than offering yours, is that an employee who helps find the solution to a problem will more readily accept the changes which that solution will require. In addition, there is always the likelihood that the employee may have a solution that is better then yours.

To elicit an employee's suggested solution, simply ask, "What ideas do you have for developing a solution to this situation?" or, "What suggestions do you have for increasing your performance in this area?" or "What else can you do?"

But be cautious here. The employee's response might be, "Well, I guess I'll just have to try harder!" The problem with this solution is that even though it communicates a willingness to change, it says nothing about how that change will occur. You will find it is very difficult to later follow up an "I'll-try-harder" solution. It is better for you to say, "Well, I appreciate your willingness to try harder. But how do you see yourself doing that?" Or, "What things can you do?" When you get specific solutions, you can better follow up and provide appropriate feedback. Surprisingly enough, in Step 3 an employee will bring up an area of concern (a performance problem) more often than a positive performance, or an "I don't know" response.

Now let's look at the second most frequent response to the leader's request or a topic of discussion: a positive performance statement.

Positive performance. When you ask, "What topics would you like to discuss first today?", the employee may bring up something that he or she feels especially proud of. When this happens, immediately provide specific positive feedback—e.g., "I'm glad you mentioned that! I've noticed several instances where you've done extremely well. For example . . ." (describe events). The reason for providing specific feedback is to increase its positive impact to the employee as well as to give believability to the compliment. If you can describe specific times and situations, the employee knows that you really have noticed his or her positive performance.

No response. Occasionally an employee may choose not to respond to your question, "What topics would you like to talk about first?" This sometimes happens with a new employee who is still anxious or an employee who has had bad experiences with past performance appraisal interviews. If you feel the cause of the reluctance is nervousness, then take the initiative and comment positively on a strength you have noticed. This will help reduce the tension the employee may be feeling and sets the stage for a productive interview. After you have discussed the employee's positive performance however, then do follow up again with, "What other topics would *you* like to discuss?"

4. Discuss concerns not mentioned by the employee.

After dealing with the topics the employee has brought up for discussion, it is now time for you to bring up any of your concerns that have not already been mentioned by the employee. This step uses a four-step sub-model as follows:

  a. **Describe the employee's specific performance**. First, you introduce the topic by describing in specific terms the employee's actual performance. A specific statement helps reduce arguments with the employee because it describes behavior, not personality. For example, don't say, "You make too many errors!" (what is "too many"?); or "You're always late!" ("always" is probably not true). Instead, specify the behavior—e.g., "There were six errors made on the January report."; or, "The record shows that you have been fifteen minutes late five times during the past thirty days."

  b. **Describe the expected standard of performance.** Next, you need to state exactly what the employee should be doing that he or she is not doing—or what the employee should not be doing that he or she is doing. Try to avoid nonspecific statements like "You've got to improve your production.", "I expect you to improve your attitude!" or, "You need to reduce the number of errors you're making." Examples of better performance standard statements are: "I expect a minimum of ten percent increase in your production", "This job requires attendance at or before eight o'clock each morning", or "The performance standard for this job is zero defects."

c. Ask employee to identify cause(s) of the situation. As suggested in Step 3, it is important to probe for the cause of the problem for the following reasons:

- Employee identification of causes helps in later acceptance of solutions.
- The employee may see causes not seen by you.
- Identifying the most probable cause increases the quality of the solution.
- It keeps the discussion focused on the cause of the problem in order to prevent premature focus on solutions.

To help the employee analyze the cause of the problem, ask, "What do you think is the cause of this situation?" or, "What other causes do you see?" Note that in the first question the word selected was "situation," not "problem." Employees tend to react less defensively to analyzing situations rather than "problems."

d. Ask employee for his or her suggested solutions. Here again it is important to ask the employee for his or her solutions. If the employee is going to play a role in making needed changes, it is better to gain acceptance by guiding him or her to identify the solution.

You and the employee should explore each solution to reach one that will correct the problem. You also can make suggestions based on your general knowledge or experience that might improve the quality of the solution. Then encourage the employee to select the solution(s) that will be employed.

Because of the difficulty of handling too much change at once, select only a few solutions. You are looking for quality and degree of improvement in important areas, not small improvements in many. After selecting a solution or solutions, you and the employee will develop an action plan for each solution, in Step 5.

5. **Develop written action plans for carrying out key solutions in a specific time period.**

Some solutions will not need action plans. For example, the employee who is constantly tardy doesn't need a full-blown action plan to get to work on time. But for more complex solutions, a written goal statement with step-by-step plans will greatly increase the likelihood that the employee will accomplish the positive change.

If this is the first time a particular employee has written an action plan, you may have to put on your "training hat" and assist in writing a planning statement. However, be careful who holds the pencil! If you write it, it's your plan, not the employee's. Letting the employee write a planning statement encourages ownership, acceptance, and future results.

But even though you want it to be the employee's plan, you can increase its quality by offering your suggestions or assistance. You can provide help by saying: "I wonder if this might be something you could consider doing . . . ?", "What can I do to help?", or "What would you like me to do?"

6. **Give specific feedback on any positive performance that has not already been discussed.**

A performance appraisal interview provides you with an excellent opportunity to give employees positive feedback on their accomplishments. You should plan to spend a significant amount of time on this step so as to balance the interview between the employee's needs and strengths. To provide positive feedback that is meaningful to the employee, use the following model (similar to the one presented in Chapter 5 on motivation):

a. **Describe the employee's specific behavior and illustrate with examples.** By being specific and giving examples, we make our feedback credible. Also, the employee then knows exactly what he or she did that you like and appreciate. This will increase his or her motivation to repeat the behavior in the future.

b. **Give reasons why the employee's strength is important.** When you plan for this meeting, analyze why a particular strength of the employee is important to you, the organization, and to him or her. By giving all the reasons why the employee's strength is important, you reinforce the desired behaviors.

c. **Spell out your future expectations.** By spelling out your expectations of continued high performance, you inform the employee that you expect such performance in the future.

d. **Express your appreciation.** Most employees have a need to feel appreciated by their leaders.

e. **Develop written action plans for further using the employee's strengths (if appropriate).** Leaders often spend much time discussing how an employee can improve, and developing written action plans for improvement in particular areas. Similarly, we should spend time discussing an employee's strengths, and even develop written action plans for better using those strengths if possible. Leaders sometimes overlook the fact that good performance can be made even better—thus building on an employee's strengths.

7. Summarize the interview and discuss ratings.

In Step 7, highlight the key areas discussed to ensure clear understanding. Misunderstandings result when two people think they clearly understand what was said and agreed upon, when in fact they don't. In addition, if you summarize the key points each of you made in the interview, then both of you will have a solid feeling of accomplishment.

After you have summarized the highlights of the discussion, share with the employee your perception of his or her ratings. If you discuss ratings first in an interview, the employee cannot see the reasons for your ratings. The employee may then become defensive, and you will find yourself defending the ratings. But by summarizing the interview and discussing your ratings at the end of it, you will focus attention more on the job performance, rather than on the ratings.

8. Set follow-up dates.

Now set follow-up dates with the employee, and mark the date and time on your calendar in the employee's presence. This shows that his or her performance is important to you and clearly commits you to follow up and the employee to meet expectations as agreed upon.

9. Thank the employee.

Thanking the employee for the time and energy he or she devoted to preparing for and taking part in a performance appraisal interview is simple common courtesy—and will be greatly appreciated.

If you want to experience greater effectiveness and success in conducting performance appraisals, this tested nine-step process is for you. But it will require that you give it the needed time and effort to prove itself in your experience. Any human interaction process tends to look easy when reduced to its key steps on paper. Some hard work is necessary when training yourself to a new system, however. If some step in this process doesn't seem to work for you, feel free to alter it. Shape the system to fit your needs. But give it a full and honest try before judging it. If you do, you will find this basic nine-step method as effective for you as it is for the successful leaders who utilize it.

On the following pages you will find a *Preparation Guide,* and *Leader's Checklist* to copy and use in planning for and conducting your next performance appraisal interview.

LEADER'S CHECKLIST
CONDUCTING YOUR
PERFORMANCE APPRAISAL

1. Preparation

- Give employee a copy of the performance appraisal form and discuss it with him or her 2 to 3 weeks before actual interview

- Ask employee to complete a copy of the form before the interview

- Reserve an area for the interview where you can control interruptions

- Review incident files, and analyze specific areas to be discussed in the interview

- Tentatively analyze causes and solutions, and create tentative action plans

- Tentatively fill out the performance appraisal form on the employee

2. Introduction

- Put the employee at ease
- Reduce physical barriers to communication
- Stress your role as a counselor, not "judge"

3. Determine topic(s) employee wants to discuss

- If employee brings up an area of concern:
  - Ask questions to help employee be specific
  - Ask questions to explore causes
  - Obtain employee's solution(s)
- If employee brings up area of positive performance:
- Provide positive feedback

- If employee does not offer topic:
  - — Comment positively on strengths you have noticed
  - — Ask again for topic

4. **Discuss concerns not mentioned by employee**

   - Describe employee's specific performance
   - Describe the expected standard of performance
   - Ask employee to identify causes of the situation
   - Ask employee for his or her suggested solutions, and discuss

5. **Develop written action plans for carrying out key solutions in a specific time period**

   - Let employee select key solutions for development
   - If necessary, assist the employee with writing a planning statement
   - Offer suggestions or ideas as employee develops specific steps that he or she will take over the next six months

6. **Give specific feedback on any positive performance that has not already been discussed**

   - Describe the employee's specific behavior and illustrate with examples
   - Tell him or her why it was important to you, your organization, and to the employee
   - Spell out your future expectations
   - Express your appreciation
   - Develop action plans for the employee's strength if appropriate

7. **Summarize interview and discuss ratings**

8. **Set follow-up dates**

9. **Thank employee**

PREPARATION GUIDE
Preparing for Your Actual
Performance Appraisal

In each step below, write what you would actually say or do when you conduct the interview with your employee. Feel free to look at the text for ideas on what you can say in each step.

1. PREPARATION
   Have you met briefly with the employee one to two weeks in advance to prepare him or her for the interview by:
   a. Giving him or her a copy of any form(s) that will be used in the interview? _____
   b. Discussing the form(s) with the employee? _____
   c. Asking that the employee prepare for the interview by filling out the form(s) before the meeting? _____
      (Don't ask to see the form(s). They are to be used privately by the employee.)

   Have you prepared for this interview thoroughly by:
   a. Reserving an area where you can control interruptions? _____

   b. Reviewing incident files on this employee and carefully analyzing specific areas to be discussed during this session? _____

2. INTRODUCTION
   What will you do? _____

   _____

   What will you say? _____

   _____

3. DETERMINE TOPIC(S) EMPLOYEE WANTS TO DISCUSS
    What are you going to say to encourage the employee to talk first?

    _____

    _____

    When employee brings up area of concern:
    a. What question(s) will you ask to determine cause(s)? _____

    _____

    b. What questions will you ask to determine his or her solution(s)?

    _____

    _____

    What questions will you ask to obtain a second or even third issue
    for discussion from this employee? _____

    _____

4. DISCUSS CONCERNS NOT MENTIONED BY EMPLOYEE

    a. Describe the employee's specific performance _____

    _____

    b. Describe the expected standard of performance _____

    _____

    c. What questions will you ask to determine cause(s)? _____

    _____

    d. What questions will you ask to determine his or her solution(s)?

    _____

    _____

4. DISCUSS CONCERNS NOT MENTIONED BY EMPLOYEE
   (Used when there are two concerns. Repeat Step 4 if there are two concerns.)

   a. Describe the employee's specific performance _____
   _____

   b. Describe the expected standard of performance _____
   _____

   c. What questions will you ask to determine cause(s)? _____
   _____

   d. What questions will you ask to determine his or her solution(s)?
   _____
   _____

5. DEVELOP WRITTEN ACTION PLANS FOR CARRYING OUT
   KEY SOLUTION(S) IN A SPECIFIC TIME PERIOD

   a. What questions will you ask the employee to get him or her to
   relate his or her key solution(s)? _____
   _____

   b. What will you say to get him or her to write an action plan?
   _____
   _____

6. GIVE SPECIFIC FEEDBACK FOR ANY POSITIVE PERFOR-
   MANCE THAT HAS NOT ALREADY BEEN DISCUSSED

   a. What specific example will you use to describe the positive
      performance? _____

      _____

   b. What reasons will you give this employee why the positive
      performance was important?
      To you? _____
      To the organization? _____
      To the employee? _____

   c. What can you say to let him or her know that you expect this
      positive strength in the future? _____

      _____

   d. What will you say that is genuine in expressing your appre-
      ciation? _____

      _____

   e. How can this employee's strength be even better utilized?

      _____

      _____

7. SUMMARIZE THE INTERVIEW AND DISCUSS RATINGS

   What will you say to lead into the actual summary? _____

   _____

8. SET FOLLOW-UP DATES

   What will you say? _____

9. THANK EMPLOYEE

   What can you say that is genuine? _____

   _____

15
Employee Career Counseling

At the turn of the century, an entire generation of young people grew up reading a series of novels written by Horatio Alger. The books were titled *Strive and Succeed, Making His Way, Struggling Upward, Do and Dare,* and *Helping Himself.*

In almost every case, these books had a plot that went as follows: A young boy had either an absent father, or a father (often a minister) who was kind and good, but not concerned with the practical side of life. The family was always poor. And there was usually a rich villain who was going to foreclose on the mortgage—a princely sum like $500, in a day when you could buy a house for $600.

But the ending always turned out happily. In the Horatio Alger stories, "happy" meant that the boy earned the money to pay the mortgage because he was honest, hard working, kind, and loved God, his mother, and his country. The central theme was: "If you are willing to work hard, success will come automatically because of the grand opportunities that exist in this country."

Today the Horatio Alger story is, unfortunately, largely untrue. This is so because the facts of life in the business world are quite changed. We still view the individual as fundamentally responsible for his or her success or failure. But the maxim "Hard work will ensure success" has by now become more myth than truth. Look at the facts. In the 1950s and 60s, the chances of being promoted were 1 in 5. Today the odds are 1 in 30. In other words, you are six times less likely to be promoted today than you would have been in the recent past.

Future expectations are formed by past experiences. A whole generation—our parents—grew up with remarkable opportunities. Their children are now our employees, and they have similarly high expectations. They were told: "Work hard. Stay in school. Go to college. Get your degree. Do these things, and you will succeed!" As a result, they expect responsible jobs with opportunities for advancement. The truth is, however, that they are not going to find the same opportunities that our parents did in the past. We need to manage differently! And one solution is a career development system that can greatly help your employees overcome career obstacles and achieve success.

Career Development Systems

Good organizations know that their employees are their strength. Today you will find such organizations helping their employees build careers that make them more and more valuable to the organization.

Here is a picture of the way the parts of a modern career system fit together. As you can see, the central focus is on career counseling and career action plans.

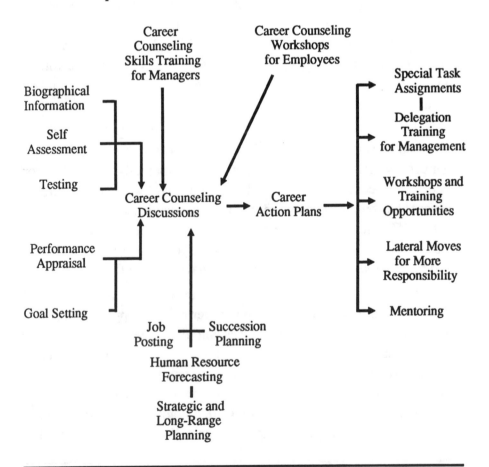

Organizational Strategies

Organizations are built on a foundation of strategic planning. This planning is usually conducted by top management in order to define the organization's mission or vision. From the organization's definition of what it is about—its mission—a long-range plan is developed.

After the organization completes its long-range planning, it can then forecast its human resource needs. When the forecasting is complete, the organization can then do succession planning to determine who needs to be trained to do what in future jobs. Finally, the organization communicates its human resource needs to its employees by job-posting.

Even if your organization does not do forecasting or succession planning, you can still take responsibility for your employee's career development. The first step for you is to help your employees figure out where they are going, what knowledge and skills will be required, and then determine what they need to get there.

Useful Strategies for Determining Employee Needs

To explore employee developmental needs, you will need to analyze their past experience to determine their strengths, knowledge, skills, and values. This information will be very useful in helping them make sound career development decisions.

For example, if you look at my background you will discover that in nearly every job I've had, I have enjoyed making presentations. Even in high school, my only "A" was in Public Speaking. (Where I went to school, it was socially unacceptable to make too many "A's"!) Therefore, if you were assisting me in my career planning, you would focus on my strength and skills in making presentations.

Job History Form. One way to organize information about employees is to ask them to fill out a *Job History* form. They will begin by listing each job they have held, starting with their present position (a maximum of five). A major job change within one organization is counted as a new job.

Next, the employees break down each job into its major tasks, and enter the details on the form. Then they show their level of personal satisfaction for each task. Finally, for those tasks rated very high or very low in satisfaction, they note the reasons why they liked or disliked each one. This list will provide clues and themes to the key things they want in a career—as well as the things they wish to avoid. The following is an example of a job history describing one of my past positions:

JOB HISTORY

1. Job	2. Major tasks	3. Satisfaction 5 = High Level 1 = Low Level	4. Why did you like or dislike this specific task?
Department Manager	Team Leader	3	
	Long Range Planning	4	
	Handling Budgets	1	I hate dealing with budgets because I am
	Writing and Creating New Programs	3	not very good at it!
	Making Presentations to Executives	2	
	Acting as Resource Person for Technical Questions	5	I enjoy being the "expert" and helping people.
	Speaking at Local and National Conventions	5	The recognition I receive feels good to me. I also like being competent.

5. **What generalizations (themes) can you make about yourself from your job history analysis? What are the key things you want in a job, and what things do you wish to avoid?**

   1. I like the mentoring role.

   2. Recognition for work well done is important to me.

   3. I would strongly dislike working with numbers.

On the next two pages is a *Job History* form that you may copy and use.

JOB HISTORY (page 1)

1. JOB	2. MAJOR TASKS	3. SATISFACTION LEVEL 5 = High 1 = Low	4. WHY DID YOU LIKE OR DISLIKE THIS SPECIFIC TASK? (For only the highest and lowest satisfaction levels—5 and 1.)

Copyright I.T.C., Inc.

JOB HISTORY (page 2)

1. JOB	2. MAJOR TASKS	3. SATISFACTION LEVEL. 5 = High 1 = Low	4. WHY DID YOU LIKE OR DISLIKE THIS SPECIFIC TASK? (For only the highest and lowest satisfaction levels—5 and 1.)

5. WHAT GENERALIZATIONS (THEMES) CAN YOU MAKE ABOUT YOURSELF FROM YOUR JOB HISTORY ANALYSIS? THAT IS, WHAT ARE THE KEY THINGS YOU WANT IN A JOB; AND WHAT THINGS DO YOU WISH TO AVOID?

Life History Form. In addition to the *Job History* form, the employee should also fill out a *Life History* form. This form will also ask him or her to identify major skills and interests.

To use a *Life History* form, employees begin by listing five key positive events in their lives, either job-related or personal, that resulted mostly from their own efforts. For each event, they list the skills or abilities they used. Then, the employees honestly indicate specific reasons why each of the events was important to them.

Next, they examine each of their skills and abilities, and make a new list of the most important ones. Finally, they analyze the reasons why each positive event was personally important to them, and list the underlying values shown in the event. That is, what did the employee like or enjoy about each situation?

To illustrate the use of this form, let's take as an example a life event that was significant to me. The teachers in my elementary school thought I was strange. I could read at an astonishing speed. But I absolutely could not spell. As a matter of fact, after failing the sixth grade, I almost became a grammar school dropout.

It wasn't until I was in college that I learned I had a condition referred to as "dyslexia." Many years later I felt honored when I was asked to give the commencement address to a special high school graduating class of 12 students—who were all dyslexic! Here is the way I analyzed this positive event in the format described above.

LIFE HISTORY

1. Positive event	2. List your skills/abilities that resulted in this event	3. Why was this event importamt
I gave the commencement address to a high school class of dyslexics	— Speaking before groups — Writing skills (not spelling!) — Knowledge of how to conduct a needs assessment (I interviewed each of the 12 students prior to writing the speech)	— Recognition; I felt needed — Satisfaction in helping others personally

4. From #2 above, list your most important skills and abilities	5. Identify your underlying values
Speaking before groups	— I like being in a situation where I can help others and am perceived as being exceptional — I enjoy the resulting recognition

It is difficult to perceive the power of *Life History* and *Job History* forms until your employees have had an opportunity to experience them. On the following two pages is a *Life History* form that you may copy and use with your employees.

LIFE HISTORY (page 1)

1. POSITIVE EVENTS (minimum of 5)	2. LIST YOUR SKILLS/ABILITIES (THAT YOU ENJOY) THAT RESULTED IN THIS EVENT	3. WHY WAS THIS EVENT IMPORTANT TO YOU (Be honest and specific)

LIFE HISTORY (page 2)

1. POSITIVE EVENTS
(minimum of 5)

2. LIST YOUR SKILLS/ABILITIES (THAT YOU ENJOY)
THAT RESULTED IN THIS EVENT

3. WHY WAS THIS EVENT
IMPORTANT TO YOU
(Be honest and specific)

4. FROM #2 ABOVE, LIST YOUR MOST IMPORTANT
SKILLS AND ABILITIES.

5. FROM #3 ABOVE, ANALYZE THE REASONS WHY THESE
EVENTS WERE PERSONALLY IMPORTANT TO YOU, AND
SEE IF YOU CAN IDENTIFY YOUR UNDERLYING VALUES.

Testing

There are a number of tests or questionnaires that can help you to determine your employee's career interests and needs. Examples of such tests are John Holland's "Self-Directed Search," the "Myers-Briggs Type Indicator," and, for supervisory or management positions, the "Leatherman Leadership Questionnaire." Tests such as these can usually be obtained through your organization's personnel department.

There are two main kinds of tests to help people determine career interest and needs. The more common tests are called "perception" questionnaires. "Knowledge-based" questionnaires are less common.

Perception Questionnaires. Perception tests are used to determine which topics in a list are perceived as being career development needs. For example, a questionnaire that begins by asking the employee, "Which of the following topics do you feel are important for your future development?" belongs to this class of test.

Perception tests are easy and quick to complete. They can be filled out by the person being tested, the boss, or a peer.

Unfortunately, perception tests also have very serious limitations. For example, some topics from a career development test might be selected as important when, in fact, they are not truly the employee's needs. When topics such as "communications," or "time management" appear in a list, they are almost guaranteed to be selected as critical. This is because they are what we call "umbrella" terms. In other words, terms like "time management" are labels that cover a number of different sub-topics. If any of the sub-parts are important to you, you will mark "time management" as important. But other parts may not be important to you at all.

Also, what people think they need, and what they really need, may be quite different. For example, you may have little competence in managing your performance appraisal interviews, and yet not know that you need help in this area. It often happens that entire organizations often don't know that they don't know how to conduct performance appraisals effectively!

Knowledge-Based Questionnaires. Knowledge-based tests, on the other hand, are used to determine your employees' actual knowledge in specific job task areas. For example, the following is a typical knowledge-based question:

> The primary responsibility for career development rests with the:
>
> A.   Employee's immediate supervisor.
> B.   Personnel department's establishment of career development programs and procedures (e.g., mentoring, training programs, career planning systems).
> C.   Employee.
> D.   Chief executive of the organization, since his or her support is essential for the success of any career development program.

As with perception tests, knowledge-based tests are easy to administer. But unlike perception tests, knowledge-based tests, when properly developed, provide very accurate information. Also, they reveal exactly what the person knows, rather than what the individual thinks he or she knows.

Performance Appraisal Systems

Another source that can help you identify your employees' needs and strengths is a performance appraisal—when it is properly done. If you are honest and accurate in your feedback to your employees, if the appraisal system is designed to allow the employee to be a part of the discussion, and if the performance appraisal form includes information about their future, then good career development information can be obtained.

In order for the performance appraisal interview to be meaningful for employees—and the organization, the employees must have an opportunity well in advance to discuss their job responsibilities with their supervisor (as much as one year prior to the interview, if possible). This pre-interview discussion is important in order to reduce the chances that employees are appraised on issues or factors they didn't know were going to be included. Here, there should be a full discussion of the job's tasks, the standards for each task, their authority level for the task, and a careful analysis made of any problems that might impede their performance.

In addition, supervisors and managers must be able to give their employees honest and straightforward feedback when appraising them. Leaders must also be willing to spend time in the appraisal interview discussing not only employees' past and present performance, but their job future as well. And last, the performance appraisal form that is used should address such issues as career planning, and setting future developmental goals and objectives.

As a part of a well-rounded performance management system, some organizations use a formal goal-setting process where employees, with their leader's help, write job-related goals and objectives, and then create plans to reach their objectives. This type of information, even though it is focused on an employee's present job tasks, can provide further career development data.

Career Development Workshops

Most performance appraisal systems fall short of the desired standard. Therefore many organizations have encouraged the employee to accept responsibility for his or her own career development by setting up career development workshops for them. In these workshops, employees complete work sheets much like the *Job History* and *Life History* forms presented earlier, and design action plans for their personal development.

Such workshops not only assist employees in identifying their knowledge, skills, and values, but will also show them that they are not alone in their career development needs. A payoff for the organization is that employees often find that they have far better opportunities within their organization than outside of it.

Leader-Employee Career Counseling Sessions

One of the best ways you can help your employees with their career development is to conduct individual career counseling sessions. You can help employees to:

1. Determine whether their organizational goals are realistic.

2. Identify their strengths and determine whether they are important for future positions.

3. Identify areas of needed improvement.

4. Communicate career job alternatives.

5. Create action plans for continued development covering both strengths and needs.

Now let's consider some important strategies to guide you in conducting a career counseling session with your employee. First we will look at an eight-step procedure for conducting a career counseling session with an employee, and then we will describe each step in detail. The eight key steps are as follows:

1. Prepare for the meeting.

2. Open the interview.

3. Obtain the employee's perceptions of his or her knowledge, skills, and values.

4. Discuss the employee's perceptions.

5. Explore career choice alternatives.

6. Create an action plan.

7. Conclude the interview.

8. Follow up.

1. Prepare for the Meeting.

Make an Appointment with Your Leader. Not only should a leader prepare for a career counseling meeting, but so should the employees. Therefore, you should meet briefly with each employee well in advance of the session and advise him or her of the date, time, location, and meeting objectives. Tell him or her that you would like to discuss career goals, and share ideas on the kinds of developmental activities he or she should undertake.

If appropriate, encourage the employee to consider all possible alternatives for his or her career development. In other words, the focus should not be just on promotional opportunities, but on such issues as job enrichment, special projects or assignments, and lateral moves. For example, you might say something like:

> "I'd like to meet with you in two weeks and spend some quality time reviewing the jobs you have held in the past, where you are today, what you might want to do in the future, and how you might get there. In short, one of the objectives of this meeting is to create a written action plan that can help you reach your own realistic career objectives.

> "A word of caution: the purpose of this meeting is to help you explore your own career goals, not to announce some sort of promotion. So, between now and when we meet I'd like to encourage you to think of a wide range of career alternatives. That is, consider things like how we can make your present job more challenging. Are there special jobs or tasks that you would like to take on? And what kinds of training do you feel you need to prepare you better for your future? It's important for you to consider a wide variety of possible goals, because it's a statistical fact that there are more and more highly qualified people available for fewer and fewer openings.

> "In most organizations, the chances of being promoted today are about six times less than they were a decade ago. It used to be that a promotion was the only measure of success on

the job. But today we need to measure success in other ways—like how happy we are doing what we have chosen to do. Or how productive we are. We can no longer use promotions as the major measure of whether or not an employee is successful. So it seems to me that the astute employee will explore a wide range of possible career outcomes, rather than be limited simply to the idea of 'promotions.'"

Then give the employee a copy of the *Job History* and *Life History* forms, and ask him or her to complete them in advance of the meeting. You could say:

"Now to prepare for this meeting, I'd like you to fill out these forms. They will help you identify the knowledge, skills, and abilities you have, and also enable you to determine the kinds of things you really enjoy doing, as well as the things you don't like doing. I think you'll find that they will give you and even better understanding of yourself—and also give us good information for our meeting.

"On the *Job History* form, list five jobs or positions you've held in the past, starting with your present job, and working backward. The *Life History* form focuses more on significant events in your experience, not only on the job, but in other areas of your life as well. See what you can do. And if you have any questions, come see me."

You will also need to determine if the employee already has a career development action plan (few employees do). If so, ask him or her to bring it to the meeting. It is also advisable to urge the employee to come prepared to do most of the talking, since the responsibility for career planning is the employee's, not yours. You might say:

"Please come prepared to do most of the talking in this meeting, since it will be a discussion of your career. My role will be to listen, ask questions, and offer suggestions to help you develop a written career plan."

Taking time to properly prepare the employee for such a meeting is essential. If we expect the employee to do most of the talking, he or she needs time to reflect on the topics that will be discussed. Last, it is a good idea to reserve a private area where interruptions can be controlled.

On the following pages is a handout that can be reproduced and given to your employee to aid in preparing for the career counseling interview.

EMPLOYEE GUIDE TO USE IN PREPARING FOR A CAREER COUNSELING INTERVIEW

Fill out Job and Life History forms. After setting a meeting date with your leader, fill out both a *Job History* and *Life History* form. These forms will help you identify your knowledge, skills, and abilities, and also enable you to determine the kinds of things you really enjoy doing as well as those you don't.

Use the *Job History* form to list five jobs or positions you have held, starting with your present job and working backward. Use the *Life History* form to list significant events in your experience.

Develop Alternative Career Goals. Then, considering your talents and skills, as well as the things you like and don't like doing, try to identify where you want to be in the future. Within reason, the more alternative career goals you bring to your counseling session to examine, the better your decisions will be. This means looking ahead at many possibilities, including job enrichment in your present job, special projects, or lateral moves for more exposure or challenge.

A good strategy is to brainstorm a list of possible career goals. The idea is to create a list of goals on paper—without judging the possibility they can be achieved. When your list is complete, then delete those goals that seem impractical, combine the remaining ones where possible, and add to the list new ideas that come to mind.

Create a Career Plan. When you have identified the direction you would like to go (even a tentative one), begin to develop a step-by-step plan to reach your goal. A useful *Career Goal Planning Work Sheet* is found on the last page of this handout. Make several copies of this work sheet for use in your planning.

Analyze Risk. A key question in planning is to ask: "If I do this, what can go wrong?" This is an important question you need to ask yourself—and others—as you prepare your plan. The idea is to try to develop preventive and contingency actions you can take if problems do occur. "Preventive" action includes those things you can do now to reduce the possibility that a problem will occur. "Contingency" action is what you will do to stabilize your plan if the problem occurs anyway.

You may wish to develop several possible career plans for your meeting with your leader. One is your primary plan. The others can be used if your primary plan proves to be unrealistic for your organization. Your career plan is tentative at this point. To implement a plan, it must meet not only your needs, but the organization's needs as well.

CAREER GOAL PLANNING WORK SHEET

1. Write your goal statement: _____

   _____

   _____

2. List the steps in your plan to achieve this goal (do not number or date the steps yet):

Step Number	Step	Completion Date
_____	_____	_____
_____	_____	_____
_____	_____	_____
_____	_____	_____
_____	_____	_____
_____	_____	_____
_____	_____	_____
_____	_____	_____
_____	_____	_____
_____	_____	_____
_____	_____	_____
_____	_____	_____

3. Identify potential problems with your plan by asking: "What can go wrong?"

   _____

   _____

   _____

   _____

   _____

4. If possible, develop solutions (preventive and/or contingency actions) for any identified potential problems and incorporate these solutions into your plan as new steps.

   _____

   _____

5. Finally, number the steps in your plan, and determine a completion date for each step.

The day of your interview with your employee has arrived. The next step for you as the supervisor or manager is to:

2. Open the Interview.

Before the meeting with the employee, arrange the meeting area so that the employee feels as comfortable as possible. If meeting in your office, seat both yourself and the employee in front of your desk. An even better place to hold the interview is in a neutral meeting area such as a conference room. Your intent should be to put the employee at ease by reducing the physical barriers to communication.

When the employee arrives for the meeting, greet him or her warmly. Then again state your role, time constraints (if appropriate), and the meeting objectives. An illustration of what could be said follows:

> "I'm pleased to have this opportunity to discuss with you your career goals. In today's meeting, I see myself as being a coach, a listener, and a possible resource for you, as you explore your alternatives. This is your meeting, and you're in charge.

> "As I see it, your objective is to explore your strengths, as well as areas where some improvement may be helpful. And to discover what you like to do—and don't like to do. We also need to look at career alternatives, and to create an action plan for implementation."

In addition to explaining your role and the meeting objectives, you should also stress that there are no guarantees that what is planned will actually happen. However, by creating a well-conceived written action plan, the employee can increase the probability of reaching his or her goal.

Last, unless you have a photographic memory, you may need to take notes so that you don't forget important ideas that are discussed. It is courteous to ask the employee's permission to take such notes during the meeting.

3. Obtain the Employee's Perceptions of His or Her Knowledge, Skills, and Values.

In this step, you will begin the process of obtaining information from the employee. A good way to begin is to ask the employee to summarize the strengths highlighted by his or her *Job History* form, and determine the types of tasks that have been satisfying and dissatisfying. Then ask for a summary of knowledge, skills, and values highlighted by the *Life History* analysis.

It is important that you help the employee do most of the talking by maintaining eye contact, listening carefully, and not interrupting. You can also rephrase the employee's comments throughout the meeting, which not only ensures that you understand what the employee said, but also demonstrates to the employee that you are listening carefully. You can also encourage the employee by giving verbal prompts as he or she speaks—e.g., "That's interesting," "Please continue," and "Could you give me an example?"

4. Discuss the Employee's Perceptions.

Here you need to provide feedback on what the employee has said. For example, you might wish to reinforce any areas of agreement on the employee's perceptions of his or her strengths, as well as to state (rephrase) areas of needed improvement. In addition, you may also need to provide your honest observations on areas of need—and strengths--that the employee did not mention.

Last, don't challenge the employee's values. If the employee says, "Money is the most important thing to me!", don't respond, "You mean that money is even more important than your family?" Determining what the employee values is the objective, so it is not appropriate here to challenge his or her values.

5. Explore Career Choice Alternatives.

Within reason, the more alternatives the employee has available to examine, the better will be the final decision. This means that the employee should be encouraged to look at many different possibilities, such as job enrichment of his or her present job, special projects, and/or lateral moves for more exposure or challenge. It may even be appropriate for you to assist the employee in exploring opportunities outside the organization.

A good strategy is to ask the employee, with your help, to brain-storm a list of possible career alternatives. The idea is to create a list of alternatives on paper without judging their viability. When the list is complete, then delete those alternatives that seem impractical, com-bine the remaining ones where possible, and even add to the list new ideas that come to mind. Last, help the employee select an alternative (or alternatives) that best meets the needs of both the employee and the organization.

6.   Create an Action Plan.

After selecting one or more appropriate career alternatives, the next step is to assist the employee to write an action plan. But be careful: watch out who holds the pencil! If you write the action plan, it will be yours, not the employee's. You can begin this step by saying:

> "Why don't you start by writing out a general goal statement
> that includes one of your key alternatives? This statement
> should clearly describe what you want to become, or to do,
> and in what length of time you hope to accomplish this."

If the employee has more than one career choice alternative, then he or she may need to write out a goal statement for each. And in some cases, there is one major alternative for which other alternatives become sub-steps, or sub-goals, in the final action plan.

After writing a goal statement, the employee should next develop a list of actions that need to be taken to reach the goal. Again, the employee should explore, with your help, a number of different types of actions, such as mentoring opportunities, training programs, coach-ing by you, special tasks assignments, and even temporary lateral moves where necessary. Each of these actions or steps can then be dated, and listed in sequential order. At this point it may be necessary to revise the original goal date to meet the time requirements of the individual action (activities). For example, you could say to your employee:

> "Why don't you start by writing out a general goal statement for now. Then, after you finish the plan you will have a better feel for how long this will take to achieve, and can write in a date by which you would like to accomplish your main goal."

Before finalizing the plan, you and the employee should analyze the list of activities, or actions, for potential problems. This is important, because if you can identify potential problems now, you may anticipate likely causes and solutions.

You can develop solutions of two kinds: 1) preventive solutions, that will reduce the probability of the problem ever occurring; and, 2) contingency solutions, that will reduce the severity of the problem if it does occur. These preventive and contingency actions can then be included as a part of the original plan. The time to consider problems and solutions is in the planning stage, where it will greatly increase the chances of successfully reaching the goal. When the plan is completed, it may be necessary for you and the employee to establish follow-up meetings. Select key milestones, and use these dates to plan meetings to review the employee's progress toward completing his or her goal.

7. Conclude the Interview.

In this step you need to encourage the employee to continue to accept responsibility for his or her career development. In addition, check for any unasked or unanswered questions, and offer to answer any questions arising in the future. Last, if it fits your management style, you might wish to thank the employee for his or her efforts in creating the career plan.

You could say:

"This is your plan, and its success is primarily dependent on you. I'll help in any way that I can. But for the most part, you're going to have to make it happen. I have confidence in you and know that you will give it your best effort.

"Is there anything you have not asked, or that we have not considered?"

"I appreciate the work you did in filling out the *Job History* and *Life History* forms, and the time you've spent with me today. I feel very good about what we have accomplished together."

8. Follow up.

Sometimes we get so busy in our management job that we don't make time to follow up with the employee. Understandable—but a potential disaster! We have seen that today it is necessary to do career counseling with our employees. Career counseling is now something that is not just "nice to do," but is mandatory.

In addition, if we do spend the time necessary to help the employee develop an action plan, and then ignore the employee's future efforts, the employee will have a legitimate reason to believe that you and the organization don't really care. Don't "talk a good game," and then fail to follow through with what needs to be done. Career counseling is too important for the productivity and future of your employees, your organization, and you!

16
Managing Change

Change causes problems. In fact, the field of problem solving states that all problems result from change. Not only do you have to deal with external problems resulting from change, you will also deal with your emotions. Fear, anxiety, and worry can all occur from changes.

These emotions usually come from apprehension about the unknown. You're not certain what's coming, or whether you can handle it. You're not sure you want to give up where you are. You may fear that you are going to be less comfortable with the future than you are with the present.

Human beings tolerate change in different ways. While some feel overwhelmed even by the thought of making a change, others seem to thrive on it. Whatever your tolerance, this chapter is for those who must cope with change. You will see how to increase your tolerance for change—and how to manage it to your benefit.

Many changes are positive. But some changes don't seem to benefit you directly. You may feel that a change leaves you with fewer benefits, and that it is something you will have to suffer through.

Your ability to manage change is linked to your feeling of being in control, and to the personal benefits you see in making the change. Your challenge is to discover the ways that a change will benefit you. Or, if there are no apparent benefits, you will need to find strategies to control the negative effects of the change.

Let's first look at the major causes of change, and then examine some strategies that can help us manage changes that affect our lives.

Causes of Change

There are two major categories of change, external and internal. External changes are those that originate outside your organization. These are the ones that can cause you the most mental distress because they often create a feeling of loss of control. For example, if the economy turns downward and your organization starts to lay off workers, it may be difficult for you to maintain the morale of your employees.

Internal changes are those that result from an organization's own initiatives. For instance, if your organization decides to relocate its operations, you can be assured that you and your employees will deal with major changes.

External Changes. There are seven major causes of external change:

1. New technology

2. Governmental regulations

3. Variable economy

4. Job mobility

5. Personal relationships

6. Constant increases in wage levels

7. Union activity

These external changes cause major problems. But they can also create positive opportunities! Opportunities to do things differently-- and better. Let's examine each of these causes.

1. New technology can create havoc within any organization. Although it is rare that new technology results in industry-wide disruption, it may cause great distress in a particular organization. Even if your employees don't lose their jobs, they may feel anxiety over the possibility of being retrained or moving to another job.

But, new technology can also result in jobs that are even more secure. Suppose your organization decides to reorganize its reporting procedures, and therefore installs a new system of computers to speed the flow of information. As a result, your employees must be given hundreds of hours of training to teach them how to use the new equipment. This additional training and their new skills will make them even more valuable to the organization.

2. Governmental regulations can also have great impact on organizations. Affirmative action, tax regulations, automotive emission and gas consumption regulations, waste water disposal guidelines, and safety regulations are all examples of laws and regulations that have created major changes, resulting in problems within organizations.

But even changes in governmental regulations can produce opportunities. For example, look at what has happened to the automobile industry. Continued change in the government's regulations concerning automotive gasoline has resulted in the development of high-efficiency engines that are among the best in the world. The net effect of this has been to help save jobs by making the U.S. more competitive in world markets.

3. Variable economy. Inflation, stagnation, depression, third world debt, balance of payments, national debt, and competition from a world market are all economic realities of our time. Since you have little chance of preventing these problems, you can reduce your anxiety when they occur by taking action ahead of time to protect yourself.

Note that I said "when," not "if," they occur. Large-scale economic changes have happened, are happening, and will continue to happen. You know that you will experience some, or even all, of the global economic problems mentioned above, and that they will have a profound effect upon your organization.

Thus it is to your benefit to do those things now that will help you cope with such problems when they occur. In your personal life, for example, increase your savings rate, cut back on high-interest charge accounts, and reduce your expenses. On the job, make yourself and your employees ever more valuable to your organization by increasing the quality and quantity of your group's output. The people who survive swings in the economy are those who are the least dispensable to their organization. You'll find it is much easier to make such changes now than after trouble comes.

4.   Job mobility has both positive and negative consequences. It's great to attract high quality applicants from other organizations. It's not so great to lose your people to other organizations. Therefore, it is not enough to attract good people; you have to figure out ways to keep them. For the most part, employees don't leave organizations for financial reasons. There are some people, of course, who are always hungry for more money. But even when employees earn fair wages they may leave because another job offers an opportunity for more responsibility, greater challenge, and better leadership! In other words, today's employees today are often more committed to their professions than to their organizations. The leaders of these highly mobile employees may need to implement training programs to help create challenging environments that attract and keep good people.

The challenge for you is to select good people from the mobile market. Then keep them by using the strategies outlined in the chapters on training and motivation. For example, you might give your new employees helpful information on the people they will be working with—i.e., what they do in their jobs, and their hobbies and outside interests. This will help them establish links of interest so that it will be easier to make friends. The more they know about their future jobs, their organization, and the people they will be working with, the more comfortable and effective their transition will be.

5.   Personal relationships. Another major external factor causing change—one that we must all cope with—is in the area of personal relationships. Marital problems, separation, divorce, alcohol or drug-dependent family members, children leaving home, death—all these are examples of external situations that can cause untold stress and change in our lives. The best strategy to deal with such changes is to encourage your employees to get professional help and, if possible, group support. It is far better for your employees to seek help than to try to "tough it out" by themselves. There are many things one can do to cope positively with severe stress in personal relationships, but experience shows that trained resource people outside the situation often make a critical difference.

6. *Constant increases in wage levels* may result in employees who can afford to take frequent unofficial 3-day weekends. This will require that you clearly tell your employees the organization's expectations concerning time off, keep careful records of attendance, and immediately deal with problems when they occur.

7. *Union activity* is another major external factor that may have high impact upon the way you carry out your leadership role. Unionization often results from poor management—management that "talks" about leadership, but doesn't do it. This indicates that it is far better to have a pro-active stance that reduces the probability of having a union election. In other words, if an organization and its leaders treat their people fairly, the chances are that a union will not successfully win an election.

If your organization already has a union, then stressful changes can occur each time a contract is up for renewal. Here, lack of information about contract issues, or how they are to be interpreted can cause stress. The better an organization communicates to its leaders the key issues, the more prepared the leaders will be in handling any changes that may be required.

Internal Changes. External forces can cause internal organizational changes—sometimes sweeping ones. But internal initiatives also cause major changes within an organization. These actions fall into three categories: personnel changes, job changes, and organizational changes. Let's look at each of these in turn.

Personnel changes can have a strong impact on your employees' ability to cope. Suppose you receive a promotion and your employees get a new boss, or one of your group's fellow workers leaves the organization, or you hire a new employee to work in your group. These changes can be difficult to manage.

When bosses change, people become understandably apprehensive. What will the new boss be like? What will be his or her expectations of them? This problem is even more difficult if the employees had an extremely good relationship with their old boss.

There are things you can do to help your employees constructively cope with personnel changes. For example, new bosses have histories—they come from somewhere. The odds are that the new boss was promoted from within the organization. If so, it is often easy to obtain background information on the new leader for your employees.

Special problems can occur if the new boss came from your section and is now the leader of what were his or her co-workers. Here it is especially important that you spend time with both the new leader and the employees to help them manage this transition. If the leader is new to leadership responsibilities, you may need to help him or her see the difference between the new job and the old one. And you must manage the feelings of other employees who wanted the job. The key here is to be sensitive and aware that both the new leader and the employees will have strong feelings about this change. Your job is to listen—and to help them manage their feelings.

Losing a valued co-worker also can be distressing. Close relationships that develop on the job are normally altered when one individual leaves. You have at least two options to manage the change that occurs when an employee loses a friend through resignation, termination or transfer. First, you can help the two employees deliberately plan outside activities or develop common interests that have nothing to do with work. This will allow them to maintain a continuing relationship, though they no longer work together. Or, if your employee must give up the relationship, it is important to permit him or her to grieve this loss. For example, I once had a wonderful boss, an ex-football player who was a mountain of a man with a heart of gold. And I liked him a great deal. But because our boss-subordinate roles had not allowed for a friendship off the job, we could not maintain our relationship when I resigned my position and took another job. I permitted myself to experience fully the sadness and deep sense of loss that this change caused. And my open acknowledgment of my feelings helped—though I miss him still.

Another type of change occurs when you hire a new employee. Most new employees are anxious about their new jobs, and feel great discomfort about the strangers they will be working with. Your job is to help them overcome their anxiety in order to manage the change as smoothly as possible.

Since you know that this person is probably nervous and anxious about the new job, don't say, "This job is simple. You'll catch on in no time." Rather than relieving tension, this can make it worse. By stating that the job is "easy" you are, in effect, saying that the person is not very smart if he or she has trouble. Better to say something like, "I know that most new jobs appear difficult. But I am confident that you can manage it."

You can also help new employees overcome some of their anxiety by finding out what their outside interests are. Then as you introduce them to others in your section or department, suggest "links" of common interest.

Job changes can also have major effects on employees. Such changes range from the addition of a new job task, to a new job due to promotion or transfer. The key word here is "new." The more a new job is unlike the old one, the greater the employee's anxiety will be. So if you assign an employee to a completely new job, you can expect him or her to feel anxious about it.

A key strategy here is to make all of the tasks of the new job clearly visible. That is, take the time to describe the employee's job tasks on paper. Then review each task with the employee, and devise an on-the-job training plan. This will take some of the mystery out of the unfamiliar assignment and reduce the employee's anxiety. It will help him or her to see that what, at first, may appear to be an overwhelming job is really a series of particular tasks that he or she can handle successfully.

Organizational changes often cause employees deep concern about their future. Some changes that affect the organization, like external technological or economic ones, have already been discussed. But there are also internally caused changes that organizations make. They may want to be more competitive, introduce a new product or service, increase their profits, reduce operational expenses, or pay bigger dividends to their stockholders. Or management simply may want to look good in the eyes of a new administration. Whatever the organizational change, your employees are almost certain to be affected by it in some way.

There are several types of organizational change. New equipment, new processes, and new policies and procedures can all cause major organizational changes that affect your employees—and you. The best way to help your employees is to be assertive about your right and their right to know what is going on. Speak with your boss, the personnel department, or even your boss's boss. Most of your employees' concerns about organizational changes are due to not being kept informed. The more they can find out the specifics of a change from informed people, the better they will feel, and function. Here, of course, you must be careful about the "rumor mill." Organizational changes tend to produce strange rumors. So make every effort to obtain your information from those people who, in fact, know the facts—and then communicate what you find to your employees.

Guidelines for Managing Change

Several guidelines stand out clearly when you ask how to manage change well.

- First, changes frequently involve significant personal benefits. Your job is to identify those benefits and to discuss them with your employees in order to create within them a genuine, productive acceptance of the change.

- Second, don't *you* become paralyzed by change. Determine what aspects of the situation you can control, and take positive action on these parts. Even the effects of a change that appear most negative can sometimes be turned to your advantage when you creatively take charge in the areas you still control.

- Finally, seek the assistance of others. Even the simple act of talking to someone who is a good listener is sometimes all that is necessary to reduce your anxiety to a manageable level and free your energy.

Above all, even if an organizational change seems overwhelming or impossible for your employee to accept, don't let him or her quit in a huff! Ask that he or she take time to think through the reasons for staying with the organization. If the employee still wants to leave, encourage him or her to find another job before resigning. Remind this employee that it is much easier to obtain another job while still holding one. The plain fact is that an employee is seen by prospective employers as more valuable if he or she has a job, than if not.

I know that many leaders would allow an upset employee to go ahead and quit—especially if the employee were only an average performer. But the best policy is always to treat employees the way we would wish to be treated. Remember two things: it may be easier to turn the employee around than to hire and train a replacement. And if the employee leaves anyway, you want him or her to say good things about you and the organization.

Using "Force Field Analysis" to Manage Change

I used to write books in longhand. And then came computers. Talk about major change! So I bought the simplest word-processing program I could find, and sat down to use it. A computer expert obviously wrote the instructions, using words I had never heard of to explain things I couldn't picture. I became so frustrated that I almost gave up. The fact that the word processing program had a built-in word speller to help me overcome my spelling problem was the only reason I stuck with it. And I finally learned how to use it.

Let's look at this example to illustrate the use of what is called "Force Field Analysis." Force field analysis is a tool that will help analyze change in order to 1) gain personal control over changes and 2) to bring possible benefits of change—sometimes unperceived at first--into the present.

The first step in force field analysis is to list on one side of a vertical line all the reasons—or "forces"—that support the change. Then list all the opposing forces—reasons against changing—on the other side of the line. Next, use opposing arrows to represent the competing forces, with longer arrows indicating stronger forces.

FORCE FIELD ANALYSIS

Changing from Longhand to a Word Processor

Forces (Reasons) For Changing	*Forces (Reasons) Against Changing*
	Anxiety over not knowing how to use word processor
Much faster	
	Initial learning time required
Many fewer spelling errors	
	Cost of program
Don't want to appear "behind the times" to my staff	
	Fear of appearing slow to learn
Easier to make changes in a document.	
	Lost data when power is out
Electronic storage takes less space	

Now that I've learned how to use a word processor, I'll never go back to writing in longhand. But notice that I had an overwhelming reason (my need for a spell-checker) to continue my efforts to master this new process.

Force field analysis helped me decide to make this change by graphically showing me the factors that were influencing my feelings about the change. I could see at a glance all the positive reasons for accepting this change as well as the ones against it. Next, I could begin to minimize the effects of the opposing forces through specific actions. For example, I could reduce the learning time required by having someone who already knew how to use the program to instruct me. His help also could reduce my anxiety over not knowing how to use this new program—and my fear of appearing to be a slow learner. A "force field" chart will help you and your employees deal openly with feelings about change. It can also increase your employees' acceptance of the need for change. This technique is especially helpful if the employee must cope with changes that appear to have little value. Help your people accept the possibility that the organization (or others) had what it believed were good reasons for the change—no matter how idiotic it might seem to them! Thus your job is to help your employees discover the reasons for change—and its possible benefits.

To analyze a specific change, start by sketching a force field chart as just shown. Then, with your employee(s), list as many benefits and disadvantages as you can. If the benefits side looks sparse, there may be additional reasons why the change was introduced. So try to get more information. Go and ask your boss. Ask peers whose opinions you respect. Talk to others outside your organization, if the change is not confidential, to get their views.

And remember your goal: to discover with your employees other positive reasons for the change—not to affirm present discomfort with it. Find out the reasons for change so that you can better support it from a knowledgeable position.

If your employees can support or at least accept the need for a change, your next step is to help them look for ways to control the opposing forces (negative effects) coming from the change. This will enable them to cope with change—constructively, creatively, and—as is often done—to their advantage.

Remember the two major objectives in managing change with your employees: 1) help them look for the benefits; and 2) help them take control. On the following page is a work sheet to use for managing the changes that affect you and your employees.

MANAGING CHANGE WORK SHEET

1. Write a brief description of the change that concerns you or your employees.

   _____

   _____

   _____

   _____

2. Using the "force field" chart below (use easel paper if you are working with a group), list the reasons, or forces, that support the change on the left side, and the opposing forces on the right. Place an arrow over each force, with the length indicating the strength of the force (reason).

Forces for Changing	Forces Against Changing

3. What information do you need to further complete the chart above?

   _____

   _____

   _____

   _____

4. Who has the needed information?_____

   _____

   _____

5. What are the major benefits of this change for you or your employees?

_____

_____

_____

6. What specific actions can you take toward the opposing forces (negative results) that will minimize, or even reverse, their effects, putting you or your employees in better control?

_____

_____

_____

7. What additional actions will you or your employees need to take to make this a beneficial change?

_____

_____

_____

_____

_____

_____

17
Leading Your Employees

Times are changing! In a world of global markets, scarce resources, tougher competition, the winds of change are being felt every-where. Your employees are changing too. They are better educated, more highly specialized, and have gained greater mobility. And they cost more—more to find, more to train, more to replace.

And how about you? Are *you* moving with today's changes? Do you understand what's happening in our organizations? Do you know your employees real needs? Do you know about leading your employees effectively in the often-bewildering tasks they face? And do you really understand that every change is an opportunity to do something better—a chance to grow in your leadership skills?

This book is written for you! As it states at the beginning, it is for leaders who are looking for common sense, down-to-earth techniques for handling the great variety of employee needs that occur every day. It is a very special "how to" book, with step-by-step instructions on how to manage any employee problem. It provides practical sugges-tions, tested strategies, proven methods.

So this book is not about theories that don't relate to the job, or leadership "styles" and "personality." Instead, it is written to show ex-actly what to *do* to lead effectively. Its sixteen chapters cover virtually every important employee problem situation—your needs as well as theirs. And detailed, reproducible on-the-job work sheets are presented throughout to help you apply what you have learned.

We have seen a number of key principles running throughout this book. I would like to end by listing, as simply and clearly as possible, some of the most important ones.

If you want to be a truly effective, helpful, leader:

1. Prepare before every important interaction with your employees. (In nearly all of the step-by-step leadership models I have presented, step one is: prepare!)

2. Do the job *with* your employees—not by yourself.

3. Lead your employees; don't order them around.

4. Keep everyone informed.

5. Talk "with" employees, not "at" them.

6. Trust your employees with responsibility. They want to be challenged.

7. Set high standards—for employees tend to fulfill their leader's expectations.

8. Involve your employees. It will raise their morale, stimulate their creativity, and increase their commitment.

9. Look for what was done well, not always for what is wrong.

10. Make your feedback specific, not general, and positive as well as corrective.

11. Follow up—to provide needed, timely guidance; to ensure that what is planned happens; to make performance matter.

If you will follow these principles you will succeed in leading your employees. And they and your organization will thank you!